Dictatorships in Twenty-First-Century Latin America

Dictatorships in Twenty-First-Century Latin America

Venezuela, Bolivia, Nicaragua, Ecuador, and El Salvador

Osvaldo Hurtado

Translated by Barbara Sipe

ROWMAN & LITTLEFIELD
Lanham • Boulder • New York • London

Published by Rowman & Littlefield
An imprint of The Rowman & Littlefield Publishing Group, Inc.
4501 Forbes Boulevard, Suite 200, Lanham, Maryland 20706
www.rowman.com

86-90 Paul Street, London EC2A 4NE

British Library Cataloguing in Publication Information Available

Library of Congress Cataloging-in-Publication Data

Names: Hurtado, Osvaldo, author.
Title: Dictatorships in twenty-first-century Latin America: Venezuela, Bolivia, Nicaragua, Ecuador, and El Salvador / Osvaldo Hurtado; translated by Barbara Sipe.
Description: Lanham, Maryland: Rowman & Littlefield, 2023. | Includes bibliographical references and index.
Identifiers: LCCN 2022033686 (print) | LCCN 2022033687 (ebook) | ISBN 9781538171073 (cloth) | ISBN 9781538171080 (paperback) | ISBN 9781538171097 (epub)
Subjects: LCSH: Latin America—Politics and government—21st century. | Dictatorship—Latin America—History—21st century. | Authoritarianism—Latin America—History—21st century. | Political culture—Latin America—History—21st century.
Classification: LCC F1414.3 .H87 2023 (print) | LCC F1414.3 (ebook) | DDC 980.04—dc23/eng/20220823
LC record available at https://lccn.loc.gov/2022033686
LC ebook record available at https://lccn.loc.gov/2022033687

Contents

Preface

The invitation I received from the University of the Americas (Universidad de las Américas, UDLA) and the Biarritz Forum Network to participate in the conference "Latin America: Two Models, One Region," held in Quito in 2011, offered me the opportunity to present my reflections on the new forms of authoritarianism that were emerging in the region.

Unlike in the nineteenth and twentieth centuries, in the twenty-first century those who disregarded democratic institutions and set up dictatorial governments were not military leaders or military institutions but rather civilian presidents elected by the people to govern their countries in accordance with their constitution and the law. At the end of the millennium, this new expression of traditional Latin American authoritarianism surprisingly appeared in democratic Venezuela, led by a colonel who had attempted to overthrow the constitutional government of President Carlos Andrés Pérez. It did not take many years for Evo Morales in Bolivia, Daniel Ortega in Nicaragua, and Rafael Correa in Ecuador to follow in the footsteps of Hugo Chávez. They were later joined by Nayib Bukele in El Salvador.

Although they did not abolish the constitution in place—as the dictators of yesteryear used to do—upon assuming the mandate for which they were elected by the citizens, they discredited it with the argument that it was not truly democratic, which is why it should be changed, so that the people would have a constitution that would respond to their own interests and not those of the dominant groups. What they actually did was impose constitutional norms and institutions that would allow them to accumulate all the powers of the state in order to govern without the checks and balances of a democratic regime. The presidents who took other paths achieved similar outcomes by reforming, disregarding, manipulating, or reinterpreting constitutional norms at will, as a function of their interests.

It was surprising and paradoxical that the return of the atavistic and cyclical Latin American authoritarianism, with all its evils, should took place at the height of democracy and freedom during the region's two-hundred-year-old republican history. For the first time, dictatorships had disappeared, and democratic institutions ruled in all the countries of the region with the sole exception of Cuba. In view of this significant political progress, many had thought that, unlike what had happened in the past, democracy was back to stay.

Encouraged by the interest aroused among public opinion by my novel approach, I expanded the original essay, which gave rise to the book *21st-Century Dictatorships: The Ecuadorian Case*. It was published in Quito in 2012 by Paradiso Editores, despite the threats and coercion to which Ecuadorian publishing houses were subjected by the government in power at that time.

Several reasons led me to delve into greater depth in the study of this new expression of the old Latin American authoritarianism: the need to unravel and explain the political process whereby a democratic system became dictatorial and constitutional presidents became autocratic caudillos; the academic usefulness of conceptualizing it by analyzing its characteristics, similarities, and particularities; the civic advisability of having citizens and political and social leaders appreciate the value of democracy and freedom and become aware of how much they counted in people's individual and collective welfare; and the conviction that under no circumstance and with no excuse, not even that of carrying out economic and social transformations, could a constitutional president disregard the democratic order, violate its institutions, subjugate all the powers of the state, and affect human rights.

While I was conducting the research, studying the findings, and writing the manuscript, members of my family and people close to my political and academic work asked me to abandon the reckless idea of exposing the authoritarian behavior of the powerful and untouchable President Rafael Correa. They were certain that I would be judicially persecuted, morally disparaged, and stigmatized in the eyes of citizens—and that I could eventually be imprisoned or exiled. The Corporation for Development Studies[1] might also be subjected to similar harassment, for which Correa could rely on obsequious prosecutors and judges willing to diligently obey his orders. This is what had happened with journalists and the few political and social leaders who had dared to denounce the abuses, arbitrariness, and corruption of high-level government officials.

None of these troubling predictions came true because, when my book reached bookstore shelves, the government preferred to ignore it. It probably thought that censorship was more likely to publicize it, with a consequent increase in readership. Perhaps the government also feared that the unjustifiable persecution of a respected former president would unleash a national and international scandal that would undermine the democratic image that the government was determined to project.

In part I of this book, I specify the concept of democracy that has inspired and guided my research and study of the authoritarian phenomenon; I examine the political process whereby democratic governments elected by the citizens become autocratic; and I review the events that led to the establishment of dictatorial regimes in Venezuela, Bolivia, Nicaragua, and El Salvador, during the governments of Chávez and Maduro, Morales, Ortega, and Bukele. In part II, I analyze the means used by Ecuadorian president Rafael Correa to disregard the constitutional order and replace it with another, which would allow him to control all branches of government. In part III, I study how democratic institutions gradually lost independence, substance, and authority and ended up becoming appendages of the Presidency of the Republic. In part IV, I describe the role played by the international community, study the causes of the resurgence of authoritarian caudillismo, and examine the disparate political paths followed in recent years by the countries studied herein.

Due to the contemporary nature of the events, the main sources consulted were documentary: information published in newspapers and magazines, broadcast on television and radio, or posted on the Internet. During the confinement caused by the coronavirus pandemic, these sources proved not only extremely useful but also vital. I also used the notes I began to take when Hugo Chávez was elected president of Venezuela and Rafael Correa appeared on the political scene in Ecuador. Unlike the former, Correa was a young protester who, despite having had the singular opportunity to learn about the exemplary European and American democracies, lacked democratic principles and values.

The content of this book is limited to the political sphere and specifically to the effects suffered by democratic institutions, public liberties, and human rights. For this reason, I do not deal with the works, programs, and projects carried out by the aforementioned governments, nor do I deal with the economic and international policies they implemented. However, due to its political repercussions, one exception is my consideration of the rampant phenomenon of corruption.

Dictatorships in Twenty-First-Century Latin America is the third book I have written while fighting political battles against authoritarianism. *La victoria del No* (1986) and *La dictadura civil* (1988) were both published during the government of President León Febres Cordero. Just as in the past, besides observing Correa's government from an academic perspective, I have participated in the political debate and censured its authoritarian excesses. I have done that as well with the governments of Chávez and Maduro, Morales, and Ortega. In view of this type of involvement, I have taken special care so that this text will reflect the work of the researcher, with more than fifty years in the profession, rather than the positions of the politician impugning the dictatorships of the twenty-first century. In any case, it will be up to the readers to draw their own conclusions about the objectivity and validity of my analyses.

When I wrote the first manuscript between 2011 and 2012, for scholars, political leaders, and public opinion in Latin America and other regions of the world, the governments studied herein were democratic, and no one would have thought about labeling them dictatorial. Few questioned their systematic abuses of power, not even their effects on human rights and the freedoms of expression and protest. Some even went so far as to justify their excesses, with the excuse that Latin America finally had leaders willing to renew discredited policies, improve the democratic system, carry out a profound social transformation, and put the state at the service of the neediest. Fortunately for the future of Latin American democracy, this is not what many of them now think.

Two decades after the rebirth of Latin American authoritarianism, the repressive system implemented in Venezuela, Nicaragua, and Bolivia continues to thrive and, in the case of the first two, has become tyrannical. It has even extended to the Republic of El Salvador, and the Brazilian government is no stranger to some of its manifestations. In Ecuador, on the other hand, democratic institutions were reestablished by President Lenín Moreno, despite the fact that his predecessor had anointed him to ensure the preservation of the dictatorial legacy.

Such has been the advance of the authoritarian wave in the American hemisphere that even the world's oldest and soundest democracy did not manage to escape its pernicious scourges during the government of President Donald Trump. However, unlike what happened in Latin America, democracy managed to save itself in the United States, thanks to the strength of its institutions, as seen in the independence of election officials and the civic behavior of its leaders and most of its citizens.

Meanwhile, Belarus president Aleksandr Lukashenko, Hungarian prime minister Viktor Orban, Polish prime minister Mateusz Morawiecki, Russian president Vladimir Putin, and Turkish president Recep Tayyip Erdogan have all succumbed to the temptation of authoritarianism.[2] In those countries and many others, the rule of law has either declined or disappeared.

Just like Cuba, Latin America's twenty-first-century dictatorships justified and backed the invasions of Ukraine territory by Russian Federation troops in an undeclared war launched by Russian dictator Vladimir Putin in February 2022. This inhumane position of the dictators of Bolivia, El Salvador, Nicaragua, and Venezuela was reaffirmed at a session of the United Nations General Assembly when they did not vote in favor of the resolution approved by more than two-thirds of the countries from around the world, demanding the "immediate and unconditional" withdrawal of the attacking army. Venezuela could not vote because it was in arrears in its payments to the international organization.

Quito, April 2022

NOTES

1. The think tank I founded after completing my term in office as president of Ecuador in 1984, to research and debate the country's economic, social, and political problems.

2. I have not included Brazilian president Jair Bolsonaro on this list because, even though he uses authoritarian discourse and attitudes, he has not attempted to undermine the constituent elements of democracy and the rule of law.

Acknowledgments

I would like to express my special gratitude to the Corporation for Development Studies (Corporación de Estudios para el Desarrollo, CORDES). As has occurred with the other books I have authored since leaving office as president of Ecuador, thanks to CORDES I have been able to have the time and means I needed to undertake the study of the dictatorial anomaly that has affected the people of Venezuela, Bolivia, Nicaragua, Ecuador, and El Salvador during the twenty-first century.

In this task, the collaboration of Patricio Donoso Hurtado was key. In addition to being a diligent and insightful researcher, he reviewed the citations and footnotes, compiled the bibliography, and made helpful observations on the manuscript. These contributions made him an invaluable first editor of this text. Unfortunately, he died a few months after the presentation of the first edition in Spanish, as the result of the sudden onset of a terminal cancer.

I would also like to thank Carlos Sánchez Berzaín, Edmundo Jarquín, Asdrúbal Aguiar, and Beatrice Rangel for generously taking a pause in their day-to-day responsibilities to read and comment on the chapters referring to their home countries of Bolivia, Nicaragua, and Venezuela, as well as for their patient willingness to answer questions in order for me to be accurate in my analysis of the facts. For many years, all four of them have been aligned with defending the ideals of democracy, freedom, and human rights in Latin America.

And, of course, I must thank Jorge Castañeda, Abraham Lowenthal, and Moisés Naím, who graciously agreed to present this book to Spanish-speaking readers.

I also occasionally relied on collaboration from CORDES researchers Daniel Baquero, José Mieles, and Diego Guerra and from University of Navarra student Macarena Pachano.

Finally, I would like to express my appreciation to my dear friend and fellow scholar Nick Mills and to translator Barbara Sipe for their support in producing this English edition of the updated version of my original book.

PART I

New Forms of Dictatorship

Chapter 1

The Concept of Democracy

Democracy is not only the concept of "government of the people, by the people, and for the people," in keeping with Abraham Lincoln's authoritative definition. It is also a political system made up of a network of institutions designed to divide power, prevent its excesses, oversee its legal and honest exercise, regulate citizens' participation in public affairs, and guarantee their rights and freedoms. These and other elements of the democratic system make up the rule of law, defined by each political society in its constitution and in the laws approved by the people or their representatives in assemblies and congresses.

The main characteristics of democracy are mentioned briefly below:

- In the exercise of their functions, democratic governments and the authorities that represent them are subject to a set of legal norms whose rules they must respect and guarantee, as must individuals, the organizations they form, and society in general.
- Power is limited, divided among the executive, legislative, and judicial functions, and it is subject to various forms of control (checks and balances) in order to prevent and correct any deviations and abuses that may occur.
- The judiciary is independent of the other branches of government, is not subject to government interference or tutelage of any kind, and acts independently of economic interests and political influences.
- The freedoms, rights, and guarantees of individuals, minorities, and the different organizations they form are fully guaranteed, as well as citizens' equality before the law.
- Because they are responsible for their actions, the authorities must be accountable to the people through the legislative function, the oversight agencies, and media scrutiny.

- Also guaranteed are ideological and political pluralism; social, cultural, economic, and ethnic diversity; and the multiple ways societies express themselves.
- Ideologies, parties, and political leaders alternate in the exercise of government, without marginalization or exclusion, to ensure a pluralistic democratic society and renewal in the public sphere.
- National and local authorities are elected in periodic, free, and competitive elections, by means of citizens' secret ballots collected in a transparent manner by impartial and independent election boards.
- The people are consulted on transcendental matters of general interest, through plebiscites and referendums, and have the power to revoke the mandate of the authorities they have elected.

At the end of the twentieth century, several factors—the tragic experience of some Latin American countries during the military dictatorships of the 1970s and 1980s, the need to break the pernicious vicious circle of democracy–dictatorship, and the rarity of the democratic system in almost all Latin American and Caribbean countries—led the governments of the hemisphere to conceive of a legal instrument that would oblige states to implement and defend democracy. Approved on September 11, 2001, by a special session of the OAS General Assembly, held in Lima, that instrument was called the Inter-American Democratic Charter. The thirty-six countries that adopted it, from the Caribbean and the north, center, and south of the Americas, pledged to respect and comply with it. Then-president Hugo Chávez Frías signed this charter in representation of Venezuela. Its most important provisions are as follows:

Article 3

Essential elements of representative democracy include, inter alia, respect for human rights and fundamental freedoms, access to and the exercise of power in accordance with the rule of law, the holding of periodic, free, and fair elections based on secret balloting and universal suffrage as an expression of the sovereignty of the people, the pluralistic system of political parties and organizations, and the separation of powers and independence of the branches of government.

Article 4

Transparency in government activities, probity, responsible public administration on the part of governments, respect for social rights, and freedom of expression and of the press are essential components of the exercise of democracy. The constitutional subordination of all state institutions to the legally constituted civilian authority and respect for the rule of law on the part of all institutions and sectors of society are equally essential to democracy.

Article 5

The strengthening of political parties and other political organizations is a priority for democracy. Special attention will be paid to the problems associated with the high cost of election campaigns and the establishment of a balanced and transparent system for their financing.

Article 6

It is the right and responsibility of all citizens to participate in decisions relating to their own development. This is also a necessary condition for the full and effective exercise of democracy. Promoting and fostering diverse forms of participation strengthens democracy.

Article 7

Democracy is indispensable for the effective exercise of fundamental freedoms and human rights in their universality, indivisibility and interdependence, embodied in the respective constitutions of states and in inter-American and international human rights instruments.

These principles, institutions, and norms, on which the democratic system is based, are present in representative democracy, also known as liberal democracy, and have guided the exercise of Latin American governments in recent decades, with the exceptions of Cuba, Venezuela, Bolivia, Nicaragua, and Ecuador and later El Salvador, as will be seen in the following pages.

Meanwhile, democracy has been the backdrop for the significant development achieved by some nations around the world during the twentieth century and thus far in the twenty-first century. The peoples of Europe, North America, Oceania, and Japan achieved prosperity under its protective umbrella, and more recently the countries of Central Europe, Asia, Latin America, and Africa. The fact that the U.S. democracy is the oldest and most stable on the planet is due to the remarkable economic and social progress achieved by its people and to its status as a leading world power since the mid-twentieth century. Democracy made it possible to rebuild Japan and the European countries devastated by World War II and led as well to the economic miracles of Italy, Spain, Ireland, the Baltic countries, Chile, and the so-called Asian tigers: South Korea, Singapore, Taiwan, and Hong Kong.

Furthermore, India—the planet's second most populous nation—has begun to leave behind the extreme poverty of its inhabitants, thanks to the country's sound and stable democracy.

The economically and socially advanced nations worldwide are those that have enjoyed the most years of democracy, while the backward ones correspond to countries that were governed by dictatorships for a long time. Examples of these in Latin America are Haiti, Nicaragua, Honduras, Paraguay, and Bolivia; in Africa, most nations. The dictatorial regime that has accompanied the governments of Chávez and Maduro has had much to do with the tragic economic and social regression of the formerly prosperous Venezuela and with the poverty affecting four-fifths of its population. Chile, Uruguay, and Costa Rica—Latin American countries in the low-corruption segment—are at the same time the most stable democracies in the region. The successful African economies of Ivory Coast (Côte d'Ivoire), Ghana, and Botswana have been led by democratic governments. This is not a quirk of history but the result of lessons learned from the human tragedies wrought by European fascisms and the tyrannical dictatorships that ruled and plundered some Third World countries. In the twenty-first century, two-thirds of the earth's inhabitants have chosen to live under the wide umbrella of democratic institutions.

The case of populous China, governed by the powerful and lifelong secretary-general of the Communist Party, is often cited to deny this virtuous relationship between democracy and development. In barely four decades, China has gone from being a poor and backward society in which millions of Chinese starved to death to being the world's second largest economy. Thanks to this achievement, it has managed to massively reduce poverty to an extent unprecedented in the history of humanity: by approximately 700 million people. Although there are many reasons for the anomaly of China, such as the adoption of the capitalist economic model and the substantial contribution of foreign investment and technologies, it is possible that in the future the personal fulfillment of its citizens will require the mediation of democratic institutions. In any case, although it is significant in terms of its economy, geography, and population, China is an exception. Other nations in the same region, such as Hong Kong, Taiwan, and Singapore, developed years earlier and came to figure among the most prosperous in the world, without sacrificing democracy and losing freedom.

The following anecdote illustrates the Chinese economic miracle. When I made an official visit to China in the summer of 1984 and met with visionary Deng Xiaoping, the leader who laid the groundwork for the extraordinary progress made by his country commented to me, "Mr. President, you come from a rich country. Mine is a poor country."

In the first decades of the twentieth century in Russia and other Eastern European countries—and during the following decades in Italy, Germany, and Spain; at the start of the twenty-first century in Venezuela, Bolivia, Nicaragua, and Ecuador; and twenty years later in El Salvador—parties, intellectuals, social organizations, and political leaders seized power with the discourse that they intended to build a new and better democracy. Instead, what they did was establish single-party, single-minded dictatorships led by autocrats who intended to rule eternally while despotically oppressing the citizens. During their long terms of office, instead of perfecting representative democracy or establishing better-quality democracy, they implemented dictatorial, totalitarian political regimes that caused their peoples all kinds of suffering. In Europe, Nazism led to World War II, and in Latin America the dictatorships of Nicolás Maduro and Daniel Ortega have committed all sorts of crimes.

In light of the aforementioned democratic principles and precepts, the following pages will analyze the process whereby democracy was replaced by a dictatorial system during the governments of Chávez and Maduro, Evo Morales, Daniel Ortega, Rafael Correa, and Nayib Bukele. Indeed, the rule of law, division of power, judiciary independence, accountability, political pluralism, alternation in government, and election transparency disappeared during their prolonged terms in power. These shortcomings were compounded by restrictions on rights and freedoms, particularly freedom of expression, alongside serious and egregious violations of human rights in Venezuela and Nicaragua.

Chapter 2

From Military Dictatorships to Civilian Dictatorships

In Latin America, until the dawn of the new millennium, when twenty-first-century socialism appeared, the military had been the executors and beneficiaries of coups. Taking advantage of the power of the military structure and the privilege of having a monopoly on arms, they disregarded constitutional order, ousted presidents elected by the people, assumed all the powers of the state, and installed dictatorial governments.

During the nineteenth century and the first half of the twentieth century, dictators came to power in two different ways. Some removed constitutional presidents, shut down the national congresses, and set up autocratic governments, usually headed by one or more military commanders. Others, after being elected by the people, set aside the constitutional order, proclaimed themselves supreme leaders, and remained in power indefinitely by means of fraudulent elections. Although they were in a position to govern at will, issue whatever laws they wished, and impose their all-powerful will, they nominally retained the constitution they had trampled on as long as it did not oppose their political objectives, or they convened constituent assemblies that, in addition to confirming them as heads of state, drew up constitutions to their liking, sometimes approved in referendums. Some despots managed to stay in power for many years and intended to rule for life, such as Juan Vicente Gómez in Venezuela, Alfredo Stroessner in Paraguay, Porfirio Díaz in Mexico, and the Somoza dynasty in Nicaragua.

In the second half of the twentieth century, the dictator-caudillos were replaced by military juntas, made up of the most senior officers of the armed forces, who were entrusted by that institution to govern on its behalf. Those established in Peru and Ecuador took power driven by the need to carry out economic and social reforms that would benefit the popular sectors. Those established in Argentina, Brazil, and Uruguay did so to combat guerrilla groups seeking to form revolutionary Marxist-Leninist governments. The one

9

that took power in Chile sought to overthrow that type of government elected by the people. These latter governments incurred serious human rights violations that included the torture, murder, and disappearance of thousands of opponents. Some dictatorships voluntarily returned power to civilians by calling for general elections, most notably the Ecuadorian dictatorship in 1979.

Fidel Castro's dictatorship in Cuba was different from all the previous ones in the history of Latin America, except for the fact that, like other Latin American caudillos, he ruled his country for life, for almost half a century. Although he resigned in 2008 and transferred power to his brother Raúl, he continued to be the top government authority until his death in 2016.

In 1959, a small group of young and inexperienced guerrillas accomplished the military feat of defeating Cuba's regular army and overthrowing dictator Fulgencio Batista. Instead of reestablishing democracy, a goal for which many Cubans had fought, Fidel Castro established a supposed proletariat dictatorship, which in reality was a dictatorship of himself and the Communist Party. As in any regime of this nature, none of the institutions of representative democracy existed, and the freedoms, rights, and guarantees of a democratic society were eliminated. Until the last executions carried out in 2003, more than three thousand individuals had been executed for being "enemies of the Revolution," initially without any judicial proceeding and later without a fair trial. Many more suffered imprisonment, torture, and all kinds of persecution for having committed the "grave crime" of dissent. Now, seventy years after the Cuban Revolution began, a country once considered one of the most advanced in Latin America is among the poorest and most backward.[1]

Until the appearance of the Bolivarian dictators of twenty-first-century socialism, General Augusto Pinochet had been the last Latin American dictator. With the backing of the military and the police, he overthrew the constitutional government of President Salvador Allende (1973) in a bloody coup, proclaimed himself supreme leader of the nation, dissolved the national congress, banned political parties, and ruled Chile for seventeen years. The military junta he presided over ordered a commission to prepare a draft constitution with a transitory provision in which he was named president of the republic for a period of eight years. These proposals were submitted to a popular vote and were approved by more than two-thirds of the voters in the 1980 referendum, in part due to unpleasant memories of the government of President Salvador Allende, who had plunged Chile into economic, social, and political chaos and whose revolutionary followers had waged a bitter class struggle in an attempt to replace the democratic government with a proletariat dictatorship. With the acquiescence of the media, the positive results of the management of the economy, and certain improvements in social welfare, Pinochet sought to be reelected for eight more years. He was defeated in the 1988 plebiscite in which he ran as the only candidate, and the result was accepted. Christian Democrat leader Patricio Aylwin was elected to replace him as constitutional president, supported by the Socialist Party and other political organizations of the center-left. Due to his old age and subsequent death, Pinochet was never convicted for illicit enrichment, the torture and death of more than two thousand people, and the "disappearance" of more than one thousand others—crimes carried out by the military and police security apparatus of the dictatorship.[2]

The collapse of the Unidad Popular socialist project in Chile was followed by the Salvadoran guerrillas' integration into democratic life; the defeat of guerrilla welfare (*foquismo*) in Argentina, Uruguay, and Brazil; the failure of the Sandinista experiment in Nicaragua; and the dismantling of the powerful Peruvian guerrilla group Sendero Luminoso ("Shining Path"). By the end of the century, with the exception of the Colombian FARC, all the revolutionary guerrilla movements had been integrated into the democratic life of their countries. In view of the demise of the various Marxist-Leninist revolutionary projects that the ultraleft social and political organizations had tried to impose by force in Latin America, Marxist ideas came to occupy a marginal place in the region's political debates.

It did not take many years for revolutionary projects to return to Latin American politics once former military coup leader Hugo Chávez was elected president of Venezuela. Under the name of twenty-first-century socialism, in scarcely five years Chavismo spread beyond Venezuela to countries in the Andean region and Central America, with the election of Presidents Evo Morales in Bolivia, Daniel Ortega in Nicaragua, and Rafael Correa in Ecuador.

Venezuelan president Hugo Chavez, upon assuming power in 1999, disregarded the constitutional order under which he was elected. This is what the presidents of Bolivia and Ecuador also did at the time (but not the president of Nicaragua, who used other means to achieve the same end). They then announced their decision to found a new, "participatory" democracy by issuing a constitution to be approved by a constituent assembly. What this legal body actually did was create an authoritarian legal institutionality that would be used by the Bolivarian presidents to control all the powers of the state. Once the rule of law was abolished and an autocratic regime was established in its place, they governed their countries as they pleased, and indefinitely, just as the caudillo-dictators of yesteryear had done. Those who proceeded in this way were not ambitious military leaders nor high-level commanders from the armed forces, but rather civilian politicians[3] elected by citizens to govern their countries while respecting constitutional mandates, abiding by laws, and applying sound practices.

These surprising political events, which would lead to the return of recurrent Latin American authoritarianism, occurred at a time when, with only one exception, democratic institutions ruled for the first time in all Latin America and many believed that they would remain forever.

It is often said that the authoritarian political model analyzed in the preceding pages was influenced by the ideological conceptions, political definitions, and strategic approaches of the so-called Sao Paulo Forum.[4] There is no evidence that this group played a role in the gestation and development of the political processes that brought Hugo Chávez, Evo Morales, Daniel Ortega, and Rafael Correa to power. Rather, the propitious economic, social, and political conditions of each country and the fortuitous appearance of shrewd, demagogic, populist, and charismatic leaders played a role. So did the widespread support of the balkanized Marxist Left, which was very limited in terms of electoral representation but very strong in political activism and social mobilization. Finally, the ideas that members of the Left had been defending and promoting since the beginning of the twentieth century—as detractors of American imperialism, opposed to the market and economic openness and in favor of statism and redistribution of wealth—also came into play.

Hugo Chávez did not invent the political model whereby democracies were transformed into plebiscitary dictatorships under the leadership of a civilian caudillo elected by the people through the malicious use of democratic institutions. This had been conceived and instituted decades before by the autocrats who ruled Italy and Germany in the early twentieth century. The Latin American manifestations only added certain vernacular elements to the European fascist model, such as traditional caudillismo, atavistic paternalism, utilitarian clientelism, profitable populism, and the old anti-imperialism.

Fascism was conceived and implemented in the 1920s in Italy by *duce* Benito Mussolini and in the 1930s in Germany by *führer* Adolf Hitler, supported by the vertical and hegemonic Fascist and Nazi Parties. In these countries, as in Bolivia, Ecuador, Nicaragua, and Venezuela in the late twentieth century and early twenty-first century, rulers elected by the people transgressed democratic institutions and, after debasing these, established dictatorships that allowed them to perpetuate themselves in power and rule dictatorially.

The Italian and German peoples, driven by economic and social demands and motivated by nationalist proclamations, placed absolute power in the hands of Mussolini and Hitler by plebiscite. These rulers then used that power to eliminate citizens' freedoms, violate human rights, carry out the Jewish holocaust, and unleash the Second World War, in which fifty-five million people died, half of them civilians.

The dictatorships of the twenty-first century also have a certain similarity to Spain's Falangism, a partisan instrument used by Francisco Franco to wield absolute power and rule for decades until his death. Its constituent elements were a reverential cult to the caudillo; unconditional respect for his authority; a political monopoly of a single party; trade union verticalism; control of the media, information, and public opinion; subordination of all manifestations of national life to the interests of the government; and the restriction of citizens' freedoms, rights, and guarantees.

The political model used by the dictatorships of the twenty-first century to get rid of the constitutional order and obtain the approval of one that would grant them excessive power, by calling a constituent assembly in charge of drafting a constitution tailored to their ambitions, had been tested years before in Peru by President Alberto Fujimori. In 1992, two years after being elected in free elections, with the excuse that the established legal order prevented him from "making the changes Peru needed," he dissolved the National Congress and dismissed the judiciary and the Constitutional Court by means of a self-coup. He then summoned a Constituent Congress, which he ordered to draw up a constitution to his liking, approved in a 1993 referendum with 52 percent of the valid votes. In that constitution, the legislative and oversight powers of the congress were reduced, and the immediate reelection of the president was authorized. When Fujimori was about to finish his second term, in order to run for a third, by decree he manipulated the constitution so that his first election would not be taken into account. His government ended abruptly in 2000, when he was forced to leave the country after the discovery of the corruption network that he had set up to persecute, extort, and bribe opponents, journalists, and the media in order to put them at the service of his political interests. He was sentenced to twenty-five years in prison for embezzlement, interference in private communications, violation of human rights, and various abuses of power, and for being the "perpetrator by proxy" of the murder of citizens.[5]

NOTES

1. The Cuban dictatorship will not be studied herein since it corresponds to a political model different from those of the twenty-first-century dictatorships. Castro's power did not originate in citizens' votes, was not supported by them, and did not rely on democratic institutions to become an absolute power and govern for life.

2. The military did not kill Allende, as initially posited. Years later his suicide was proven, based on testimony given by his physician. In the months and years following the coup, opposition leaders were assassinated, including former army commander General Prats and former socialist minister Orlando Letelier. Forty-five years later, after a long judicial process, it was also discovered that former Christian Democrat president Eduardo Frei Montalva had been assassinated as well: as he recovered from

minor surgery in a Santiago hospital, members of military intelligence injected him with bacteria that led to a fatal case of septicemia.

3. Since Chávez was no longer an officer in the armed forces, he can be considered a civilian politician.

4. Called by Brazilian president Lula da Silva and the Workers Party (Partido de los Trabajadores, PT), the Sao Paulo Forum met in that city for the first time in 1990. Forty-eight Latin American and Caribbean leftist organizations that self-identified as socialist, democratic, popular, and anti-imperialist took part. They agreed to seek alternatives to imperialism and neoliberal capitalism as well as responses to the wake of suffering, misery, backwardness, and antidemocratic oppression derived therefrom. Apparently, the idea to create this forum came from Fidel Castro and was conveyed to Lula da Silva during a visit the latter had made to Havana a few months earlier.

5. Fujimori was pardoned by President Pedro Pablo Kuczynski, alleging humanitarian reasons. That pardon was revoked in 2018, but Fujimori was placed under house arrest rather than sent back to prison. In 2022, the pardon was reissued by the Constitutional Court.

Chapter 3

Dictatorships of the Twenty-First Century

By the end of the twentieth century, Latin American revolutionary projects had lost the charm they once held among intellectuals, student movements, workers' organizations, progressive sectors, and citizens inspired by the utopia of building egalitarian societies. Powerful reasons were at play: the failure of the armed road to power taken by Marxist-inspired insurrection groups, the economic collapse caused by Nicaragua's Sandinista movement, the collapse of the Soviet Union and its satellite socialist governments, the economic and social stagnation of Cuba, and the visionary Deng Xiaoping's adoption of capitalist economics for the communist government of China.

Ignoring these realities and spurred by their voluntarism, Chávez, Morales, Ortega, and Correa, the new leaders of the Latin American Left, set out to show the world that the idea of economic and social egalitarianism had not died with the fall of the Berlin Wall.

It was not a political cadre seasoned in a revolutionary struggle that resurrected the failed political projects of the Latin American radical Left and that gave Marxists, neo-Marxists, and left-wing Christians the opportunity to climb out of the ideological and political pit into which they had fallen and to take power in their countries. Rather, the lifeline came from the highly criticized military establishment, until then reviled by the revolutionaries for being an ally of oligarchies and imperialism.

Without their even having imagined it, the power of the state suddenly fell freely into revolutionaries' hands. Unlike what had happened in Cuba, they won it at the ballot box through large popular votes. The first who managed to achieve this unexpected political feat was Colonel Hugo Chávez Frías, who was elected president of Venezuela in 1998 with support from leftist sectors and other political inclinations, some even antagonistic. Nevertheless, both then and later he affirmed that ideologically he was taking a "third way," neither socialist nor capitalist. He criticized Marxism as a "dogma of the past" and declared himself to be a nationalist and a revolutionary.

This surprising victory of the revolutionary political forces soon extended beyond the borders of Bolivar's homeland and was emulated by the coca-growing Indigenous leader Evo Morales in Bolivia (2005), by former Sandinista guerrilla member Daniel Ortega in Nicaragua (2006), and by young university professor Rafael Correa in Ecuador (2006).

In all four countries, the twenty-first-century socialists faced major challenges. Rich Venezuela had enormous oil and mineral deposits, and the price of crude oil was recovering on the international market, but social inequalities were significant, and democracy had lost the support provided by a sound party system. Bolivia also possessed vast mineral and gas resources, but it was the Latin American country with the highest percentage of Indigenous populations, who were largely marginalized from progress even though there was now a political leader from this ethnic group. Ecuador also had coveted oil and was soon to produce gold, silver, and copper; its party system had collapsed; and a well-organized and influential Indigenous movement was operating in the social arena. Nicaragua, one of the poorest and most backward countries in Latin America, had a majority revolutionary party, the Sandinista Party, which, despite not having achieved the social transformation offered in its government, had managed to regain power in the next elections.

In the external sphere, a positive international environment was offering high prices for the exports of the four countries. Such a context was more than propitious for those who intended to transform these societies from their foundations up. Unlike what had happened with the democratic governments that had lacked economic resources, they would have enormous assets to finance and carry out their revolutionary projects and programs.

Moreover, they were encouraged by the voluntarism that usually accompanies those who, having had no governmental experience, believe that anything is possible with power. When it came to implementing the transformations they had offered the people, they believed that their commitment and daring would suffice to overcome all the problems, difficulties, and obstacles that might stand in their way—among these, the constitutional, legal, political, moral, economic, and international restrictions that usually condition the exercise of democratic governments.

Unlike the European Left, much of the Latin American Left had not abandoned its objections to representative democracy, nor had it resolved to conduct its political struggle within the confines of republican institutions. Many continued to discredit representative democracy as bourgeois, oligarchic, merely formal, at the service of the ruling class, and contrary to the interests of the people. Therefore, once in power, they were determined to replace it with an open, popular, and participatory democracy to be designed in constituent assemblies convened for that purpose. In the constitutions they planned to prepare, they would lay the legal foundations for the economic and social transformations offered to the voters, which would have been impossible to achieve with the constitutions in place. However, this was not the case with Ortega, who opted to reform the constitution in effect for different, quite personal, purposes, since it had been dictated by the Sandinistas when they took power in the late 1970s.

Riding the popular wave unleashed by the caudillos' election wins, and outside the constitutional order in place, they called for popular consultations for the citizens to approve convening a constituent assembly. They won these resoundingly, as well as the elections subsequently held to form it, with a parliamentary majority that allowed them to impose their ideas without hesitation. Since the new constitutions had to be tailored to the interests and ambitions of the president of the republic, following his instructions, provisions were approved granting him excessive powers, which he would eventually use to subordinate all the institutions of the state to his authority.

The texts contained in the new constitutions did not result from a pluralistic democratic debate held by the parties represented in the constituent assembly, but rather from the dogmatic imposition of the government majority, sometimes without even a parliamentary debate and usually by means of unanimous voting by a show of hands. Therefore, the constitutions issued were the expression not of the ideological plurality inherent to democratic societies but rather of the political project of the ruling party and the ambitions of each of the emerging caudillos.

Spanish academics from the Center for Political and Social Studies (CEPS for its acronym in Spanish) of the University of Valencia were involved in defining the new institutions for the constitutions of Venezuela, Bolivia, and Ecuador. They advised the members of the constituent assemblies, wrote their speeches, supported their positions, and even drafted some constitutional provisions themselves.[1]

In the referendums called for that purpose, the people approved these antidemocratic constitutions by majorities as large as two-thirds of the voters—not because of what the constitutions said and not because of their desirability, but because of the blind trust placed in the leadership of those who had asked the voters to approve them. Moreover, citizens were told that if the revolution did not have a new constitution, it would be impossible to eliminate social injustices, implement economic reforms, and attend to the needs of the poor. Instead, however, the broad powers assigned to them in the new constitutions were used by Chávez, Morales, and Correa to circumvent laws, subjugate the legislative function, take control of the justice system, subordinate oversight bodies, restrict rights and freedoms, limit or abolish political pluralism, evade accountability, manipulate electoral processes, hinder political alternation in office, and exercise unlimited power.

As the new constitutions soon ended up bothering them, despite having been drafted according to their wishes, these presidents disregarded them as often as they wished. They interpreted the texts in a self-serving and malicious manner, ordered submissive congresses and assemblies to make ad hoc reforms, or simply ignored the constitutions and proceeded as if the constitutional provisions did not exist. The tenor of the constitutional provisions was one thing, and the meaning and interpretation given to them by those in power was another. The new caudillos even went so far as to modify constitutions through lower-level legal norms contained in laws passed by the legislative bodies or in regulations and presidential decrees. In short, as had occurred when the military dictatorships were in power, a constitution was in force as long as it did not conflict with the revolutionary objectives of the governments. For all these reasons, it is not an exaggeration to say that the constitutions became ornamental legal norms that could be violated or interpreted according to the political interests of the twenty-first-century dictators. As a result, one of the essential elements of the democratic system disappeared: the rule of law.

In this way, the dictators were weaving a web of laws and regulations in which they trapped the democratic institutions. They were able to do so thanks to the excessive powers granted to them by a new constitution or, in the case of Nicaragua, by reforms made to the one previously in force—sometimes through obsequious legislative bodies and at other times through presidential vetoes and executive decrees, permitted in Venezuela under "enabling laws."

This was followed by the political subordination of the ordinary and constitutional justice systems and of the oversight bodies, including the attorney general's office and the comptroller's office, as well as by self-censorship or state censorship of the media and the co-optation of social and civil-society organizations in order to serve government interests.

Thus, through the systematic demolition of democratic institutions, the presidents of Venezuela, Bolivia, Nicaragua, and Ecuador created a system of political, economic, social, and cultural domination of an autocratic nature, which allowed them to govern at will. Alongside the disappearance of the democratic state, restrictions were imposed on freedoms, rights, and guarantees enshrined in the constitutions, or these were subject to discretionary application since one yardstick was used to measure fellow party members or supporters of the revolutionary cause and another was used to judge the government's opponents and critics.

Driven by the ambition to remain in the presidency forever, the new caudillos first established the immediate reelection of the president of the republic, previously prohibited by the constitutions, and then sought indefinite reelection. They thereby eliminated political parties' and leaders' alternation in power, an important democratic institution incorporated into constitutions in order to combat caudillismo. They did this through ad hoc constitutional reforms or twisted interpretations of the constitution by congresses, courts of justice, or constitutional tribunals dependent on the will of the ruling caudillo. They did not desist from their antidemocratic aims, not even when the citizens rejected them in popular consultations. They justified this arbitrary procedure with the argument that the revolution would be truncated if they were not reelected. They even claimed that indefinite reelection was a "human right"[2] of presidents in office. Something similar had been said and done by Latin American dictators in the nineteenth century and by some in the twentieth century.

Like the other caudillos in Latin America, those from the countries being examined herein would surely think it a folly—not a lesson in democratic integrity—that the first president of the United States, after governing his country for eight years, would have refused to seek a third term in office even though he could have been reelected as many times as he wished, perhaps even for life.

So that threats to the freedom of suffrage could be disguised, covered up, and legitimized, these caudillos set up electoral tribunals and courts composed solely or mostly of militants and sympathizers of the ruling party, willing to obey and execute orders. Instead of complying with the constitutional, legal, and moral obligation to safeguard equity in election processes, the integrity of voting, and transparent ballot counting, these bodies were interested in ensuring the triumph of the presidential candidate and of the other government-aligned candidates aspiring to national or local offices.

The norms guaranteeing equity in the candidates' financing, publicity, and proselytism in election campaigns were shelved, and ballot counts were no longer reliable. Moreover, electoral fraud, which had disappeared from Latin American election processes for many years, began to occur once again. In addition to these abuses, public funds and goods, state employees, and official propaganda were used to promote the government's presidential candidate and other candidates from his party. Behind this web of arbitrariness and abuses lay the Leninist political axiom that power, once obtained, cannot be questioned and, worse yet, ceded to adversaries. The ruling caudillo and his party could not lose a presidential or legislative election for any reason, nor could they lose in consultations or referendums.

In order to ensure their stay in power, they placed multiple obstacles in the way of those who could eventually become an electoral alternative and challenge them for the presidency. By means of legal trickery, they disqualified parties and candidates that could defeat those of the government, issued laws and regulations that harmed and hindered their opponents' work, arranged for fiscal investigations and persecutory trials, and mounted publicity campaigns to discredit them. For the allocation of congressional seats in plurinominal elections, the system disproportionately rewarded the lists of candidates who took first place in the voting. Thanks to this undemocratic arbitrariness, the official party, with one-third of the votes, was able to obtain more than half of the members in the national congress or assembly; with 50 percent, an absolute majority.

From this it can be concluded that under the twenty-first-century dictatorships the popular will was not only altered during ballot counting but also before and during the electoral campaigns. Despite these malicious procedures, if there was even a hint that the government candidate could be defeated, explicit electoral fraud occurred by manipulating the computerized systems. Upon noticing that the opposition's presidential candidate was leading the voting, election officials dependent on the will of the government halted information on the results, claiming damages in the electronic system that processed them. Hours later, when the system was reestablished, the official candidate was ahead in the count and was declared the winner.[3]

As had occurred during Latin American military dictatorships in previous decades, some opponents were victimized by criminal actions through the repressive government apparatus. More often, the government preferred to annihilate its opponents morally, through smear campaigns mounted by the government propaganda apparatus, with which they were professionally and morally discredited, their reputations tarnished, and their credibility in public opinion undermined. They were portrayed as defenders of the old order and spokespersons for the interests of the oligarchies, determined to prevent the curtailing of privileges and the realization of the economic and social changes sought by the people. Once the government had succeeded in silencing critics and opponents, whatever they said or denounced was questioned or simply dismissed by the citizens—regardless of how fair, true, and documented it was.

The ideological, partisan, and programmatic diversity of the pluralistic democratic society was ignored. Critics and opponents were treated as enemies who had to be silenced and not as citizens with the right to take part in the discussion of public affairs. Their remarks about the government were portrayed as conspiratorial acts or hoaxes aimed at distorting or paralyzing the government's revolutionary programs.

Opponents and critics were persecuted judicially and administratively through processes that the government forged against them for the purpose of silencing or intimidating them. They were charged with criminal offenses, tax fraud, noncompliance with labor laws, and other misdemeanors. For this, the twenty-first-century dictatorships relied on prosecutors, judges, and other officials who, instead of administering justice, proceeded according to orders they received from the authorities regarding the content of rulings and sentences. The same thing happened with those who participated in protests and demonstrations, some of whom were imprisoned, tortured, and murdered by the repressive government apparatus.

Because all the state offices were being controlled and there were no independent justice systems, courts, or officials, those who did not agree with the government could not defend themselves and could not get false accusations retracted and abusive sentences overturned. Since the defendants could do nothing in trials that did not respect due process, it was impossible for them to invalidate the arbitrary rulings and sentences of judges and other authorities and officials. In the judicial proceedings held in the interests of the government, all the procedural levels ended up ruling according to the instructions given by the dictator and his emissaries, and these instructions were sometimes shamelessly issued publicly. In light of the vulnerability and helplessness that opponents and critics felt, many (thousands in Venezuela and Nicaragua and hundreds in Bolivia) opted to seek refuge in silence or to go into exile.

This is how the governments of Venezuela, Bolivia, Ecuador, Nicaragua, and later El Salvador, originally elected by the citizens in fair and free election processes, became dictatorships. Political regimes in which the constituent elements of the democratic system (rule of law, division of power, independence of the justice system, political pluralism, alternation in power, accountability, civil liberties, and free elections) have disappeared cannot be called by any other name.

The intelligence services in the hands of the armed forces and the police were replaced by repressive and persecutory political bodies under the authority of the president of the republic. Instead of preventing and prosecuting criminal actions against individual and national security, private property, and public assets, these bodies focused their attention on the activities of those whom the government considered its critics, opponents, or enemies: political leaders, social leaders, journalists, businessmen, and civil-society activists. Violating constitutional guarantees and ignoring express prohibitions in the laws, they tapped phone calls, intercepted correspondence and electronic communications, sent anonymous intimidations, made threatening phone calls, brutally repressed protests and demonstrations, expelled people from streets and squares, imprisoned and tortured people, and carried out criminal assaults.

The control and manipulation of public opinion, through harassing official propaganda and the malicious use of social networks, became one of the government's most important policies since the president's popularity depended on his ability to remain in power and on his candidates' election wins. For this purpose, his merits, capacity, and achievements were inordinately praised;

freedom of expression was restricted or eliminated; news was distorted or falsified; and opponents were vilified. Through the concession or withdrawal of advertising contracts paid for by the government and through punitive laws that required the payment of heavy fines or indemnities, self-censorship reigned in the press, television, and radio. These circumstances led to the bankruptcy of some media outlets. All of them were forced to join the president's regular TV and radio broadcasts or to broadcast self-serving official propaganda, sometimes aimed at defaming critics and opponents. Finally, the government formed media empires by expanding the scope and number of government-owned magazines, television and radio stations, and newspapers and by expropriating private media.

Of paramount political importance was the manipulation of the people's needs and frustrations by preaching a kind of class struggle, supposedly between rich and poor, exploiters and exploited. This Marxist discourse of the Chavista presidents came to fruition as a result of economic disparities, ethnic differences, social injustices, and individual and collective resentments that had existed for centuries among broad sectors of the population. According to this discourse, with the rise of political leaders unfettered by the past, committed to popular needs, and determined to confront the ruling classes, the caudillos claimed that the exploitation of the poor would end, social justice would be implemented, and economic equity would be achieved. Inequalities would disappear, and there would never again be families with unsatisfied needs, let alone poor and indigent. In fact, this was not what happened in Venezuela, Nicaragua, Ecuador, and Bolivia, as will be seen below.

As noted previously, the Chavista presidents eliminated ideological and political pluralism, imposed a single way of thinking, surrounded the governing party with privileges, limited the rights of other party organizations, and hindered their participation. Twenty-first-century socialism was defined as the ideological expression of the people's interests and the government party as the one responsible for executing the social revolution contained in its maxims and proposed by its leaders. Other political, social, and civil-society organizations, which were stigmatized as enemies of the revolution, were persecuted, divided, or dissolved. Something similar has begun to happen in El Salvador, for different reasons, related to the authoritarianism in which caudillo governments tend to end up.

Although other political parties and movements were tolerated and allowed to participate in elections, they were subjected to constraints on their legal recognition, their proselytizing activities, and their electoral participation. The opposition parties were excluded from the most important offices of the state, and their members and sympathizers were barred from being members of ordinary courts, electoral tribunals, and constitutional courts, among other state entities. In electoral events, the participation of opposition candidates with possibilities for winning was prevented or hindered, and some who managed to run were disqualified even after being elected. In other words, the socialist caudillos of the twenty-first century used democratic institutions to govern undemocratically.

In this sectarian political environment dominated by dogmatism, intolerance, and intransigence, it was not possible to have a rational debate on public affairs, as is usually the case in democratic societies. This was not even possible in the parliament represented by a congress or an assembly, that is, the very forum that was entrusted with such responsibility through a constitutional mandate and that should bring together all ideologies and parties with popular representation. Different points of view, different figures, contrary ideas, and different realities presented or defended by the opposition and civil society were not refuted by the government using logical reasons, evidence, numbers, arguments, and facts that contradicted them. The president and his spokespersons, instead of refuting them, chose to impugn their opponents, making personal accusations and recurring to moral disparagements that had nothing to do with the subject of the debate or the issue under discussion. They also used a wide range of pejorative adjectives, which on occasion became insults. OAS Secretary General José Miguel Insulza, Latin American and U.S. presidents, and anyone who criticized the twenty-first-century dictators' behaviors and decisions were all targeted by such language.

Aware that the weapons were in the hands of the military and that they would need them to quell protests, impose their arbitrariness, and perpetuate themselves in power, the caudillos sought to politicize the military so that they would become the armed wing of their revolutionary projects. This is what happened in Venezuela and Nicaragua, countries where the military became the main support of the governments of Chávez, Maduro, and Ortega, but not in Ecuador and Bolivia, despite political pressures exerted on the military institutions, alongside constant harassment and the manipulation of promotions. In El Salvador, Bukele has raised the salaries and increased the benefits of members of the military and has used them to reinforce his intimidating political actions. The dictators took the class struggle to the barracks, promoting confrontations between officers and soldiers with accusations that the former enjoyed privileges while the latter suffered from all kinds of shortages.

Convinced that the people had entrusted them with the mission to profoundly transform their countries, the new caudillos gave government administration a messianic character that led them to count national history from the date on which they assumed power. According to the caudillos, until then governments had done little or nothing to encourage the progress of society: major physical infrastructure projects, the need to drastically reduce illiteracy and poverty, and the improvement of the well-being of the popular and middle-class sectors had been ignored. They obstinately overlooked the economic and social advances achieved over almost two hundred years, particularly in the second half of the twentieth century. They did not even acknowledge the relentless efforts made by political parties and leaders to perfect and consolidate democratic institutions. In the same way that they reduced national history to the date on which they began their mandates, they pretentiously announced that they would "refound" Venezuela, Bolivia, Nicaragua, Ecuador, and El Salvador.[4]

In order for this egomaniacal preaching to be accepted by the citizens, especially by children and young people attending primary and secondary schools, they ordered the publication of textbooks and pamphlets that distorted history and turned education into an instrument of propaganda and indoctrination.

The cult of personality for the ruling caudillo among followers and publicists depicted him to citizens as an exceptional person, full of virtues, merits, skills, knowledge, and strengths. Unlike ordinary mortals, he was intelligent, wise, courageous, honest, sensitive, caring, self-sacrificing, hard-working, infallible, and humanitarian. Thanks to these unique attributes, he was in a position to know, in a visionary way, what the people's needs and problems were and how they should be addressed and solved. Furthermore, he was always right in what he said and did, never wrong, which is why his decisions and pronouncements could not be discussed and, worse yet, criticized. In the submission of party leaders and even of high-level government officials, the utilitarian consideration that they would lose the power, pecuniary income, and privileges they had achieved if they did not venerate him also came into play. In order to honor him, monuments were erected, and museums were set up to perpetuate his memory and remind visitors of the unequaled legacy he was leaving to the homeland.

Contributing to the deification of the twenty-first-century caudillos was their reluctance to surround themselves with competent, enlightened, and honest people, and their proclivity to have individuals of little merit, limited knowledge, limited talent, no experience, and fragile moral principles at their side. Those who met these requirements had a clear path for ascending to the high-level positions of vice presidents, ministers, parliamentarians, magistrates, governors, diplomats, and directors of public enterprises. Aware of how difficult it had been for them to occupy a public function in previous governments, and grateful for the distinctions bestowed on them, they felt obliged to show deference and become unconditional servants of the "boss." The latter, for his part, felt safe and confident by having such individuals at his side, since none would dare to dispute his leadership and they would always be ready to second anything he said, ordered, or did, no matter how foolish it might be.

The leaders of the official party and social groups, as well as government officials and militants of the revolutionary project, were subject to a rigid ideological and political verticality, due to their intellectual and psychological dependence on the caudillo. Moreover, in general they did not have their own opinion, or if they did have one, they did not express it in internal discussions and even less in public ones, especially when a decision was made or a political, economic, or international line was set, no matter how wrong or immoral it was. Some acted in this way because they believed that by expressing their points of view they would be giving the government's enemies ammunition that could be used against them, others because the unbridled fanaticism that clouded their minds and alienated their thinking made them distort the facts, ignore realities, and bury the ideals for which they had previously fought. For these reasons, they were willing to agree with whatever the leader said or did, no matter how absurd, wrong, illegal, harmful, immoral, or criminal it might be.

These limitations prevented the political parties that accompanied the Bolivarian revolution and the Sandinista revolution from being deliberative entities. Their members did not freely elect their leaders, did not renew them periodically, and did not nominate candidates for local and national elections, nor did they meet regularly to analyze the conduct of the government and its officials. In fact, they ended up becoming simple conveyor belts for the governing caudillo, for the orders given by his political operators, or for the transportation of people to support rallies. This is what happened with the Movement towards Socialism (Movimiento al Socialismo, MAS) of Bolivia, the Lofty and Sovereign Homeland Alliance (Alianza PAIS, AP) movement of Ecuador, New Ideas (Nuevas Ideas) of El Salvador, the Sandinista National Liberation Front (Frente Sandinista de Liberación Nacional, FSLN) of Nicaragua, and the United Socialist Party of Venezuela (Partido Socialista Unido de Venezuela, PSUV).

Nonetheless, the discourse of Chávez, Morales, Ortega, Correa, and Bukele—which offered to establish a new democracy, different from the elitist, bourgeois, and merely formal democracy they had inherited, a new democracy in which the people would participate directly in government decisions—did not become a reality. Neither did the promise that they would turn the people into authors of their own destiny through their permanent participation in government decisions. On the contrary, they concentrated power and decision making, even secondary decision making, in the president of the republic, so ministers and other high-level officials became mere executors of authoritarian orders.

The twenty-first-century dictatorships have demonstrated just how true is John Dalberg-Acton's dictum that "power corrupts and absolute power corrupts absolutely." They have created political, legal, economic, and judicial conditions for corruption to displace laws and oversight bodies, proliferate, and become institutionalized. Presidents, vice presidents, ministers, judges, magistrates, prosecutors, comptrollers, superintendents, managers, and legislators were no strangers to the misappropriation of public funds. Officials who had the power to approve contracts for public works, the acquisition of goods, and the provision of services demanded the payment of bribes on a regular basis. The following situations contributed to this: the exponential increase in public spending; the broad responsibilities and powers given to the state; the restrictions on freedom of the press; the loss of independence among prosecutors, judges, and oversight authorities; the extinction of the oversight function of congresses and assemblies; the persecution of those who investigated and denounced acts of corruption; widespread impunity; and the bad example of the highest-ranking government officials. Therefore, those who profited from public funds were certain that they would never be investigated, judged, and convicted as long as they remained loyal to the ruling caudillo—so much so that Rafael Correa, his vice president, and several ministers and senior officials could only be investigated, prosecuted, and convicted for corruption after he left office.

The new caudillos were also capable of saying anything, no matter how false, inane, slanderous, hurtful, ignorant, misleading, malicious, or stupid it might be. They were capable of openly denying what they had said or done and of contradicting themselves the next day or even in the very same speech or statement, and they were capable of irately defending a position and then saying or doing the opposite. They denied evidence, ignored realities, and distorted facts. They criticized opponents' actions, behavior, and practices even though they themselves had done the same. They complemented and praised someone and then harshly criticized him. They taunted those who held well-justified positions or made accusations based on reasons, arguments, facts, and numbers. They made insults a weapon against critics and adversaries, sometimes other heads of state—many of these insults too brazen or lewd to publish. They mocked and humiliated ministers, officials, and collaborators, sometimes publicly, and blamed them for their own mistakes and failures. In sum, these twenty-first-century demagogues have lacked, and continue to lack, intellectual honesty.

Finally, the twenty-first-century dictatorships were populist, socialist, and anti-imperialist; the one in El Salvador, only populist:

- Populist, because they practiced demagogy, paternalism, clientelism, and the generous giving of gifts and benefits with ulterior motives; they stimulated and manipulated social resentment and citizens' irresponsibility; they promoted subsidies, many of them retroactive; they encouraged the squandering of public funds and managed the economy in an irresponsible manner.

- Socialist, because they broadened the responsibilities of the state, disproportionately expanded public spending, nationalized efficient private-sector production activities, increased regulation and control, drove away domestic and foreign private investment, fostered an illusory egalitarianism, promoted wealth redistribution policies, and discarded the successful market economy.
- Anti-imperialist, because they fought against the United States, scorned the world's leading economy, forged ideological alliances contrary to national interests,[5] swelled the ranks of the outdated Third World mentality, underestimated multilateral cooperation organizations, and rejected free trade.

At the Fourth Summit of the Americas, held in Mar del Plata in 2005, Venezuelan president Hugo Chávez, with his anti-imperialism discourse and gestures and support from Presidents Lula Da Silva, Néstor Kirchner, and Tabaré Vázquez, was responsible for the failure to agree on the American Free Trade Area (AFTA in English and ALCA in Spanish) proposed by U.S. president George Bush and maintained by Presidents Bill Clinton and George W. Bush. "ALCArajo" [a play on words meaning "to hell with ALCA"] was the expression that Chávez used when proclaiming his diplomatic victory.

After that frustrating incident, the United States and Canada abandoned their continental economic integration project, which would have contributed a great deal to driving development in the Latin American region—as has indeed occurred with the bilateral agreements since signed with Colombia and the Central American countries.

Years later, this irrational, sectarian, and antiquated anti-imperialism would spread beyond the borders of Venezuela, Nicaragua, Bolivia, and El Salvador, when those countries were willing to overlook the criminal invasion and abusive territorial conquest of peaceful Ukraine by Russian dictator Vladimir Putin in February 2022. The leaders in those countries did not care that the territory of a peaceful nation was being invaded, that the invader was failing to comply with a United Nations order to withdraw its military forces from the occupied territories, and that the cruel bombardments were severely affecting the human rights of the civilian population.

These supposedly anti-imperialist policies had already distanced the twenty-first-century dictators from the international democratic community and hampered their ability to take advantage of the positive international economic environments of the first decades of the twenty-first century. They also exacerbated the economic and social crises that were unleashed when this environment became unfavorable. Particularly illustrative is the case of

Venezuela, due to the catastrophic deterioration of the population's living standards caused by the huge increase in inflation, the poverty of almost its entire population, and the largest exodus in the history of Latin America. The country that became the richest on the subcontinent during its democratic governments has now become the poorest and most backward.

With their votes, citizens put the twenty-first-century dictators in office and kept them in power by reelecting them repeatedly. Sectors claiming to be progressive and leftist, including intellectuals, technocrats, members of civil society, and leaders of social and political organizations, promoted, supported, tolerated, and justified their outrages. Large, medium, and small businessmen financed their election campaigns and joined the ranks of the government—many attracted by sizeable contracts often tainted by corruption. In popular consultations, the people overwhelmingly approved rejecting the constitution in place, breaching the democratic order, convening constituent assemblies, and implementing authoritarian constitutions as well as reforms along the same lines. Few political and social leaders, journalists, and media outlets criticized, condemned, and fought against the abuses of power and the restrictions of liberties, rights, and citizen guarantees—especially in the early years.

Despite the efforts made by Chávez to extend the Bolivarian Revolution and twenty-first-century socialism to other Latin American countries, he was unable to go beyond the aforementioned countries. This was mainly because domestic economic, social, and political conditions were not propitious and also because the triumphant populist leaders he tried to seduce rejected him and chose to respect democratic institutionality. This is what happened with Lucio Gutiérrez in Ecuador (2003) and Ollanta Humala in Peru (2011). Brazil's Lula de Silva and Dilma Rousseff, Argentina's Néstor and Cristina Kirchner, and Uruguay's Tabaré Vázquez and José Mujica, despite having been political allies of the governments of Chávez, Maduro, Morales, Correa, and Ortega, respected democratic principles and adhered to their practices while governing their countries.

It took two decades for the Chavista political model—whereby a democratic government elected by the people becomes dictatorial through the malicious use of republican institutions—to emerge from the socialist cloister in which it was confined. It was not a Marxist revolutionary who adopted it but rather a young populist politician coming from the business world. Just months after taking office, the president of the Republic of El Salvador, Nayib Bukele, who had been elected by a large popular vote, decided to take the rugged authoritarian trail blazed by Chávez.

The concept of the authoritarian model implemented by the twenty-first-century dictatorships having been examined along with its constituent elements, the following chapters will study the governments that adopted it in Venezuela, Bolivia, Nicaragua, and El Salvador. The case of Ecuador will be analyzed in more detail in the second and third parts of this book. As mentioned in the preface, the study of each country will be limited to matters related to the operation of democratic institutions and the fate of the rule of law and civil liberties.

NOTES

1. Among others, Roberto Viciano, Albert Noguera, Decio Machado, Martínez Dalmau, and Marco Aparicio. Their contribution was not altruistic; they received sizeable remunerations.

2. On June 7, 2021, the Inter-American Human Rights Court ruled that an indefinite presidential reelection is "not a human right."

3. Through fraudulent actions, Nicolás Maduro managed to "defeat" Henrique Capriles in 2013 and then be reelected in 2019, Lenín Moreno defeated Guillermo Lasso in 2017, and Evo Morales defeated Carlos Mesa in 2019.

4. Chávez showily exhumed the remains of liberator Simón Bolívar to demonstrate that he had been poisoned by the oligarchy and to claim that the two of them physically resembled each other due to shared ethnic ancestors.

5. Usually with autocratic tyrants in Asia, Europe, and Africa: Kim Jong-un in North Korea, Vladimir Putin in Russia, Alexander Lukashenko in Belarus, Recep Tayyip Erdogan in Turkey, Muammar Gaddafi in Libya, Robert Mugabe in Zimbabwe, and Bashard al-Assad and his father in Syria, among others.

Chapter 4

The Governments of Hugo Chávez and Nicolás Maduro

I am the Law, I am the State, I am the People.

—Venezuelan president Hugo Chávez Frías (1999–2013)[1]

They will never be a political power in Venezuela . . . as long as the anti-imperialist, revolutionary, and Bolivarian armed forces exist.

—Venezuelan defense minister Vladimir Padrino López (2014–)[2]

Hugo Chávez Frías was born in 1954 in the bosom of a modest family of schoolteachers in a town in the state of Barinas. Together with other young comrades in arms, on December 17, 1982, under the shade of the historic Samán del Güere tree, Captain Hugo Chávez Frías swore to liberate Venezuela. To this end, within the armed forces, he formed a clandestine political organization called the Revolutionary Bolivarian Movement (Movimiento Bolivariano Revolucionario).

Ten years later, in 1992, with dozens of middle- and low-ranking officers and hundreds of soldiers under his command, Chávez tried to overthrow President Carlos Andrés Pérez through an armed assault on the Miraflores Palace, with the tragic result of thirty-two dead and ninety-five wounded. The presidential escort defeated the insurgents and forced them to surrender; this response by the loyal military saved the Democratic Action (Acción Democrática) government and Venezuelan democracy and prevented the establishment of a military dictatorship.

The rebels were arrested and accused of the crime of rebellion for attempting to depose the constitutional president through violence and arms. Chávez acknowledged the defeat, admitted his responsibility, and regretted that "for now" the "objectives" of the "Bolivarian military movement" could not be "fulfilled." He as well as other officers of his rank were charged with the intellectual authorship of the coup attempt. Shortly thereafter, almost all the insurrectionists were freed by President Carlos Andrés Pérez, who also ordered their reinstatement in the armed forces. Two years later, in 1994, Chávez and the rest of the leaders of the conspiracy recovered their freedom, thanks to a pardon granted by President Rafael Caldera that did not include their reincorporation into the ranks of the army. In 1998, Chávez won the presidential election.

The new Venezuelan leader exhibited many of the characteristics of the Latin American caudillos of the nineteenth and part of the twentieth centuries and particularly garnered a certain personality cult or hero worship. Therefore, in the economic and social transformation he proposed, Colonel Chávez's messianic conviction that he had been called by higher forces to lead a revolution that would refound Venezuela and change the fate of its inhabitants was going to weigh more than the ideas, programs, and party that would accompany his political struggle.

In the pursuit of this ideal, Chávez initially distanced himself from Marxism and then said he would seek a third way; ultimately, he anchored himself in twenty-first-century socialism. At the same time, he declared himself a Marxist and made Fidel Castro his mentor and Cuba his example to follow. In spite of this ideological wandering, what actually took place during the governments of the Venezuelan caudillo was plain and simple Chavismo.

A good part of the Venezuelan ruling class was tolerant of the military coup leader even though he had been involved in criminal offenses, had attempted to overthrow a constitutional president, and had caused the death of some thirty comrades in arms. Many justified the insubordination and quite a few endorsed the insurrectionist's political project.[3]

Chávez was supported by the electoral movement Fifth Republic (Quinta República), which he had founded, and by other leftist organizations, mostly of a Marxist orientation.[4] However, mainly thanks to the leadership role he had acquired by trying to overthrow a president who had lost his popularity, Chávez was elected president in 1998 and reelected in 2000, 2006, and 2012.[5] The fourth term never began because he died the following year due to a cancerous tumor. He also triumphed in regional and legislative elections, and in almost all the referendums he called, except for the one in 2007 regarding several constitutional reforms, whose major questions had to do with the indefinite reelection of the president and the transformation of Venezuela into a socialist society. Both of these proposals were rejected by the electorate.

During the electoral campaign, Chávez had announced his unbridled intention to refound Venezuela through profound economic and social transformations that would begin with issuing a new "Magna Carta" (constitution). Since 1991, jurists and politicians had also cited the desirability of convening a constituent assembly in order to reform the Venezuelan political system, which had declined in recent years, but naturally within the legal framework of the 1961 constitution and the election laws in place, which included involvement by the National Congress (Brewer-Carías 2018, 32–36).

Upon taking office as president, Hugo Chávez did not swear to submit his actions to the current constitution; he declared that it was "at death's door" and announced that it would be replaced.[6] For this purpose, he called for a constituent assembly, the convening of which would be consulted directly with the people. Since the 1961 constitution did not contemplate such an institution, the Supreme Court of Justice was asked to analyze the legal validity of the president of the republic's proposal. It did not do so and instead issued an ambiguous decision; since it was open to diverse interpretations, President Chávez's prevailed. Citing a provision of the Organic Law of Suffrage and Political Participation, which provided for holding consultative referendums, the day he took office (February 2, 1999), Chávez issued a decree requesting that the people approve the convening of a constituent assembly.[7] This first manifestation of the authoritarianism with which he would rule Venezuela for many years was endorsed by the National Electoral Council even though Chávez was not calling for a consultative referendum, as foreseen by the laws in place, which stipulated that, after being voted on, the people's opinion would have to be validated by the National Congress, which would require it to issue a constitutional reform.

The first question on the referendum read: "Do you call for a National Constituent Assembly for the purpose of transforming the State and creating a new legal system that allows for the functioning of a Social and Participatory Democracy?" A second question asked voters to approve the "bases" on which its members would be elected and work to fulfill the responsibility entrusted to them. Both proposals were overwhelmingly passed by the citizens, the first by 88 percent and the second by 82 percent.

In the elections held to form the Constituent Assembly, the lists of candidates from political organizations close to the government won 52 percent of the votes. However, they accounted for 95 percent of the members, partly due to the fragmentation of the opposition, but above all due to the application of an inequitable system for the allocation of seats. This system, ignoring the democratic principle of proportional representation and the electoral rights of minorities determined in the constitution, disproportionately rewarded the majority political party. This undemocratic and somehow fraudulent configuration of the Constituent Assembly left almost half of the voters (48 percent) without representation and gave President Chávez, his party, and allied organizations absolute control.

Since the Constituent Assembly was a nonexistent institution in the 1961 constitution, its attributions were not regulated. This void led to disputes with the congress regarding the respective competencies. These disputes were solved by means of a dialogue between their governing bodies, which concluded with the reciprocal recognition of the spheres that each one would cover. This process was so constructive that they arrived at a harmonious distribution of the offices that they would occupy in the Legislative Palace.

However, it was not many days before deputies and senators found access to their offices blocked by members of the national guard and activists of the nascent Chavismo. In the end, the legislators' democratic courage outweighed the violence with which they were received and the beatings they suffered, even female senators and deputies, when trying to break through the blockade and recover their seats in congress. The outrage inflicted on the legislative function led to a national and international scandal that forced Chávez to retract his decision to shut it down by means of the government's violent crowds. The congress was therefore able to continue meeting without major setbacks until the Bolivarian Constitution was written—but without being able to do anything to ensure respect for its legislative and supervising powers, stop the march of the autocratic project of Chavismo, and defend republican institutions.

The Chavista members of the Constituent Assembly used their overwhelming majority to enshrine the ideological and political postulates of twenty-first-century socialism and the Bolivarian Revolution, despite what other sectors of the political society might think. This was the first sign of the pattern with which they would govern Venezuela, violating the democratic principle that the constitution is a law for all the inhabitants of a country, not only some. The draft of the constitution finally approved by the Constituent Assembly, which Chávez hailed as "the best in the world," was "prepared and corrected" by him, according to Asdrúbal Aguiar (2012, 296).[8]

The organic part of the constitution underwent significant modifications with respect to that of 1961. It strengthened the authority of the president of the republic by establishing the possibility of immediate reelection, extending the presidential term to six years, allowing the president to dissolve the National Assembly, and empowering him to summon the people to popular consultations on a variety of matters. However, in a way, it weakened the president's authority by authorizing the revocation of his mandate by the citizens. It created a fourth power (in addition to the three classic ones: executive, legislative, and judicial), which it called the "Citizens Power," "to prevent governments and presidents from committing abuses." This power was exercised by the Republican Moral Council, composed of the comptroller, the attorney general, and the ombudsman.

Considering the impact it had on Venezuelan democracy, the Constituent Assembly's most important constitutional reform was to grant the president of the republic the power to legislate by decree in any matter after an enabling law had been issued by the National Assembly, whereby the latter surrendered its most important and most characteristic attribution: to legislate on behalf of the people, with the participation of different parties and ideologies.

The institution of enabling laws existed in the 1961 constitution but was restricted to exceptional situations and economic and financial matters. Thanks to these safeguards, over almost forty years the congress had enacted only six enabling laws, which gave rise to 172 laws by decree. So it was an institution that presidents had used only when Venezuela was experiencing critical economic and financial circumstances.

During his administration, Chávez used this privilege regularly even though he had a legislative majority willing to attend to his requirements. This power was granted to him by the National Assembly on four occasions, for a total of four years and six months, that is, one-third of the thirteen years he held office as president. In practice, in violation of the constitutional and democratic principle of the division of power, he stripped the assembly of its exclusive power to legislate. Through this legal instrument, he issued 215 laws, from which no area of national life, public or private, escaped. Many of these laws were aimed at increasing his already immense power to the detriment of other state functions and bodies.

By means of these laws, he subordinated the armed forces, police forces, and intelligence services to his authority; changed the structure of the state; gained control of autonomous, departmental, and municipal agencies; expanded the public sector of the economy, especially in the oil, electricity, mining, steel, and telecommunications fields; limited rights, liberties, and constitutional guarantees; weakened the powers of the control and oversight agencies; created and increased taxes; affected property rights; and materialized the socialist principles of the Bolivarian Revolution.

In the referendum called for the people to consider the new constitution of the Bolivarian Republic of Venezuela, more than two-thirds of the voters (72 percent) voted for its approval. In this regard, it should be noted that in the three electoral events that defined the future of Venezuelan democracy—to call for a constituent assembly, to elect its members, and to hold a referendum to ratify the new constitution—the abstention of voters on the voter registry was high, between 53 and 62 percent.

For the authoritarian project of the president of Venezuela, the political decisions of the constituent assembly were much more valuable, particularly those contained in the transitional regime issued before the new constitution was approved. As some jurists and political leaders had envisioned, it declared itself the repository of popular sovereignty, a definition that empowered it to "reorganize the State and create a new democratic legal order" and to place government institutions under its authority. In that context, it dismissed the holders of all powers, including the Supreme Court of

Justice, the National Electoral Council (CNE for its acronym in Spanish), the comptroller, the attorney general, and other high-level officials and replaced them with "provisional" magistrates who would later become permanent. Furthermore, it confirmed Chávez in the presidency—which he had placed at the disposal of the Constituent Assembly—and closed the National Congress, which was replaced by a legislative commission known as the "congresillo" (little congress).

For an authoritarian president on his way to becoming an autocrat, it was unacceptable for the plurality of democratic society to be represented in the National Congress and in the CNE and, even worse, that officials in the chambers of deputies and senators belonged to the budding opposition—even though these representatives had been chosen by the citizens in the legislative elections held simultaneously with the presidential elections.

High-level government officials, members of the Constituent Assembly, and the militants or sympathizers of the emerging Chavismo would soon come together to form the United Socialist Party of Venezuela (Partido Socialista Unido de Venezuela, PSUV), through the merger of all the political organizations that supported Chávez, many aligned with Marxism and all revolutionary. To the extent that its militants took over all state bodies, political pluralism disappeared, and Venezuelan democracy became, in fact, a single-party political regime.

As usually happens in political organizations of a vertical nature, in the PSUV there was no internal debate, no self-criticism, and even less participation by leaders and members in shaping doctrine and policy or in nominating candidates for different positions. On these matters, and many more referring to how political life and the government were conducted, there was only one voice, that of caudillo and protodictator Hugo Chávez, whom the members of the government and the Bolivarian Party had to listen to and follow in a disciplined manner. Those who ignored or contradicted him were marginalized, forced to make retractions, or removed from their functions. This presidential authoritarianism, the ostracism of dissenters, and the lack of democratic debate contradicted the postulates of "radical" democracy with which Chavismo proposed to replace the highly criticized "bourgeois," representative, formal, and liberal democracy.

By the end of his first year in office, President Hugo Chávez had managed to severely undermine some of the institutions that compose the democratic system, especially the rule of law and the division of power among the executive, legislative, and judicial branches of government. The executive function had grown stronger at the expense of a weakened legislative function. As if the National Assembly did not exist, Chávez legislated on all kinds of matters on his own and at his own whim, issuing laws by the dozens with the acquiescence of the Constituent Assembly.

Hugo Chávez had been elected by the Venezuelan people as a constitutional president and was to govern as such. He did not do so. He shelved the constitution that had guided decades of progress and freedom and came up with one of his own liking, which he did not respect either. The same thing happened with laws, which were frequently ignored or applied as a function of government interests, even those that he himself issued. Abuses of power became commonplace, as did the restriction of constitutional rights and guarantees, particularly free speech. This early authoritarian evolution of the government of the Bolivarian Revolution worsened as the months went by and ended with the democratic regime's replacement by a dictatorial regime.

In this persevering and obsessive empowerment of the president of the republic, the manipulation of public opinion through propaganda, tinged with a strong personality cult around the Venezuelan caudillo, was key. He was profusely advertised in the media or exhibited in murals painted along streets and on carts. Radio and TV stations were forced to be part of mass broadcasts whenever the government so ordered, so that citizens would be forced to listen to and watch his "dialogues with the people." In this way, he was present in Venezuelan homes daily and at all hours, saying and promising what the people wanted to hear, in the captivating language of the exceptional demagogue that Chávez was. Using these means, he managed to establish a direct and personal relationship with the voters and to be seen as one of their own, someone in whom the people could blindly trust.

In the hours-long weekly program *Aló Presidente* broadcast on radio and television on Sundays, he discussed citizens' problems and needs in colloquial language, reported on what he was doing to solve them, stirred social resentments and personal frustrations, and described the projects and programs he was implementing to eliminate poverty and correct inequalities. He also gave orders to ministers and officials; announced decisions he was about to make; discredited the media, journalists, and opponents and called for their exclusion from citizens' homes; identified the enemies of the Bolivarian Revolution; and justified outrages, arbitrariness, and abuses of power.

Chávez did not hesitate to grant interviews to the press, radio, and television, but instead of answering the questions he received from representatives of the media, he limited himself to saying whatever he pleased or digressed and made funny comments or wisecracks. Something similar happened in the debates on public affairs with political and social leaders, business spokespersons, and civil-society activists, to whom he preferred to respond with personal attacks and disparaging remarks.

So great was the popularity Chávez achieved, so great the power he concentrated in his own hands, and so great the subordination of those who served him, that ministers, managers, and officials in public offices found it normal, fair, and acceptable to submit to the instructions emanating from the

Miraflores Palace, even though some of their entities were autonomous by constitutional mandate. Those who attempted to exercise their functions independently, subject to legal and constitutional provisions and based on their know-how, were summarily dismissed. This is what had happened with the attorney general and the ombudsman, who were replaced by officials close to the government, circumventing the procedures established in the constitution (Brewer-Carías 2001, 272–73), despite the fact that the constitution provided that the attorney general's office, the comptroller's office, and the council in charge of organizing and supervising electoral processes should be nonpartisan, in order to guarantee the political independence of these bodies, their compliance with legal norms, and the integrity of their decisions.

The rule of law, the division of power, and other constituent elements of the rule of law disappeared. The president of the republic held omnipotent power, which breached the constitution and the laws and turned him into an autocrat. He built a solid and invulnerable wall to prevent the recovery of constitutional order. He restricted human rights and civil liberties, particularly free speech. The privately owned media were subject to daily harassment, sometimes tinged with violence by the government's siege groups known as the "Bolivarian Circles." It became seemingly impossible to reestablish democratic institutions and to reverse the unbridled accumulation of power in the presidency that began the day Hugo Chávez settled into the Miraflores Palace. In sum, almost all the constituent elements of the rule of law disappeared and led the opposition forces to the painful conclusion that the democratic regime was defenseless. Some of them believed that they would have to use other means to reestablish it.

This is what happened, apparently fortuitously, three years after Chávez took office as president, when a spontaneous citizens demonstration coincided with a military uprising that took place in Caracas. This would lead to the overthrow of Chávez.

Once this objective was achieved, the conspirators proposed to reestablish democracy and its institutions, for which they committed themselves, calling for presidential and legislative elections. That is how other Latin American and Venezuelan democrats had proceeded to depose nineteenth- and twentieth-century dictatorships that had denied them the right to live in a free society.

Chávez's folly in mocking respected administrators of the state oil company (PDVSA) and dismissing them with much ado was an opprobrious humiliation seen and heard by millions of Venezuelans. It put the authoritarianism of the president of the republic on display on a giant screen with a very high volume.

Such was the annoyance of ample urban sectors at this unconscionable behavior that Chávez's misstep ignited the fuse of a revolt that had been spontaneously brewing, mainly among middle-class urban sectors. On April 11, 2002, a twenty-four-hour general strike organized by the Venezuelan Workers' Confederation (Confederación de Trabajadores de Venezuela) and the employers' federation (Fedecámaras) became indefinite. A multitudinous march of the opposition, unprecedented in the history of Venezuela, changed course and headed to the presidential palace to demand Chavez's resignation, proposed days before by several military commanders, particularly air force generals and navy admirals. The popular protest was met with shots fired by Chavista snipers stationed in the vicinity of Miraflores, where the president was. It left twenty-six dead and sixty-nine wounded. In view of this bloody event, the high command ordered Chávez's arrest, confined him in a barracks, and obtained his resignation, which was voluntarily offered with the condition that he be allowed to leave the country (Aguiar 2012, 309). Later, the constitutional chamber of the Supreme Court of Justice would rule that there was no coup but rather an interruption of the constitutional order.

Supported by the military, the business community, opposition parties, the media, trade-union organizations, and the Catholic Church hierarchy, business leader Pedro Carmona took office as president. His government was ephemeral. Three days later, Chavez triumphantly returned to Caracas protected by loyal military commanders, among whom were officers who had accompanied him in the attempt to depose President Carlos Andrés Pérez by means of a military insurrection. Upon resuming the presidency and addressing Venezuelans on radio and television, he apologized for his mistakes, offered rectifications, and called for dialogue.

The reinstated president's moderated and constructive discourse did not succeed at appeasing his detractors and did not stop the popular protests of Venezuelan democrats. This was, in part, because President Chávez, besides not meeting any of the opposition's demands to reestablish healthy democratic practices, not only continued but also accentuated his authoritarianism. People in the streets were not placated, and protests, mobilizations, strikes, and work stoppages continued throughout 2002, many of them led by the union movement. One of these was declared indefinite and lasted sixty-two days. All of them were aimed at obtaining the resignation of the president, who had become one more of the many caudillos at whose hands Latin America had suffered for two centuries.

The failed coup exacerbated Chavez's megalomania and egomania, for when he succeeded at recovering power, his leadership grew stronger rather than weaker. He had inflicted a painful defeat on his powerful opponents (unions, the business community, politicians, the military, the media, and Catholic bishops) and received acclaim and support from his followers, as well as from some Latin American governments.

This experience also offered him the opportunity to identify and eliminate the military commanders who were averse to him and to replace them
with loyal officers, dependent on his will and sympathetic to the Bolivarian
Revolution, as well as to take control of the constitutional chamber of the
Supreme Court of Justice with judges he trusted and to increase the number of
its magistrates.[9] He also accelerated the process of politicization of the armed
forces, in order to turn them into the armed wing of the Bolivarian Revolution
and twenty-first-century socialism. He consolidated and expanded the
Venezuelan government's relations with Cuba, particularly in the fields of
policy, social control, and intelligence. He took absolute control of the powerful and prestigious state-owned oil company (PDVSA), from which he dismissed all its directors and fifteen thousand workers. Finally, in response to
the "boldness of the reactionary right wing," he bolstered socialist, populist,
statist, expropriationist, and anti-imperialist policies. Years later this is what
would unleash the dreadful economic, social, and humanitarian crisis that
would devastate Venezuela and impoverish its population.

In addition to controlling and politicizing the military so that they would
become the armed wing of Chavismo, he used information, communication,
and public opinion. These power factors have become decisive in contemporary democracies; in Venezuela, they were aligned with the defense of
democratic institutions and the repudiation of the reigning authoritarianism.

Chávez increased the number of radio and television stations by as many
as dozens in a couple of days, as well as the various forms of propaganda, all
centered on the caudillo's personality cult, for example, the gigantic murals in
cities and along highways. He set up a network of public media (press, radio,
and television) dependent on the government, which transformed information
into advertising and propaganda. He limited or eliminated the advertising of
public entities through media that he defined as enemies of the Bolivarian
Revolution, in order to affect the latter economically and bankrupt them.
He defamed journalists and persecuted them judicially and administratively;
some of them were even physically assaulted by Chavista mobs. He facilitated control over the Internet and social networks.

He forced self-censorship through coercion, threats, sanctions, and the
prosecution of journalists and media managers and owners. Such measures
were carried out solicitously by officials and judges subordinate to his authority. Faced with the risk of being found guilty, closed down, or nationalized,
some media opted for self-censorship, and those who persevered in their
democratic struggle were administratively and judicially persecuted, in
addition to suffering aggressions from the regime's assault groups. Dozens
of radio and television stations considered hostile to the government were
shut down, such as the influential Radio Caracas Televisión (RCTV), some
of them through the ploy of not having the licenses for their frequencies

renewed. Frequencies were granted to friends of the government and taken away from its critics.

In order to have an instrument to "legalize" restrictions on freedom of expression and the persecution of media, journalists, and opponents, Chávez issued the Law of Social Responsibility in radio, television, and electronic media and reformed the penal code. Among other crimes, the penal code criminalized repudiation of public officials, criticism of state institutions, and participation in unauthorized protests and demonstrations.

None of the above coincided with Chávez's constructive discourse upon recovering power or with the rectifications he had offered to make or with the calls for dialogue and democratic understandings. On the contrary, the violations of the constitution and the restrictions and abuses of the rights and liberties of citizens as well as social, political, business, and civil-society organizations worsened, and the president's power became absolute.

In order to escape from the dead end in which Venezuelan democracy was trapped, the opposition decided to play the card to revoke the mandate of the president of the republic. That option had been incorporated into the Bolivarian Constitution by Chavismo but not used thus far due to President Chávez's great popularity. The opposition managed to push it through despite the multiple difficulties used by the government to prevent it—among these, two annulments of the signatures that had been collected by the promoters of this initiative so that the Electoral Council would organize the recall voting.

With the endorsement of international observers, which included representatives of the OAS and the Carter Center, the government and the opposition agreed to form a new National Electoral Council, a "reliable, transparent and impartial" one, according to what was said at the time. Since the current one was under government control, it did not offer any guarantee that ballot counting during the recall vote would be honest. Chávez did not comply with this commitment and ordered his representatives to stop attending the meetings of the liaison and follow-up mechanism formed for that purpose.

Under such circumstances, a government-controlled body was to be in charge of the voting and ballot counting during the recall referendum, as had occurred in previous electoral events. That body's decisions could not be monitored and challenged by international observers and opposition delegates. Furthermore, without agreement from the opposition, the traditional manual voting system had been substituted by an easily manipulated electronic system whose aboveboard operation involved complex verification.[10]

In fact, at the last minute, the opposition warned that thousands of new voters had been incorporated or eliminated from the voter registry, supposedly because they had died, and more than one million had been moved to voting precincts far from their homes. Those in charge of these polling places had been replaced by militants of the Bolivarian Revolution. Such irregularities were easy to forge because the government had the identity records of those who had signed the request for the recall referendum (Aguiar 2005). All this also benefited from the artful use of state institutions, resources, money, and personnel to promote the vote in favor of having Chávez remain president.

Despite these serious irregularities, several exit polls taken among voters on the afternoon of election day indicated that the recall was winning, by up to 19 percentage points according to the polling firm Súmate. However, early in the evening, before voting ended, CNE officials informed the international press that Chávez had won. At the same time, the government mounted a national and international information campaign to position the supposed victory. It prohibited international observers and opposition representatives from entering the venue where the computations were being made, and it did not comply with the agreement to carry out an immediate audit of the results that the electoral authorities were about to make official (Aguiar 2005).

In the early morning of the following day, according to the author cited previously, to the surprise of OAS Secretary General César Gaviria and of the opposition representatives, Jimmy Carter "joyfully" informed them that Hugo Chávez had won the referendum. Earlier, it had been possible to have some privately owned media be neutral in the referendum campaign, but the former U.S. president did not demand such conduct from the official media. Shortly thereafter, through a nationwide radio and television address, the CNE president informed Venezuelans of the government's "indisputable victory."

Over the following days, the official results could not be verified either, despite new indications that electoral fraud had taken place. At thousands of polling stations, despite the different number of voters, identical results for the yes and the no options appeared (Aguiar 2009). In Colombian border areas controlled by the FARC, thousands of Colombians had also been registered on the voter registry so that they could vote in the referendum.[11]

According to Article 72 of the constitution, if the number of those who voted for the recall of an official's mandate was equal to or exceeded the number of those who elected him, he was *ipso jure* out of office. This is what happened in the referendum to revoke the mandate of President Hugo Chávez, held on August 15, 2004, despite the irregularities pointed out above. However, the National Electoral Council, instead of notifying Chávez that he had been removed from office, as resolved by the Venezuelan people and as provided for by the constitution, abstained from doing so. It simply ignored the aforementioned article and argued that since the number of no votes had been higher than the number of yes votes, he should remain in office. These fraudulent election procedures became common in future electoral events.

Such practices were logical and explicable in a political regime that, due to its Leninist nature, would never, for any reason, leave power voluntarily, not even in the case of suffering an electoral defeat. If such a defeat were to occur, it would be disregarded and transformed into a victory because the higher interests of the Bolivarian Revolution would demand it. This is what would happen in the years following the death of popular leader Chávez, during the government of the unpopular Maduro.

The frustration and discouragement of those who had gone to the polls to vote for the termination of Chávez's presidential mandate would be pathetically expressed in the 2005 parliamentary elections, when more than 80 percent of registered voters abstained from voting (Aguiar 2012, 327). This was probably because many citizens had come to the conclusion that their vote was worthless in the dictatorial regime implanted by Chavismo.

Once his presidency had been saved by means of an electoral fraud and the violation of a clear constitutional provision, Chávez announced the beginning of "a new stage." There was not a new stage, however. As of the events described above, the reigning authoritarianism worsened, the autocratic Chavista regime was consolidated, and economic and political relations with Cuba deepened. In effect, Venezuela became the economic benefactor of the Cuban Revolution, Fidel Castro became Chávez's influential advisor, and the island's intelligence services became the Venezuelan government's sage guide. How right was Fidel Castro when he told Hugo Chávez that Chávez had been "the Cuban people's best friend in all of Cuba's history."

On October 31, 2000, Fidel Castro and Hugo Chávez signed a comprehensive cooperation agreement that led to undertaking more than 1,500 social projects in Venezuela, with the participation of more than 150,000 Cuban professionals, mainly doctors, nurses, teachers, and agricultural technicians. The economic benefits received by the Cuban government were enormous. Cuba retained part of these professionals' salaries for its budget and at first received 120,000 barrels of oil per day free of charge and later 50,000 barrels, with a total value of more than twenty billion dollars.

In order to regain Chávez's diminished popularity, the social programs of Cuban inspiration called "Bolivarian Missions," which had been implemented in the marginal shantytowns of the cities, were expanded and bolstered. Since they attended to the felt needs (food, health care, education, housing, subsidies) of the populations living in the impoverished "ranchos," the aid received was appreciated by the beneficiaries. Furthermore, these programs were politically profitable since they were clientelist and were populistly managed by government activists who facilitated the transportation of demonstrators to support rallies and of voters to polling places.

Chávez was also worried about the possibility of losing power due to uncontrollable popular protests or demonstrations or a military insurrection. In order to avoid these risks, he entrusted the Cuban advisors with strengthening and training the government's intelligence services, especially those of the armed forces. To this end, specialized groups were formed to monitor

possible dissidence in the military and to repress destabilizing popular protests. In this context, Chávez dismissed commanders and officers who did not
like him, proclaimed himself commander-in-chief, wore the corresponding
insignia, and dressed in uniform so that he would be seen by his subordinates
as the authority whom they had to respect and to whom they had to be loyal
and obedient.

Meanwhile, Chávez expanded the ties he had established with the FARC,
housed their fighters in Venezuelan territory, and used them to carry out
covert operations and to make incursions into drug trafficking. He did the
same thing with other national and international criminal and terrorist fac-
tions, with the justification that, by virtue of the fact that they were "fighting
against U.S. imperialism," they were his allies. The government likewise
established a covert relationship with delinquents and criminal gangs, which
it used to set up paramilitary and parapolice organizations called "collectives" (*colectivos*). They were made up of militarily organized "patrols" and
"brigades" whose function was to repress protests and demonstrations and to
extort, mock, and victimize opponents. Chávez also began militarizing citizen
security. This process was later accentuated by Maduro and would lead to
extrajudicial executions that became a sort of public policy.

At the same time, Chávez deepened his repressive policy regarding constitutional rights, guarantees, and liberties and accelerated the replacement of
the democratic regime with a dictatorial one. Using his omnipotent power,
he judicially persecuted those who criticized his abuses. He removed from
office public officials who belonged to opposition parties or who had signed
the petition to revoke his mandate. He prevented opposition leaders who
might win from running for office or at least made it difficult for them to
do so. Leaders of social movements and business associations, particularly
civil-society organizations represented by NGOs, were subjected to judicial,
political, and economic harassment when for many years they had worked
freely in the fields of ecology, academia, and social promotion among popular sectors.

Personally and through the propaganda apparatus he had mounted, Chávez
undertook smear campaigns to discredit his opponents and critics, as well
as persecution and imprisonment that led to the first political prisoners. To
make the threats, discrimination, retaliation, and sanctions look "legal," he
filled the attorney general's office and the justice system with his faithful. For
him, those magistrates and officials who blindly obeyed his instructions and
did not hesitate to violate the constitution and the laws to please him were
"patriots." In these proceedings, evidence was fabricated, false witnesses
were used, and due process guarantees were ignored.

Ultimately, Chávez got himself reelected twice, with the argument that
the first election should not be taken into account since it had taken place

before the Bolivarian Constitution was in force. After declaring himself a twenty-first-century socialist in 2005 and a Marxist in 2009, he called for a referendum so that the people could voice their opinion on the adoption of that ideology and its policies.[12] Although the proposal was rejected by the voters, Chávez took measures to move Venezuela's economy in that direction.[13] The same thing happened with the Venezuelan people's vote against the indefinite reelection of the president of the republic. Chávez filed it away and, when electoral conditions were favorable, called for a new referendum, which he won thanks to the manipulation of the electoral process and the weariness of citizens frustrated because their will as expressed in the ballot boxes was powerless to change the autocratic nature of the government and to stop the abuses of power.

By then, many Venezuelans had reached the conclusion that the popular will expressed at the ballot boxes was incapable of changing the dictatorial order, either because electoral fraud subverted results or because the citizens' voices were ignored by the government, which, instead of rectifying its direction, not only persevered in its dictatorial practices but also expanded and reinforced them. So the more elections, consultations, and referendums held in Venezuela, the more democracy shrank and the dictatorship intensified. All this occurred in a country that most likely held the most voting events worldwide: in a little more than two decades of Chavista governments, there have been twenty-nine electoral events and fifteen referendums.

Having become a habitual and compulsive legislator, Chávez issued every law he could think of, making use of the enabling laws approved by the National Assembly. As had always happened in Latin American governments such as his, he ended up turning the government of the Bolivarian Revolution into a den of corruption in which his daughters, other family members, and close collaborators profited. Curiously, Chavez had once said that "being rich is bad, inhuman."

Convinced that after Bolívar no one had been more valuable in the history of Venezuela and certain that he would rule for life, Colonel Hugo Chavez managed to be reelected for a fourth term. However, he could not take office due to unexpected health problems caused by a cancerous tumor that led to his premature death on March 5, 2013.

By then, because he had subjected all the powers of the state to his autocratic will and done away with citizens' rights, liberties, and guarantees, he had ceased to be a constitutional president and had become the dictator of Venezuela, one more of so many since liberator Simón Bolívar established the republic.

Hugo Chávez was succeeded by Vice President Nicolás Maduro Moros, whose political career he had carved. As a leader of a bus drivers union in his youth, Maduro enlisted in Chavismo early on and soon won the caudillo's goodwill due to his own modest social background, active party militancy, and absolute loyalty. In order to train himself ideologically and politically, he was sent to Cuba at a time when, for the Latin American Marxist Left, Fidel Castro was the incarnation of the revolutionary ideal and an enlightened example to follow in order to put an end to economic differences and establish social equality.

Sponsored by his mentor, Maduro was a member of the National Assembly and the Constituent Assembly and served as the minister of foreign affairs and vice president of the republic. When his death was imminent, Chávez arranged for Maduro to succeed him as the acting president, despite the fact that the right to succession corresponded to the president of the National Assembly, Diosdado Cabello, as provided by the constitution.

Nominated as a presidential candidate in the 2013 elections, Maduro lost or was on the verge of losing.[14] Since Maduro lacked the shrewdness, charisma, rhetoric, and popularity of his predecessor, it was not very helpful for him to put the power of the state and its propaganda apparatus to use in his favor. The growing popular discontent and the candidate's scant appeal would carry more weight in the voters' decision. According to many, Maduro triumphed thanks to the electronic manipulation of the results by the National Electoral Council, which, upon perceiving that the results might be negative, suspended information on the partial vote tallies. (Later, the same strategy would be used in Ecuador and Bolivia.) When ballot counting resumed, the trend changed, Maduro was declared the winner, and the electoral authorities refused to recount the votes as requested by the opposition candidate. According to the questionable official vote count, Maduro surpassed candidate Henrique Capriles by only 1.5 percent, a close win for the government and one that had not occurred in any of the previous elections.

The loss of Chavismo's electoral hegemony, unbeatable for three lustrums, was confirmed in the parliamentary elections of 2015, which were widely won by the opposition, represented by the Mesa de la Unidad Democrática (MUD), with 64 percent of the seats in the National Assembly. It triumphed even though its candidates had to overcome countless obstacles during the electoral campaign while those of the government had plenty of advantages, as had invariably happened in elections and plebiscites held previously.

This resounding victory gave hope to those in Venezuela and abroad who had been fighting for the reestablishment of the democratic order, which had been disregarded, trampled on, and degraded first by Chávez and then by his successor. They thought that the National Assembly would put an end to authoritarianism, reestablish democratic institutions, and eventually replace Maduro. However, it did not take long for them to discover that the government was not going to respect the attributions of the National Assembly, much less relinquish absolute control of power since, in the event of losing that power, those who held it could be removed and prosecuted for crimes involving human rights violations, violations of public morals, and drug trafficking, among other crimes. Constrained by this worrisome risk, Maduro decided to "sterilize" the National Assembly—there was talk of surrounding it with a cordon sanitaire—regardless of the unconstitutionality and illegality of the means employed, just as had been happening since the authoritarian Chavismo took power.

In the end, the government acted shrewdly by neither failing to recognize the National Assembly nor dissolving it. Instead, the government took away its powers, ignored its decisions, prevented their implementation, and politically corralled it with the complicity of the constitutional chamber of the Supreme Court of Justice. Since the latter unconstitutionally and abusively declared that the National Assembly's decisions were null and void (Aguiar 2012, 798, 800), it could not legislate, appoint the heads of the various state bodies, oversee the acts of officials in the executive function, and sanction those who violated the constitutional order and abused their power, not even those who were involved in acts of corruption.

The National Assembly's power to legislate was stripped when Maduro issued enforceable executive decrees, using the so-called enabling laws approved by the previous legislature. Due to these obstacles, the National Assembly's presence in examining and resolving on public affairs became ornamental. It ended up becoming a political forum in which the outrages that the government inflicted daily on Venezuelan democracy were denounced and debated without any effect whatsoever on the existing, ironclad power structure.

The opposition, frustrated by the dictatorship's siege against the National Assembly and encouraged by the electoral success achieved and by the massive popular mobilizations of support carried out in Caracas and other cities, in 2016 decided to play the card to revoke the mandate of the president of the republic, as it had previously done with Chávez.

The process of gathering the signatures of support required for the respective recall referendum to be held under this constitutional resource was suspended de facto by the government, alleging that the signatures had been obtained with irregularities. This was the same challenge made previously by Chavista organizations. Aware of his certain defeat because of the electoral triumph obtained by the opposition in the legislative elections, Maduro did not hesitate to impose his dictatorial will, as Chávez had done so many times before. This abuse of power, clearly unconstitutional, was legitimized by regional criminal courts and the Supreme Court of Justice, without any inquiry process to verify the impugnment voiced by Chavistas.

Disregarding the Venezuelan people's right to voice their opinion on having Maduro stay in office did not stop there. With the fallacious justification that Venezuela required a new constitution so that the government could respond to the growing challenges it faced, it called for a second constituent assembly in 2017.[15] This proposal implied replacing the Bolivarian Constitution presented by Chávez as the beacon that would illuminate and guide the Bolivarian Revolution. Such had been the worship he rendered to that constitution that he ordered citizens to read it, venerate it, and learn it as a sort of catechism through which the people should deepen their civic-mindedness. Naturally, a desire to perfect Venezuelan democracy and get it out of the mire in which it found itself was not what was behind the surprising announcement that a new constitution was needed. Rather, it was a malicious maneuver to politically deprive the National Assembly of its powers and transfer those powers to the Constituent Assembly. The government would thereby snatch the legislative function back from the opposition. That function had been recovered with the vote of the citizens, thus reestablishing the democratic institution of the division of power eliminated by the authoritarian Chávez.

The Constituent Assembly would be composed of the large number of 545 members, with the novelty that one-third would not have a territorial representation but would come from the universal vote of the citizens. There would also be representation of collectives through assembly members nominated by organizations of workers, peasants, students, businessmen, retired persons, disabled persons, community members, municipalities, and the like, many of them controlled by the government (Brewer-Carías 2018, 400ff.). For this reason and considering that the regime did not want to perfect democracy but rather the dictatorship, the opposition abstained from participating in the unconstitutionally called, and most likely fraudulent, elections of the members of the new constituent assembly. There was no popular consultation as required by the constitution, election officials depended on the dictates of the government, the electoral districts had been manipulated to favor the latter, and there was no guarantee that the voting and the ballot counting would be fair and honest.

For these reasons, and because many Chavistas believed that the main political legacy of the "eternal" leader was being affected, in the polls a wide majority of the Venezuelan people, between 66 and 80 percent, expressed their opposition to convening a new constituent assembly. This widespread rejection was confirmed on voting day, when barely one-third of the registered voters turned out to vote. To prevent this low turnout from delegitimizing the already questioned constituent assembly, the National Electoral Council, flaunting its lack of scruples, added one million fictitious voters.

The worst predictions about the shamelessly fascist task that the Constituent Assembly would be in charge of came true, as Maduro made use of it not only to usurp the power of the National Assembly but also to clinch the dictatorial state that Chávez had devised. Even though it met for almost twice as long as the term for which it had been convened, in session for three and a half years, it did not approve, and did not even review, a single article of the constitution it was supposed to discuss and issue. What it did do was to suppress the National Assembly elected by the citizens, supplant its exclusive legislative function, fulfill the requests of dictator Maduro, cover up his abuses of power, and whitewash them with a coat of "legality." Among the National Assembly powers that it appropriated, it eliminated the jurisdiction of opposition legislators and ordered their prosecution; it issued and reformed laws, decrees, and resolutions; it dismissed, appointed, and swore in magistrates and high-level state officials; and it modified election calendars.

In the 2018 presidential elections, the opposition, represented by the Mesa de la Unidad Democrática, decided not to participate. It alleged that there were no guarantees that the elections would be free and transparent, due to the government control of the body in charge of conducting them, as had already happened with the fraudulent first election of Maduro and the equally fraudulent election of the members of the Constituent Assembly. The registration of the candidacy of Henri Falcón, a former Chavista leader, contributed to "legitimizing" Maduro's election and to diminishing the voter abstention proposed by the opposition.

Maduro was reelected for a second term, supposedly with 68 percent of the votes, but this result was tainted by the abstention of 53 percent of the registered voters, the highest figure ever in a presidential election since Venezuela reinstated democracy in 1958. This occurred even though, as in the Chavista era, the government used all the means, resources, and instruments of the state to favor the official candidate, including recruiting voters in low-income neighborhoods by offering economic benefits and threatening that those who were already receiving them could lose them. Therefore, when it was time to vote, voters had to register in the offices installed next to the voting precincts in order to obtain the "homeland card" (*Magnet* 2018, 23).

In the lopsided struggle waged by the National Assembly to make the Maduro government respect its constitutional powers, the most important political initiative was to entrust its president, Juan Guaidó, with the presidency of the republic. The National Assembly based its January 11, 2019, decision on Article 233 of the constitution, according to which, in the event of the absence of an elected president (and Maduro was not), new elections were to be called. In the meantime, it was up to the president of the National Assembly to assume the presidency of Venezuela on an interim basis. Days later, Guaidó was sworn in as acting president at an open meeting held in Caracas, which was accompanied by massive demonstrations of support. No state body recognized Guaidó's authority or abided by the decisions of the

National Assembly, including the call for elections to choose a new president. Meanwhile, both the National Assembly and the designated president received broad support from the international community. The National Assembly was recognized as the holder of the legislative function, and Juan Guaidó as the legitimate president of Venezuela, by the OAS, the European Parliament, and the governments of more than fifty countries.

After achieving a Supreme Court of Justice and a National Electoral Council to its own liking and usurping the powers of the National Assembly, Maduro's government announced in mid-2020 that it would call for parliamentary elections, which would be followed by the termination of the spurious Constituent Assembly. The CNE set December 6 of that year for the corresponding elections. At the same time, in order to soften up the opposition and appease the international community, the dictator informed that in order to promote "national reconciliation" he had decided to pardon a hundred deputies, political leaders, social leaders, and other citizens who had been judicially persecuted by the government. Some of them were in prison, others in exile or in hiding, and still others subject to ongoing investigations. From this "magnanimous" pardon he excluded the most important and popular opposition leaders: Juan Guaidó, Henrique Capriles, and Leopoldo López.

Since the constitution provided for the periodic renewal of the National Assembly, in January 2021 the period for which the current National Assembly had been elected would end. However, there was no guarantee that the new elections would be free and fair. As had been common in the two decades of Chavismo, the election officials were people closely linked to the government, so there was the conviction that they would organize a new fraud. This is what had happened in the previous electoral processes in which Maduro was reelected and the members of the Constituent Assembly were elected.

After overcoming initial discrepancies, the twenty-seven party organizations grouped in the Mesa de la Unidad Democrática decided not to participate in the elections, alleging the circumstances cited above. The government's refusal to form an independent CNE that would guarantee a transparent electoral process also contributed to that decision.

Maduro not only ignored the complaints and requests of the opposition but also added a new and reckless abuse of power. The Supreme Court of Justice illicitly and abusively replaced the directors of the most important opposition parties—particularly those holding the majority, Acción Democrática and COPEI—with progovernment leaders, some of them previously expelled from the party ranks. They were charged with nominating the opposition candidates for the legislative elections. In an equally unconstitutional manner, the government substantially increased the number of members of the National Assembly (by 65 percent), created national representatives, modified the legal norms governing the electoral process, and maliciously rezoned voting districts.

On the day of the parliamentary elections, opposition voters did not turn out to vote, mainly the youth. The voting precincts were deserted despite the transportation facilities provided by regime activists, the fact that the number of polling stations had been reduced from 44,000 to 29,000 with respect to the 2018 elections, and the perverse threat made by powerful Constituent Assembly President Diosdado Cabello that whoever did not vote "will be quarantined and will not eat," referring to the "doggie bags," money, and subsidies that votes aligned with Chavismo received. So that Cabello's threat could be fulfilled, "red spots" were set up near voting precincts on the day of voting so that the voters carrying the patriotic or homeland ID card could be registered as a formality to continue receiving special compensations.

Once the electoral process was concluded, the CNE reported that 69 percent of the registered voters had abstained from voting. Meanwhile, the December 6 antifraud observation team set abstention at 82 percent, a percentage that coincided with the estimates made by polls and with data leaked to the press by election officials. Nicolás Maduro himself had made his political weakness evident by not casting his ballot in the voting precinct of a low-income neighborhood, as had been his custom, but rather voting in one installed in a barracks for the occasion.

From this it can be concluded that, although Maduro's dictatorship managed to regain control of the National Assembly in the parliamentary elections of December 2020, it offered national and international public opinion the opportunity to count the number of its supporters—barely one out of every ten citizens—and to confirm its unpopularity.

This electoral collapse of the formerly popular Chavismo has been seen by those who sympathized with the Bolivarian Revolution inside and outside Venezuela. The silence or cryptic statements of the governments of Argentina, Bolivia, and Mexico and of the former presidents invited to Caracas to observe the elections, José Luis Rodríguez Zapatero, Evo Morales, and Rafael Correa, cannot be explained otherwise.[16] The only government that celebrated Maduro's "victory" was that of Cuba.

In November 2021, elections for governors, mayors, and other high-level officials were held in the twenty-three states into which the Venezuelan territory is organized. The opposition agreed to participate despite the unfavorable conditions in which the elections would take place. The government had accentuated its internal divisions, encouraged the personal ambitions of pre-candidates, and arbitrarily disqualified rising regional leaders for whom winning was a possibility. As had happened before, it was to be expected that the government would put all the power of the state at the service of its candidates. It was also to be expected that, if necessary, the results would be adulterated. However, the opposition agreed to participate, motivated by the presence of observers from the European Union, whose independence the government had vowed it would respect, and by the National Electoral Council's incorporation of members who were not dependent on the will of the government.

The outcome was favorable for the government and discouraging for the opposition since opposition candidates managed to win in only three states. In addition to the abovementioned reasons, many others came into play in these results: voter absenteeism (58 percent), the opposition candidates' limited access to the media, the manipulation of voter registration, the fact that some political organizations were declared illegal, the imprisonment of some leaders, and the refusal of the opposition (represented by the MUD) to accept or support the candidacies of local caciques previously linked to Chavismo.

The surprising novelty was that the government candidate was defeated in Barinas, a state in which the Bolivarian Revolution had always won because it is the cradle where its "eternal" leader was born. Because of the symbolism that site entailed, the result could not be accepted by Hugo Chávez's political heirs. The CNE therefore annulled it, arguing that irregularities had been committed.

In the new voting held there, the opposition candidate won again (though a different one was running). This occurred thanks to the unified participation of the diverse forces, as confirmed by the presence of their main leaders in the electoral campaign—and even though Chavismo had deployed all the economic and political power of the state, all its leaders having taken part in the campaign and exacerbated electoral clientelism by handing out gifts to voters, including expensive household appliances. The size of the opposition victory (58 percent) and the acceptance of the result by the Chavista candidate forced the government to admit its painful electoral failure.

Despite being minor in terms of geography and population, this political episode confirmed once again that the democratic opposition is in a position to win the next presidential and parliamentary elections, regardless of the backing that the government may provide its candidates. However, an opposition victory would likely not be accepted if the replacement of Maduro's dictatorial regime by a democratic regime were at stake.

This is due to a simple ideological and political reason, the one underlying Maduro's electoral frauds and the fraud Chávez perpetrated in order to succeed in the recall referendum on his mandate. That premise is the intrinsic perennial nature of dictatorial regimes and the consubstantial amorality of Leninist politicians.

With the exception of dictator Augusto Pinochet, in recent decades no Latin American autocrat has left power voluntarily. Autocrats are unlikely to step down first of all because whoever presides over a political regime of such a nature is in a position to dictate the results he wishes to obtain in the voting to the body in charge of organizing and scrutinizing the electoral process. Second, for those who are engaged in Marxism-Leninism, no legal norm or moral principle or even the vote of the citizens may impede the march of a revolutionary process (and it turns out that Chávez died convinced that he had created a revolution and Maduro believes that he is continuing it). Third, in the event that a dictator loses power, he may end up in prison, together with his civilian and military staff, after being tried, convicted, and sentenced for crimes against humanity in an international criminal court. So those who have agreed to submit to the verdict of the citizens through an election have only done so when they were certain they would win—fraudulently if necessary.

In this unavoidable reality lies the failure of the initiatives promoted in the international arena so that representatives of the government and the opposition could negotiate and design a path that would allow Venezuela to move peacefully toward democracy. None of them succeeded in getting dictator Maduro to at least crack a window so that a slight democratic breeze could be felt, much less in getting him to consent to holding free and fair elections.

In late 2017, a bargaining process led by Norway began between the government and the opposition. Talks began in the Dominican Republic and ended in Barbados, without reaching at least a basis for agreement on any point. The negotiations sponsored by Mexico in 2021 never even got underway when Maduro demanded the prior release of Alex Saab, known as his frontman. The latter had been arrested by the United States and was to be subject to investigations for corruption. In light of a statement from a Department of State official that the United States government would be open to more flexible sanctions "if there were changes to democracy," the head of the Venezuelan delegation said that Venezuela would "never respond" to that request.

During the successive governments of Hugo Chávez—by virtue of his will to govern, the authoritarian political system he implemented, and his power to legislate through presidential decrees—the legislative and judicial functions and other government bodies fell under the command of the president of the republic. These included the National Electoral Council, the Attorney General's Office, the Comptroller's Office, and the Constitutional Court. The reins on these institutions that should have been protected by the rule of law were held so tightly that those who headed them limited themselves to processing and executing the instructions they received from the ruling caudillo, regardless of the constitutionality and morality of those instructions.

This absolute and autocratic power exercised by Hugo Chávez, a dictator who called himself president, worsened during the governments of Nicolás Maduro. For long periods Maduro has ruled by decree, using the enabling laws submissively dispatched by the National Assembly and the Constituent

Assembly. He has also institutionalized electoral fraud and made human rights violations systematic and ruthless.

Maduro has eliminated freedom of expression; brutally repressed protests and demonstrations; imprisoned, tortured, and murdered opponents; committed blatant electoral frauds; and judicially persecuted opponents, journalists, media, social leaders, and members of civil society. The peaceful massive demonstrations in favor of democracy and freedom, which brought together millions of Venezuelans, were cruelly repressed by the police and paramilitary groups organized, protected, and outfitted by the government. During the 2017 protests, hundreds died at the hands of these repressive groups, and those who were detained suffered all kinds of humiliations. According to Human Rights Watch (2018b), more than five thousand protesters were arrested and tried in military courts, and some were subjected to "savage abuses" that included electric shocks, beatings, hanging, rape and other sexual abuse, and being forced to eat human excrement.

The criminal nature of Maduro's dictatorship is evident in the following example. When opposition municipal councilman Fernando Albán returned to Venezuela, he was arrested by the government's intelligence service (SEBIN) and accused of having participated in a plot to kill Maduro. Days later his broken body appeared on the street, according to the attorney general because he had committed suicide by throwing himself from a tenth-floor window of the building in which he was being questioned. Opposition leaders said that he had died while being tortured and that the people responsible for his death had thrown him out the window in order to cover up their crime. The government and the justice system did not publish the findings of the autopsy or their supposed investigation.

In Venezuela, it is simply not possible for free and fair elections to be held to elect the president, legislators, and other high-level state officials; for the popular consultations and referendums to be transparent and their results reliable; and for the constitutional provision to revoke the mandate of the president of the republic to operate effectively. This is for the simple reason that there is no independent electoral authority but rather a group of individuals subordinated to the government and willing to submissively obey its orders. The CNE arbitrarily disqualifies opposition candidates and parties to prevent them from participating in elections. It refuses to process requests to call for revoking Maduro's mandate, or it establishes requirements and conditions impossible to comply with. It traps opposition candidates in a web of regulations and resolutions aimed at preventing their registration. It manipulates voter registration by adding or subtracting voters and arbitrarily changing their addresses, as a function of the interests of the government-aligned candidates. It legitimizes the use and abuse of public resources by progovernment candidates, as well as their privileged access to information and propaganda.

As though these restrictions were not sufficient, the CNE carries out shameless electoral frauds and proclaims the Chavista candidates as winners. It authorized the voting in which Maduro was reelected to take place eight months earlier than the date stipulated in the constitution. In 2016, it did not process a request for citizens to be called to revoke Maduro's mandate. It did accept a similar request in 2022 but set a five-day deadline for the opposition to gather more than four million signatures of support.

During his campaign as a candidate and later as president, Chávez said that he would "put an end" to the corruption supposedly present in previous governments. Maduro has repeated that statement but with less emphasis. Corruption, which in the former's government had already become one of the most critical and serious problems of the Bolivarian Revolution, became widespread during the latter's government. Today it affects all state offices, including the Presidency of the Republic, and has become the main source of enrichment of almost all government officials, particularly those in high- and middle-level positions. Another source is involvement in the trafficking of drugs and precious metals and its cover-up. On July 25, 2019, the United States imposed sanctions on Maduro's three stepdaughters for their participation in "a complex network of bribery and money laundering." In 2020, International Transparency (Transparencia Internacional) placed Venezuela among the four most corrupt countries in the world. In a speech given on December 2, 2021, Maduro admitted that in the economic realm corruption "is worse than the gringo blockade."

The dismantling of democratic institutions and the disregard of citizens' guarantees, liberties, and rights have become so significant that the government of Nicolás Maduro has been labeled dictatorial (a term that the tolerant international community did not use to refer to Chávez's government). This label is used not only by Venezuelan democrats but also by the governments of almost all Latin American, North American, and European countries and by international organizations such as the OAS (2019b) and some nongovernmental organizations.

There were more than enough reasons for Maduro to earn this label. He had been elected and reelected in fraudulent elections; prevented a recall referendum on his mandate; ignored the powers of the National Assembly; arbitrarily convened a constituent assembly; discredited opposition candidates and leaders and had them prosecuted and imprisoned; assumed all the powers of the state; granted impunity to the regime's repressive criminals; and systematically and barbarously violated human rights and committed crimes against humanity, including thousands of extrajudicial executions.

A report prepared by the United Nations High Commissioner for Human Rights, Michelle Bachelet,[17] on the Bolivarian Republic of Venezuela for the period between January 2018 and May 2019 confirmed the existence of numerous and serious violations of democratic principles, human rights, and the economic and social rights of millions of Venezuelans (UN Human Rights Council 2019a). It also mentioned the breakdown of democracy, the subordination of all branches of government to the executive function, the loss of parliamentarian immunity, and the criminalization of citizens' social protests and of the opposition's legitimate activities. In addition, it identified the various forms of violence experienced by critics and opponents of the government, such as arbitrary arrests, torture, sexual and gender-based assaults, and use of excessive force by the police and other repressive organizations against participants in protests. The report cited the violent deaths of 6,856 people, many due to the extrajudicial executions of opponents, critics, and protesters by the Special Actions Force (FAES for the acronym in Spanish) and the Bolivarian National Guard, acting as repressive agencies of the government.

Senior officers in the armed forces, particularly those viewed as potential leaders or considered opponents of the Bolivarian Revolution, have been persecuted or relieved of their duties. They have been excluded from commanding troops or elite groups, their communications have been intercepted, and their promotions have been denied or deferred. Some have died while being held as prisoners and investigated. Many soldiers and junior officers have deserted in order to avoid these dangers. According to the NGO Justicia Venezolana, 250 members of the armed forces have been tried, and 190 are imprisoned.

The independent media lost their freedom of expression and were subjected to draconian restrictions, including censures, shutdowns, and trials and incarceration for journalists and directors, in order to prevent public opinion from learning about government outrages against human rights (Human Rights Watch 2018b). More than a hundred radio and television stations and magazines have been shut down and some radio frequencies transferred to friends of the government or to the official media network. The morally most scandalous case has been the transfer of the traditional newspaper *El Nacional* to the powerful Chavista leader Diosdado Cabello, as payment of a multimillion-dollar indemnification granted by the government-allied justice system in a lawsuit brought against the newspaper's director and owner.[18] In order to survive, some private media outlets have agreed to abide by government instructions and to defend and support the government with their information and commentaries. For its part, the government has put together a network of state-owned and -operated media, mainly radio stations, and an apparatus to control social networks and to persecute those who criticize the regime.

On September 16, 2020, a United Nations Independent International Fact-Finding Mission issued an accusatory report on the human rights violations that have occurred in Venezuela since 2014. In a documented 443-page study, it holds the government of Nicolás Maduro and his interior and defense ministers responsible for a repressive "State policy" that includes "extrajudicial executions, forced disappearances, arbitrary detentions, and the systematic use of torture." These criminal operations, described as "crimes against humanity," were perpetrated "by the security forces and intelligence agencies" of the government.[19] These crimes have remained in impunity because they have been systematically ignored by the authorities.

According to the IACHR, "in Venezuela there is a context of systematic persecution and criminalization of the people perceived of as opponents." Therefore, it should not be surprising that the report of the observation team on violence in Venezuela states that twenty-six people were victimized daily in 2021 for "resisting authority," with executions carried out by police and the dictatorship's paramilitary forces (OVV 2020).

In September 2021, a United Nations Independent International Fact-Finding Mission severely questioned the independence of the Venezuelan justice system. In its report it denounced a "deeply eroded" system that has endangered "its function of imparting justice and safeguarding individual rights." It also said that the "increase in political pressures" has led prosecutors and judges, "through their acts and omissions," to contribute to "human rights violations and crimes committed by actors of the State against opponents" and that magistrates "habitually receive orders about how to rule, sometimes from high levels of the government, channeled through the Supreme Court of Justice," and for which reason many "resigned and left Venezuela for fear of reprisals." The report also declared that "the overwhelming majority of crimes against human rights have not led to investigations, trials, and convictions."

The serious, systematic, and widespread violation of human rights and the impunity of the perpetrators led the prosecutor of the International Criminal Court (ICC), British attorney Karim Kahn, to initiate an investigation to determine the possible responsibility of Nicolás Maduro and dozens of Venezuelan government officials in the crimes against humanity mentioned in the preceding pages.[20] A year earlier, his predecessor, Fatou Bensouda, had said that there was "evidence of crimes that should be investigated by the Office of the Prosecutor of the International Criminal Court," crimes committed by the repressive organizations of the government: military, police, and paramilitary groups. Thus, Venezuela has become the first Latin American country to be investigated by the ICC.

Under Maduro's government, the population's living conditions have worsened dramatically. According to Bachelet's report, shortages of essential goods and hyperinflation limit the "ability to purchase basic foodstuffs and medicines and [to obtain] timely medical care." As a result, malnutrition among the population is on the rise, overall and infant mortality is increasing, and patients are dying in hospitals (UN Human Rights Council 2019a).

Research carried out by the Institute of Economic and Social Research of the Andrés Bello Catholic University between 2019 and 2020 cites the following findings: life expectancy has regressed 3.7 years, Venezuela is the second most inequitable country in Latin America, 79 percent of the population does not receive sufficient income to cover the basic staple foods, 30 percent of children under five years of age are chronically malnourished, and 76 percent of the inhabitants live in poverty and 55 percent in extreme poverty, levels worse than those in Haiti.[21]

These catastrophic economic and social consequences have occurred in a country that in the second half of the twentieth century was the most prosperous in Latin America. After two decades of Chavista governments, the Venezuelan economy has shrunk by 70 percent compared to what it was at the beginning of the Bolivarian Revolution, even though oil prices have been high for more than ten years.

The social devastation suffered by Venezuela during Maduro's dictatorship has brought about the exodus of one-fourth of its population, an unprecedented figure in the history of Latin America, a region that has not shied away from the suffering that accompanies massive emigrations. More than six million Venezuelans, some accompanied by their children, wander the continent in search of a job that will allow them to survive. They left their country to escape the brutality of the government's repressive gangs, unemployment, poverty and destitution, lack of food and medicine, and the highest and most impoverishing inflation in the world: 200,000 percent in 2019, according to the IMF. According to the Andrés Bello Catholic University, poverty affects 94 percent of the population, and the minimum monthly wage is two dollars. It is estimated that 40 percent of families live off remittances sent to them by Venezuelan emigrants.

As will be seen in the first chapter of part IV, the international community has mobilized to reestablish democracy, freedom, and human rights in Venezuela, but with some delay since the process that undermined its democratic institutions began during the successive governments of Hugo Chávez. The OAS and some fifty countries have declared the presidency of Nicolás Maduro illegitimate and recognized Juan Guaidó as the constitutional president of Venezuela. In addition, the United States, the European Union, and other countries have imposed economic sanctions on the highest-ranking officials of the Venezuelan regime and their families.

Such is the moral character of those who govern Venezuela, and such is the criminal nature of its top officials, that the United States government has placed dictator Nicolás Maduro on the list of the criminals most wanted by its justice system, together with his minions in the Constituent Assembly, the Supreme Court of Justice, and the Ministry of Defense. It has also offered multimillion-dollar rewards for information leading to the capture and prosecution of these criminals (CNN 2020).

In the copious authoritarian history of Latin America, less draconian, corrupt, and criminal dictatorships were deposed by popular mobilizations and military insurrections. The same thing has not happened in Venezuela because the armed forces have ceased to serve the nation, the state, and democracy and have become the private army of Nicolás Maduro, recruited through perks and the possibility of enrichment.

The benefits earned through the bribery of military commanders and the co-optation of the armed forces have outweighed millions of Venezuelans' rejection of the dictatorship; the election victories of the democratic opposition; the international pressure of the United States, the European Union, the OAS and fifty countries; and the incriminating reports issued by these organizations and the United Nations on the atrocious human rights abuses taking place in Venezuela.

Members of the military receive high salaries as well as some undeserved promotions and generous benefits. High-ranking officers are in charge of lucrative ministries, governors' offices, public enterprises, and other agencies; some of them also participate in the substantial dividends left by drug trafficking and the awarding of public contracts.

Nothing is more illustrative of the moral degradation into which the military institution has fallen than the fact that the Venezuelan armed forces have two thousand active generals, more than those in the U.S. or NATO armies.[22]

NOTES

1. Quote from 2011 (Aguiar 2016, 226).

2. Quote from July 5, 2020, referring to the democratic opposition at the celebration of Venezuela's Independence Day.

3. Asdrúbal Aguiar (2009, 289) affirms that, with respect to the stay in the case against Chávez, "there were no reservations in any sector of the country," including the Catholic Church, and that in prison he was visited by people from "all the social and political sectors, from the highest to the owners of social media."

4. Movement towards Socialism (Movimiento al Socialismo, MAS), Communist Party of Venezuela (Partido Comunista de Venezuela, PCV), A Country for Everyone (Patria para Todos, PPT), and other, lesser organizations.

5. With 56 percent, 60 percent, 62 percent, and 56 percent of the votes, respectively. The 1999 constitution authorized the immediate reelection of the president, which was prohibited in the 1961 constitution and which became indefinite in the 2009 referendum.

6. He said, verbatim: "I swear to God, I swear before the country, I swear before my people, that on this dying constitution I will drive the democratic transformations

needed for the Republic to have a new constitution suitable for the new times. I swear."

7. A detailed summary can be found in Brewer-Carías (2018).

8. For details on the process of the Constituent Assembly and the 2000 elections, see Neuman and McCoy (2001).

9. Years later, control of the constitutional chamber would prove very useful to Maduro to politically and legally "sterilize" the work of the National Assembly elected in 2015 with an opposition majority.

10. Memorandum sent on April 25, 2005, by opposition representative Asdrúbal Aguiar to André Dupuy, the papal nuncio in Caracas, in the context of the government's negotiations to hold the referendum.

11. Five hundred thousand, according to Colombia's foreign minister (Aguiar 2012, 322).

12. Earlier, Chávez had said that the Bolivarian Revolution would be a new and real revolution, different from those carried out previously by Marxist groups.

13. See Vera (2008).

14. See a detailed summary in Aguiar (2018).

15. A summary is available in Brewer-Carías (2018, 369ff.).

16. In an interview done by Telesur on December 7, 2020, Correa said only that the election process had been "impeccable and successful" and that there was "an international double standard" when it came to election results because the participation in Poland's legislative elections had been only 30 percent.

17. That report was particularly relevant because Bachelet had a close relationship with Hugo Chávez while she was the president of Chile, and she was also in office at the same time as Nicolás Maduro.

18. He had reprinted a news story published by the Spanish newspaper *ABC*, which reported that Cabello was being investigated for drug trafficking in the United States.

19. Special Action Forces (Fuerzas de Acción Especial, FAES), Scientific Research Corps (Cuerpo de Investigaciones Científicas, SICPC), Bolivarian National Intelligence Service (Servicio Bolivariano de Inteligencia Nacional, SEBIN), and the Directorate-General for Military Counterintelligence (Dirección General de Contrainteligencia Militar, DGCIM).

20. Kahn has argued in hearings on accusations made by Argentina, Canada, Colombia, Chile, Paraguay, and Peru.

21. National Survey on Living Conditions in Venezuela, conducted by the Economic and Social Research Institute (IIES for its acronym in Spanish) of the Andrés Bello Catholic University (UCAB for its acronym in Spanish) in nine thousand households in 2020.

22. Admiral Craig Faller, chief of the Southern Command of the U.S. Army, quoted by the BBC World News, February 19, 2019 (BBC 2019a).

Chapter 5

The Government of Evo Morales

Political takes precedence over legal . . . ; when some jurist says to me "Evo, you're legally wrong," well, I do it anyway even if it's illegal. Then I tell the lawyers, "If it's illegal, then make it legal. What have you studied for?"

—Bolivian president Evo Morales Ayma (2006–2019)[1]

Evo Morales Ayma, a peasant leader of Indigenous origin[2] who had not finished high school due to his parents' economic hardships, entered Bolivian politics in the late 1980s. He began his activism among the peasants who illegally cultivated coca in the Chapare region, located in the Cochabamba tropics. Coca cultivation was prohibited there, although it was not prohibited in other regions where such crops could be grown for medicinal purposes and traditional uses by Indigenous populations.

During the governments of Hugo Banzer and Jorge Quiroga, protests by illegal coca growers increased due to the measures taken by those governments to combat drug trafficking, one of which was the elimination of plantations that were not permitted by law. According to the United Nations Office on Drugs and Crime (UNODC), a high percentage of these crops was used in cocaine production (n.d.).

In order to pressure the government to revise the policy and halt elimination of these crops, the local populations blocked roads, surrounded cities and towns, invaded government facilities, paralyzed economic activities, and assaulted security forces. Morales was the leader of these violent outbreaks that led to dozens of deaths and hundreds of wounded. Prevailing on the political ascendancy that this activism gave him among coca growers, he formed the first growers' organizations in Cochabamba and later the Special Federation of Peasant Workers in the Tropics (Federación Especial de Trabajadores Campesinos del Trópico). Later, with other groups of a similar nature, he founded the Unified Syndical Confederation of Peasant

61

(sometimes translated as Rural) Workers of Bolivia (Confederación Sindical Única de Trabajadores Campesinos de Bolivia, CSUTCB) and was named its coordinator.

This union representation and the prominent role Morales played in leading the coca growers' protests gave him a certain political notoriety, opened doors to the media, and made it possible to project his leadership. As a result, in 1997 he was elected to be a deputy in the National Congress. He was supported by an electoral platform formed by the Federation of Coca Growers of the Tropics and the Movement towards Socialism (Federación de Cocaleros de los Trópicos y Movimiento hacia al Socialismo), which had split from the Bolivian Socialist Falange (Falange Socialista Boliviano), originally catalogued as a right-wing movement. These two organizations later merged under the leadership of Evo Morales, with the name Movement towards Socialism (MAS).

Through Morales's access to the most representative institution of democratic political participation, he could freely express his opinions, voice the demands of his constituents, and promote political and legislative initiatives of interest to him. However, he did not stop his insurrectional actions as the leader of the coca growers. On the contrary, he continued to harass democratic governments and undermine republican institutions. A protest carried out in the peasant region under his influence during the Quiroga government left several dead and numerous wounded, mainly unarmed soldiers who had been sent to collaborate with the overwhelmed police to control the public order. The protestors assassinated two uniformed men who had been held hostage and attacked ambulances transporting wounded and tortured policemen. These events caused a national uproar.

Since he was considered responsible for these criminal acts and so that he could be criminally prosecuted, Morales was deprived of his parliamentary privilege with the favorable vote of two-thirds of the members of the Chamber of Deputies. The proceedings were soon halted due to the deliberate negligence of prosecutors and judges, who also "misplaced" the file. Thanks to this judicial connivance, Morales was not prosecuted and convicted for his terrorist actions. The voices raised in his favor—among them, those of the Catholic Church and influential Cochabamba bishop Tito Solari Capellari—had a great deal to do with this.

The fact that the state power represented by the justice system was unable to investigate, prosecute, and punish the coca growers' leader for the crimes he had committed was seen by many as a political victory for Morales. As a result, his political influence, previously confined to the rural areas of the tropics, grew and spread to the cities, the Andean region, and its large Indigenous population. Thanks to the popularity achieved in these "social struggles," he managed to take an impressive second place in the 2002 presidential elections.

By virtue of the national leadership Morales had managed to carve out, he undertook an intransigent and conspiratorial opposition against President Gonzalo Sánchez de Lozada in the latter's second term, which Morales undermined with multiple protests, generally tinged with violence. These disturbances worsened as a result of measures taken by the government to address the country's economic and social crisis. Society was shaken by a succession of strikes by urban workers and subversive actions by the peasant movement. These consisted of road blockades, sieges on cities, attacks on public and private property, suspension of oil production, food and fuel shortages, and paralysis of economic activities.

The disenchantment and frustration that these disturbing and costly events generated in the population worsened and became generalized when rumor spread that the government of Sánchez de Lozada was preparing to export gas to the United States through a Chilean port. Given the Bolivian people's traditional mistrust of their Andean neighbor, the opponents took advantage of the occasion to portray it as an act of treason. An economic decision whose advisability was being studied by the government was treated as a fait accompli in order to stir up Bolivians' nationalist and anti-Chilean feelings and to turn them against President Sánchez de Lozada.

The government was immediately cornered by a series of protests and demonstrations and multiple episodes of violence in the highlands, the tropics, the countryside, and the cities. These events led to dozens dead and hundreds wounded, among both demonstrators and members of the security forces.

In this chaotic and destabilizing social and political situation, aggravated by a police strike, an umpteenth confrontation took place in an area near La Paz. More than a thousand Bolivian and foreign tourists, who were attending a renowned folklore festival in the town of Warisata, had been besieged by peasant organizations opposed to the government. In order for them to escape and return to La Paz, security forces intervened. Along the way, the caravan was ambushed by insurgents led by Felipe Quispe, an Indigenous leader in the highlands, leaving a new toll of dead and wounded.[3]

Amid the protests and revolts, Sánchez de Lozada lost credibility in the eyes of the public and was forced to resign.

Although Morales, who was visiting Muammar Gaddafi in Libya, did not participate in these convulsive events, he was the main beneficiary of the overthrow.

It seems that this insurrectional political process, which culminated in the ousting of a democratic government elected by the people, was planned, counseled, and financed by the governments of Venezuela and Cuba and monitored by their embassies in La Paz (Sánchez Berzaín 2013, 50–54).

By then, the successful Cuban–Venezuelan strategy was already underway, whereby the revolutionary forces in Latin America would rise to power, control it absolutely, and remain in power indefinitely through election wins and constituent assemblies, not through armed struggles, which had failed.[4]

Upon resigning, the president was succeeded by Vice President Carlos Mesa, who was subjected to similar protests and destabilizing actions and in 2005 suffered the same fate as his predecessor, before he was able to complete two years in his new functions.

The successive overthrow of two presidents, the unmanageable social unrest, and the awareness that a new transitional president could not govern in such political turmoil made early presidential elections the remedy that would allow Bolivia to escape from the chaos in which it was plunged. Elections were called by the interim president and won by Evo Morales in the first round of voting, with 54 percent of the votes. He was supported by the Movement towards Socialism (MAS) and the Indigenous population, as well as by organizations of coca growers, peasants, workers, teachers, and professionals.

Morales's election reassured Bolivia and earned a widespread positive reaction, not only in Latin America. Five hundred years since the discovery and conquest of the Americas, during which time Indigenous ethnic groups had suffered all kinds of humiliation and plundering at the hands of whites and mestizos, one of their descendants was preparing to assume the presidency of the republic for the first time.

Two years before Morales's triumph, the political process that would lead to the eradication of the rule of law and the creation of an authoritarian regime had already begun. The process would not rely on the action of protesting forces, some of them self-described as revolutionary, but rather on the democratic leaders themselves.

One of the first decisions made by Carlos Mesa upon taking office as president was to grant amnesty to those who had committed various crimes during the insurrection that ended with the overthrow of President Sánchez de Lozada, among them Evo Morales. Furthermore, with the argument that "a new social pact" was necessary to carry out "a profound transformation of the State," he sponsored a questionable constitutional reform that introduced the legal figure of a constituent assembly empowered to effect a "total reform" of the constitution—a possibility not foreseen in the constitution in place at the time (Tardío Quiroga 2006).

Morales took advantage of this unconstitutional reform to convene a constituent assembly as soon as he began his presidential mandate. In the elections to form it, out of the 255 seats in dispute, the government party (MAS) and its allies obtained the majority (137). However, since this number did not reach the two-thirds required to approve the constitutional reforms, MAS was forced to reach agreements with other political organizations.

The Constituent Assembly could not escape the confrontational nature of Bolivian politics and the daily mobilizations and disturbances promoted by its social organizations. Some of them reached such magnitude that, in order to be able to hold regular sessions, the Constituent Assembly was forced to change its venue from Sucre to Oruro. The mayhem and confusion that these tumultuous events unleashed affected the Constituent Assembly's work, to the point that the vote on the first article of the new constitution did not take place for nine months. Some provisions were even discussed and approved by an outside "secret commission" without the participation of the members of the Constituent Assembly (Sánchez Berzaín 2013, 57–83). However, it ultimately fulfilled its purpose, and the new constitution was approved by 61 percent of the voters in the referendum held in 2009.

The Political Constitution of the Plurinational State of Bolivia did not contain provisions that strengthened the executive function to the detriment of the attributions of the legislative and judicial functions. Nor did it favor the control of other state bodies by the president of the republic, as occurred in the reforms made to the constitutions of Venezuela and Ecuador. Other means were used by Morales to deprive other bodies of their independence and submit them to his authority: the authoritarian exercise of power. This strategy included, for example, the manipulation and distortion of the norms contained in the constitution and in the laws; the absolute majority that he came to have in the National Congress; the retroactive application of certain legal norms;[5] and the forced dismissal of magistrates, officials, and directors from the most important public institutions, among them the justice system. All of them were replaced by people whom Morales trusted and who were aligned with his ideas and his authoritarian project.

Morales forced the resignation of officials who had been elected for a specific period and were still in office, harassing them with accusations, investigations, prosecution, and threats of dismissal, and in some cases following through. He ended the terms of incumbents with the argument that the institutions they headed or were part of had disappeared, simply because their names had changed.

More decisive was the two-thirds majority he achieved in the two chambers of the National Congress thanks to the ample win obtained in his first reelection. Despite the fact that Morales had absolute control over the legislative function and the opposition had been reduced to a minimum expression, the congressional majority deprived legislators critical of the Morales government of their parliamentary privilege so that they could be prosecuted for events that had occurred during their previous functions.

Thus, the bodies in charge of legislating, administering justice, ruling on the constitutionality of officials' acts, guaranteeing the honest administration of public funds, overseeing economic activities, and ensuring free and fair elections gradually fell under the control of the government or were placed at its service. All of them were formed and managed by members of the ruling party (MAS) or by people willing to follow the instructions of the government because of their ideological and political identification with Morales and the revolutionary commitment to participate in the construction of a new society.

With the culmination of this process to concentrate public power in a single person, many elements inherent to democracy disappeared: the division of power, the rule of the constitution and the laws, the independence of the justice system and of the control and oversight bodies, political pluralism, free and fair electoral processes, and certain freedoms and guarantees for citizens, such as freedom of expression.

The concentration of power also reduced the spaces for discrepancy, debate, criticism, and opposition in which the independent press, political parties, and social, economic, and civil-society organizations usually operate. Those who, in the exercise of their constitutional right to freedom of expression, remarked on the conduct of the government, promoted political actions against it, denounced acts of corruption, called attention to Cuban and Venezuelan interventionism, or promoted popular protests and demonstrations were subject to threats, retaliation, shutdowns, inspections, and criminal prosecutions.

Legal proceedings were generally initiated based on accusations made by government officials and the president himself, and sometimes extended to family members, associates, and companies or organizations with ties to the defendant. Since prosecutors, judges, and magistrates were politically dependent on the government and felt obliged to comply with the instructions they received in cases that were in its interest, the defendants were left in the lurch and were usually convicted. However, some escaped prison by fleeing Bolivia and seeking asylum in neighboring countries. By the end of the Morales dictatorship, it was estimated that there were more than one hundred political prisoners and more than one thousand exiles (Sánchez Berzaín 2013, 102–14).

Opponents were also discredited through the official media or through media lynch mobs mounted by the regime's propaganda apparatus.

The government intervened in electoral processes in order to favor MAS candidates and harm those from opposition parties, with the connivance of a National Electoral Court and departmental courts controlled by the president of the republic.

The arbitrary and abusive use of public resources by government candidates was widespread, as was the inequitable zoning of voting districts in order to favor MAS candidates. Despite having only thousands of voters, the districts in which MAS supporters, mainly peasants, were concentrated elected the same number of legislators as districts having tens or hundreds of thousands. In addition, the individual and universal nature of citizen suffrage was ignored since peasants were prevented from voting according to their own opinions and were forced to vote according to the opinion adopted by each community. This abuse is known as "community-defined voting." Certain officials are not elected by the citizens or appointed by state bodies, but rather by trade organizations, through a form of corporatism of fascist origin.

Meanwhile, the opponents' campaigns lost public funding, their candidates were forbidden to visit Indigenous communities, and the businessmen who contributed financially to their campaigns suffered retaliation. Even more serious was the fact that the voting results were altered when there was a possibility that the government would be defeated (Sánchez Berzaín 2013, 90–99).

With the fallacy that the appointment of the high magistrates of justice should be democratized, giving the people the power to elect them, Morales's party devised an unprecedented system for selecting judges. The candidates, in a first instance, were chosen by an absolute majority among the members of the Plurinational Legislative Assembly, that is, by MAS legislators. They were then voted on by the citizens in universal elections organized by the National Electoral Court. Since publicity campaigns for the potential judges were prohibited, voters could not assess their merits, so voters' decisions were conditioned by their political positions and affiliations. Morales supporters dutifully voted for the list drawn up in the assembly, and the opponents annulled their vote, rejecting the questionable procedure followed. The latter still managed to win in four of Bolivia's nine departments (Sánchez Berzaín 2013, 90–99). However, as the valid votes were the only ones counted, the government ended up filling the Attorney General's Office and the justice system with its associates and sympathizers. Citizen participation in the election of judges served this purpose.

The Constitutional Court and the National Electoral Court, whose members were appointed by the National Assembly, were also composed of magistrates who ideologically and politically identified with the government. The courts were not formed using a pluralist approach as usually occurs in democratic regimes. The same strategy was applied to the Attorney General's Office, the Comptroller's Office, and the Federal Prosecutor's Office, which were not filled by independent and honest magistrates either but rather by officials of the same political line.

Finally, alternation in power, an element that defines a political system as democratic, is in question since the indefinite reelection of the president of the republic has been approved, in clear violation of the constitution and under the absurd consideration that it is a human right. The Inter-American Court of Human Rights, as previously indicated, has ruled to the contrary.

The executive function's encompassing of the main institutions of the democratic state, which given their nature should be independent and autonomous, prevented them from fulfilling their obligations: to safeguard the rule of the constitution and the laws, to safeguard the division of power, to preserve the independence of justice, to guarantee free elections, to protect citizens' rights and liberties, to respect alternation in power, and to promote transparency in officials' acts. Instead, they became instruments of the political objectives of the Morales dictatorship. These objectives included judicially persecuting his critics, legitimizing the autocratic exercise of power, and satisfying his ambition to rule Bolivia indefinitely.

Evo Morales began his first government in 2006, but his term was reduced to two years by the Constituent Assembly, since the Political Constitution of the Plurinational State of Bolivia provided for new presidential, vice-presidential, and legislative elections. As it authorized the immediate reelection of the president of the republic, once only, Morales ran for a new term, which he won by a wide margin in the 2009 elections (Gamboa Rocabado 2010, 169; *Bolivia Decide* 2013).

Half of the period of this second five-year term having elapsed, Morales ordered the Constitutional Court to interpret the respective constitutional provision in his favor, so that he could run again. He argued that the prohibition on his eligibility should be applied as of the date the new constitution was issued because it had "founded the Plurinational State" to replace the defunct Republican State. By having his first election in 2005 disregarded, Morales was able to run again in 2014 and be elected for the third time.

Upon obtaining this controversial ruling from the Constitutional Court, he said that he would not seek a fourth term, in order to reassure public opinion. That statement was unnecessary since such a possibility was not provided for in the constitution. However, a year before the end of his third term, forgetting the solemn commitment he had made and ignoring the constitutional prohibition, he managed to get the National Assembly, controlled by his party, to request that the Constitutional Court eliminate the prohibition. That request was diligently reviewed and approved.

In view of the widespread questioning that this arbitrary decision caused in public opinion, he allowed the issue to be submitted to a referendum. Confident that the ploy he was using to once again arbitrarily continue in the presidency would be approved at the ballot boxes, he said that he would abide by the people's decision should the constitutional reform be defeated. It was not in vain that he had won three presidential elections in the first round of voting, with a wide advantage over his immediate contenders. However, contrary to the forecasts made by the polls and the pessimism of national and international observers interested in the future of Bolivian democracy, 51 percent of the voters voted against further reelection.

Given the Bolivian people's majority rejection of the unconstitutional reelection of Morales for a fourth term, the Bolivian opposition and international observers believed that the doors had finally been closed to his stubborn desire to be reelected indefinitely.

This was not the case, though, for he immediately concocted a new legal maneuver by getting the Supreme Electoral Tribunal to authorize him to participate in the MAS primaries, called to choose the party's candidates for the 2019 election. Once they were concluded, the Constitutional Court authorized the registration of his candidacy, alleging that the indefinite reelection of Morales was a human right that the constitution was obliged to respect. The Supreme Electoral Tribunal agreed with that argument. Afterward, half of the members of the Constitutional Court left but were later appointed to important positions in state offices.

This iniquitous behavior of three state bodies in charge of ensuring respect for the rule of law—in response to the president of the republic's demand to be allowed to be reelected indefinitely despite the existing constitutional prohibition—clearly illustrates the political subordination to which their members were subject during the Morales administrations. The subordination was so absolute and pandering that the Constitutional Court went so far as to support the aberration that indefinite reelection was a human right and thus to justify that Bolivia could well have a president for life, contrary to the country's constitution and the democratic principle of alternation in power.

In the general elections of October 20, 2019 (as in all the previous ones, replete with advantages for the government-aligned candidates and obstacles for the opponents), the difference between Evo Morales and his closest runner-up, Carlos Mesa, did not reach the 10 percentage points required by law in order for him to be declared the winner. This result, which forced a second round of voting, was announced by a polling firm authorized to take an exit poll sample; it was also based on the rapid count conducted by the Electoral Tribunal, when 84 percent of the votes had been counted.

It was the last report that Bolivians were able to hear because broadcasting of the results was immediately interrupted by an order from the Supreme Electoral Tribunal. Five days later, Morales was proclaimed president-elect, having obtained 47 percent of the votes and Mesa 36.5 percent, that is, with an advantage of more than ten percentage points.

In the following days, two OAS reports, one preliminary and the other final, rejected the results proclaimed by election officials, citing irregularities in the ballot count (OAS 2019c). The fraudulent alteration of the popular will earned angry criticism from the international community and triggered a massive protest by the Bolivian people, including social organizations that had sympathized with Morales.

In order to calm the political storm, Morales announced that a new Electoral Tribunal would be appointed, so that another election could be organized. Since this announcement failed to appease the inflamed public opinion and the heads of the armed forces and the police urged him to step down, he resigned as the president of the republic on November 10, 2019, and left the country to seek asylum first in Mexico and then in Argentina.

Unexpectedly and inexplicably, Vice President Álvaro García Linera and the presidents and vice presidents of the chambers of senators and deputies, faithful followers of Morales, also resigned—perhaps to leave a power void that would lead to chaos because, in the order of succession, it was up to one of them to replace the resigning president. In any case, with favorable votes from the MAS legislators, the resignations of the Bolivian president and the other officials were accepted.

In view of the vacancy in the executive function, Jeanine Áñez, the second vice president of the senate and sixth in the line of succession, was sworn in as interim president. This action was endorsed by the National Assembly and the Constitutional Court. At the same time, the National Assembly called for general elections to choose a new president through an impartial electoral board.

Bolivia's new interim government, weak and unrepresentative, was soon faced with social mobilizations led by Evo Morales from exile. These were similar to those he had previously led against presidents Banzer, Quiroga, and Sánchez de Lozada. Blocking roads and cutting off access to urban areas deprived the cities' inhabitants of food, goods, and services, and later even of oxygen tanks required by hospitals to treat patients affected by the coronavirus epidemic. The former left thirty-four dead and hundreds wounded, many from gunshots fired by security forces; the latter caused the deaths of forty patients in intensive-care units.

Interim President Áñez extended her temporary mandate for almost a year and ran for president, a blunder that she was forced to amend due to public criticism and negative results in the polls. She did not include a single member of the Indigenous communities in her cabinet, and that decision led to her being labeled a racist. Her government repeated practices that the opposition had accused the MAS government of, such as authoritarianism, corruption, and nepotism. Repression of the violent protests promoted by Morales supporters caused several deaths. Ultimately, due to the interim president's negligence, the presidential elections that should have been called immediately to elect a president, a vice president, senators, and deputies ended up taking place a year later.

These missteps disheartened the social and political sectors that had fought against the Morales dictatorship and affected the credibility of the transitional government, especially those who expected exemplary and transparent conduct from the opposition at a crucial crossroads for the future of Bolivian democracy. In addition, the opposition had a fragmented turnout in the presidential race, with half a dozen candidates, while MAS remained united and had support from the still popular Morales.

Thus, the dictatorship's opposition and critics themselves created the political conditions for the first-round triumph of candidate Luis Arce, nominated by the former president. Arce had served under Morales for a decade in the Ministry of the Economy. He earned a resounding win, obtaining 55 percent of the votes, with a difference of more than twenty points over Carlos Mesa, his main opponent. Thanks to this successful result, MAS obtained a majority in both chambers of the National Assembly, but not two-thirds as had been the case in the last Morales governments.

It was said previously herein that the Bolivian constitution did not contain provisions that favored the concentration of power in the presidency, to the detriment of other state functions and bodies, and that the subordination of government institutions to the president, as occurred during the Morales administrations, was due to the omnipresent exercise of presidential authority outside the constitutional framework. Using malicious interpretations of the constitution and the laws and taking advantage of the absolute majority he had in the National Assembly, Morales had managed to take over all the major institutions of the state, including the justice system, the Attorney General's Office, the Constitutional Court, and the Electoral Tribunal.

This autocratic political structure, dictatorially imposed by Morales on Bolivian democracy for more than a decade, has not disappeared in the government of President Luis Arce. It survives with two particularities: it is not Arce who directs and controls the government, but rather it is the coca growers' caudillo, and the center of power does not lie in the presidency, but rather in the National Assembly.

In the days when the government of Luis Arce was taking shape, Morales admitted that he had participated and said he had been "consulted." His influence was confirmed with the appointment of the attorney general, who was his personal attorney, and through tweets he sent giving instructions. The presidents of the two chambers of the National Assembly, other officials, and most legislators have Morales to thank for the positions they hold, and they also consult his opinions. He has assumed the leadership of the government party and controls its social bases, especially those of the coca growers. The large popular demonstrations with which he was received upon returning to Bolivia and those that have welcomed him in the various regions of the country confirm his political influence. Complacent prosecutors and judges have shelved the inquiries and criminal proceedings brought against him, some for common crimes, and have vacated an arrest warrant.[6] Nothing confirms all this more than when a former minister of Morales asked "the big boss" to take on "the political and strategic direction of the Government."

Using the power he still wields without holding any public office, Morales managed to turn his resignation from the presidency into a coup, supposedly carried out by the second vice president of the senate, Jeanine Áñez. Prosecutors and judges close to the former dictator undertook investigations against her for the crimes of conspiracy and sedition,[7] which she allegedly used to overthrow President Morales. Once she was convicted, Morales could say that this was proof that he was removed from the presidency by means of a coup and not because he ran for office again in violation of the constitution, won elections through electoral frauds, and was rejected by the citizens through large popular demonstrations. Morales also wanted to punish those who dared to call for his resignation, by persecuting them judicially.

The following facts show the malicious and persecutory nature of these criminal proceedings. Those brought against former president Áñez were initiated without prior authorization from the National Assembly, a requirement established in the constitution for the prosecution of a former president. In addition, the preventive imprisonment to which she and some former ministers and former commanders of the armed forces and the police were subjected exceeded the maximum period foreseen under the law. Events were fabricated, evidence was falsified, they were charged with fictitious crimes, and due-process norms, procedures, and guarantees were ignored.

On January 20, 2022, the Global Human Rights League documented the existence of sixty-four political prisoners in Bolivia, including former president Jeanine Áñez and her collaborators. In January 2022, Human Rights Watch director Tamara Taraciuk, in statements made to the newspaper *El País*, pointed out the Bolivian case "as the most extreme case of the political use of the justice system." The European Parliament has described Áñez as a "political prisoner," condemned her "arbitrary and illegal" detention, and requested her "immediate release" and withdrawal of the unfounded charges that have been made by the Attorney General's Office. United Nations Secretary General António Guterres has also called for "respect for due process" in the aforementioned investigations.

Paradoxically, upon being elected, President Luis Arce said that he would "put the process of change back on track" and that he would not seek "revengeful political persecutions." However, this offer was ignored by Arce once took office, as were the calls made by international human rights organizations, the United Nations, the European Union, and other countries to halt the judicial persecution of ex-president Áñez orchestrated by former dictator Morales after his return to Bolivia. The attorney general who had acknowledged the constitutional nature of Áñez's government accused her of having perpetrated a coup, and politicized lower-court judges at the will of the Bolivian caudillo sentenced her to ten years in prison, thereby violating the judicial processes laid out in the constitution and the law.

NOTES

1. "'Evadas,' 100 frases 'célebres' de Evo Morales," *El Mundo*, June 14, 2011, https://www.elmundo.es/america/2011/06/14/noticias/1308069851.html?cid=CM0803.

2. Even though Morales has indigenous ancestors, he is a mestizo, as suggested by his last names, the paternal one in Spanish and the maternal one in Aymara. He does not speak either Aymara or Quechua.

3. According to Quispe, the insurrectionists proposed to capture and kill Defense Minister Carlos Sánchez Berzaín (interview published in the Cochabamba newspaper *Opinión*, August 4, 2013).

4. The Venezuelan military attaché was arrested and forced to leave Bolivia for having attempted to bribe military commanders to oust Sánchez de Lozada. The Bolivian president complained to his Venezuelan counterpart about the intervention in Bolivian politics (Sánchez Berzaín 2013, 49).

5. Article 123 of the constitution was used by the government of Morales to persecute those it considered its enemies, many of whom had held some public position. Even though the article said that the law was not retroactive, exceptions were made for cases of corruption and for "investigating, processing, and sanctioning crimes committed by public servants against State interests" (Sánchez Berzaín 2013, 102–14).

6. After his resignation, several fiscal inquiries were conducted, and penal proceedings were brought against him for the crimes of terrorism, sedition, ecocide, genocide, and statutory rape. All of these charges were shelved when Luis Arce took office as president.

7. He has also been accused of crimes of terrorism and genocide due to the approximately thirty-three deaths that occurred during the confrontations between Morales supporters and law enforcement at the time he resigned and left the country. As a result of these crimes, some military and police commanders, ministers, and other officials have also been investigated and arrested.

Chapter 6

The Government of Daniel Ortega

Anything can happen here, except for the Sandinista Front to lose power. . . . I told Daniel Ortega that we can pay any price. Whatever they say . . . , let's do what we have to do. . . . The highest price would be to lose power.

—FSLN founder and director Tomás Borge Martínez, who held top-level positions in the FSLN governments[1]

There will be a Sandinista Front for a long time, for as long as say 100 years, for as long as say forever.

—Nicaraguan president Daniel Ortega (2007–)[2]

In the 1979 ousting of dictator Anastasio Somoza Debayle, a member of a political dynasty that had ruled Nicaragua for forty-three years, the role of the Sandinista National Liberation Front (Frente Sandinista de Liberación Nacional, FSLN)[3] was key. This political-military organization of young revolutionaries aimed to overthrow the Somoza dictatorship through the armed struggle then in vogue in Latin America and to set up a government that would emulate the economic and social transformations made in Cuba by Fidel Castro. The Sandinista political project did not include recovering freedom and reestablishing democracy.

Daniel Ortega was a militant in its ranks and had been convicted for robbing a bank to finance the revolutionary struggle. He remained in prison for seven years, until a Sandinista commando managed to free him by forcing the exchange of Ortega and eight companions for high-level government officials, relatives, and friends of the Somoza family taken hostage at a social gathering in 1974. Four years later, the dictatorship fell, dictator Anastasio Somoza (son of the former dictator of the same name) fled the country, the

Sandinista guerrillas triumphantly entered Managua, and the people cel-ebrated the recovery of democracy and freedom.

The transitional government set up to reestablish democracy under the name National Reconstruction Junta (Junta de Reconstrucción Nacional) was composed of representatives of Sandinismo (Daniel Ortega, writer Sergio Ramírez, and Moisés Hassan), of the business community (Alfonso Robelo), and of political sectors (Violeta Barrios de Chamorro, widow of politician and journalist Pedro Joaquín Chamorro, who had been murdered by the Somoza regime). Ortega was appointed its coordinator. According to Ramírez, more notable Sandinista leaders were ruled out, and Ortega was chosen because he was "the least prepared, the least charismatic, and the most boring speaker" (Varela 2021). They surely thought that those limitations would hinder his ability to project himself as a popular leader.

Alfonso Robelo and Violeta Chamorro (in English, use of her married name is more common) resigned before a year had passed, disenchanted by the Sandinistas' hegemonic procedures derived from the armed power they held, the daily disturbances created by their activists in the streets, but, above all, the close relations they had established with Cuba and the Soviet Union, whose Marxist ideas, revolutionary practices, and anti-imperialist positions they tried to replicate in Nicaragua. The authority of the Reconstruction Junta was merely symbolic, since the FSLN controlled the mobilized popular bases, and its commanders, together with the guerrilla groups, had replaced Somoza's troops and military commanders. The labels Sandinista Popular Army (Ejército Popular Sandinista) and Sandinista Police (Policía Sandinista), which these groups adopted, reflected their political alignment.

The socialist, revolutionary, and anti-imperialist positions of the new Nicaraguan government trapped it in the international conflicts unleashed by the Cold War waged by the Soviet Union and the United States across the globe. President Ronald Reagan, concerned that "international commu-nism" would take control in another Latin American nation besides Cuba, encouraged the formation of an irregular army, which would be known as the Contras (short for counterrevolutionaries), armed, financed, and advised by the U.S. intelligence agency (CIA).

The exhausting military actions and the severe economic deterioration caused by the Contras did not succeed in destabilizing the Sandinista gov-ernment and did not diminish its popularity. So in 1984 Daniel Ortega was elected president with two-thirds of the votes cast. This ample election win contributed to consolidating the Sandinista Revolution by adding democratic legitimacy to the political and military power it held and the support it had earned outside Nicaragua's borders, among progressive and revolutionary sectors in Latin America and other parts of the world.

As a result of the implementation of revolutionary policies, mainly economic, the once "prosperous" Nicaragua was plunged into a deep social and humanitarian crisis, which worsened when Ortega's term in office and the civil war ended. Annual inflation was then at 13,000 percent, thirty thousand Nicaraguans had died, poverty levels were worse, and the economic losses caused by the conflict and poor governance had risen to seventeen billion dollars. This was partly because of the onerous consequences of the civil war between the Contras and Sandinistas but mostly because of the application and consequences of policies and programs typical of socialist economies: centralized planning, careless management of public finances, expropriations, nationalization of private-sector activities, and the withdrawal of investments and business initiatives.

By the mid-1980s, these circumstances coincided with the rise of a regional consensus on the need to put an end to the serious and costly armed conflicts in some Central American countries and to reestablish the damaged democratic institutions. This idea was promoted by the Contadora Group formed by the Central American countries and supported by the other Latin American nations represented by the so-called Support Group. The consensus resulted in the Esquipulas Peace Accords (1986 and 1987), signed in Esquipulas and in the capital of Guatemala by the presidents of Costa Rica, El Salvador, Guatemala, Honduras, and Nicaragua,[4] to establish the procedures and measures to be taken to recover peace and democracy in the region.

This important peacekeeping initiative, the support it received from the international community, the widespread desire to put an end to violence, and the negative economic and social panorama faced by Sandinismo forced Ortega to agree to peace. To this end, he negotiated democratic coexistence with the opposition, which included halting military actions by the Contras and dissolving their armed forces (1990).

The serious socioeconomic problems unleashed by the Sandinistas, the onerous aftermath of the civil war, and the unified economic, social, and political sectors that made up the opposition contributed to Ortega's defeat in the 1990 presidential elections. These elections were won by Violeta Chamorro. The negative perception that most citizens had of the Sandinista government and the united front of the opposition's political organizations once again played a role in the electoral setbacks suffered by Ortega in the 1996 and 2001 elections. They occurred despite the fact that he had moderated his radical revolutionary positions and changed the symbols, colors, and slogans of his party in order to improve its image and thus win the support of voters who were suspicious of Sandinismo.

Many believed that, after three consecutive election losses, Ortega was finished as a politician, but to general surprise he made a comeback in the 2006 elections. His time would likely have been over if the democratic forces had not been divided and if the Sandinista leader had not managed to get election rules changed so that he could avoid an adverse second round of voting. Even so, in the presidential elections of that year there were doubts that his triumph had been legitimate since 8 percent of the votes were not counted and the Sandinista-controlled Supreme Electoral Council (CSE for its acronym in Spanish) never presented the final results. Electoral fraud would be more evident in the presidential elections of 2011 and 2016, also won by Ortega.

It was said that President Arnoldo Alemán's openness to negotiating the agreement that opened the doors of power for Ortega might have originated in the national interest of putting an end to social unrest. Such unrest was seen in protests and demonstrations, barricades, and strikes mounted by the Sandinistas and social organizations controlled by them (teachers, students, workers, and professionals). After losing the presidential election, Ortega had said that he would "govern from below." In addition to affecting the government politically, these actions disrupted the day-to-day work of the inhabitants of Managua, public transportation, the movement of consumer goods, and economic activities. These were problems that the capital and the country had been experiencing since Chamorro's time in office.

More than the pacification of public life, what really counted was an exchange of favors, that is, a quid pro quo that would allow the corrupt Alemán to escape justice and the ambitious Ortega to return to power.

The agreement of the two caudillos was laid out in a set of legal and constitutional reforms. The most important one was to reduce the percentage of votes that the winning candidate had to obtain in the first round of voting in order to be declared president-elect without having to go through a second round. If he reached 35 percent and surpassed the second-place candidate by at least 5 percent, he was considered the winner, as opposed to the previous requirement of 45 percent. Thanks to this reform, Ortega was able to be elected president in 2006, despite having obtained a percentage of votes lower than or equal to those obtained in his three previous failed attempts. The split in the Liberal Party also contributed to Ortega's win since it had two candidates running in the election (Jarquín 2016, 25–26).

Through a second reform, Alemán was granted the privilege of joining the National Assembly as one of its members after having served as president of the republic. A third reform divided the composition of the Supreme Court of Justice between the two majority parties, the Sandinista Party and the Liberal Party. In addition to allowing him to retain some political influence, being a deputy granted Alemán immunity in the event of criminal prosecution. Furthermore, a justice system in which half of the magistrates were from his party could be more easily influenced than one composed of judges independent from political interests.

This is what ultimately happened. Alemán was prosecuted for acts of corruption during his mandate, denounced by Enrique Bolaños, the president who had succeeded him and who was from Alemán's own party. These acts were so blatant that the National Assembly deprived Alemán of his immunity so that he could be investigated by the justice system. Ortega secured Alemán's acquittal in the Supreme Court of Justice (CSJ) by adding the votes of Sandinista magistrates to the not-guilty ruling proposed by the Liberal judges.

The Ortega–Alemán pact did not end there. It led to the resignation of the president and officers of the National Assembly, so that their posts could be occupied by Sandinista deputies, who held the majority even though they represented only one-third of the members. Ortega's political control of the legislative body extended to the CSJ, the Supreme Electoral Council, and the Comptroller's Office (Jarquín 2016, 32). Thus, before winning the 2006 presidential elections, thanks to political concessions made by Alemán, Ortega had managed to turn the most important state institutions into instruments that served his personal political interests.

When Ortega returned to the presidency of Nicaragua, Fidel Castro reportedly gave him the following advice: "Reach an understanding with the gringos, reach an understanding with the businessmen, but do not give them free elections" (Jarquín 2016, 13). Whether this is true or not, it is what Ortega did when he took office again in 2006–2007. His government was marked by peaceful and constructive coexistence with the United States, high standards for businesses, an ecclesiastic relationship with the Catholic Church, and control of electoral processes so that he would always win. Of the socialist and Marxist ideas of Sandinismo, the only thing he had kept was the revolutionary rhetoric.

Ortega suddenly became a fervent Catholic; incorporated invocations to God, the Virgin Mary, and the saints in his speeches; and described the Nicaragua he was dictatorially governing as "Christian, socialist, and [a country] of solidarity." His wife did the same thing. This religiosity led him to adopt the Catholic Church's moral position on abortion. To demonstrate his faith, he issued totally restrictive legislation on abortion, making it a crime even if the life of the mother was at stake.

He also showed himself to be a politician respectful of private property, willing to grant security and protection to national and foreign investment and to promote "harmonious" relations with the U.S. government. In this context, he advocated for the free trade agreement with the United States (CAFTA) and contributed to its implementation. Such policies encouraged economic growth, employment, and general well-being.

In the social area, in order to gain popular sympathy, he decreed free education and health-care services and the equally free distribution of medicines, school supplies, and other goods to the poorest, most destitute sectors. These programs generated political benefits for him because they addressed the felt needs of the popular sectors and because they were managed in a clientelistic manner by the territorial apparatus of the Sandinista Party.

The defeat of the opposition in the 2006 elections forced its reunification for the 2008 municipal elections. The two branches of liberalism ran together, supported even by dissidents from the Sandinista Party. As had happened in previous elections, the Liberals expected to triumph easily, especially in Managua and other cities where they had traditionally held a majority. No such thing happened. The Supreme Electoral Council altered the results to favor the candidates of the Sandinista government, a fraud that allowed it to win in 99 out of the 146 municipalities in dispute. This fraud was repeated in the next seven elections, including the presidential and general elections of 2011 and 2016, in which the dictator plainly and simply prevented the opposition from participating.

The European Union, the OAS, and the Carter Center criticized some of these anomalies, and as a result the government no longer accepted the presence of international observers, whom it labeled as "scoundrels" (Peraza in Jarquín 2016, 139).

Upon returning to the presidency, Ortega, aware of Sandinismo's minority, had the CSE make whatever arrangements were necessary to win any electoral event in which it took part. He has made use of multiple arbitrary ploys to achieve this end. He has stripped opposition political movements of their legal status, disqualified candidates with options to win, hindered the registration of their candidacies, imposed an overrepresentation of the Sandinista Party in the legislature, altered results in voting precincts, made voting records disappear during the general ballot count, prohibited the publication of results, denied the representatives of opposition parties access to voting centers, prevented the verification of results, used the economic resources of the state and its institutions, and placed a higher number of ballots in the ballot boxes than the number of voters.

Such actions, and those to be discussed below, aroused concern in the international community regarding the deterioration of democratic institutions and civil liberties in Nicaragua during the Ortega administration. Latin America, North America, and the OAS remained at the fringe of this problem.

In view of the abovementioned facts, it could be said that, when Ortega returned to the presidency, he made electoral fraud an institution of the Sandinista revolution—perhaps the most important one because his ability to remain in power would depend on it.

The exercise of absolute power, regardless of the morality and legality of the means employed, explains a remark made by one of the old Sandinistas. Three and a half years into Daniel Ortega's second consecutive government, with the proliferation of criticism for his abuses, restrictions on rights and freedoms, and the institutionalization of electoral fraud, "Commander" Tomás Borge stated, "Anything can happen here, except for the Sandinista Front to lose power." (See the full quotation in the epigraph of this chapter.)

That statement explains Ortega's connivance with corrupt ex-president Alemán. Thanks to the agreements made with him, Ortega would be elected president again, would put all the powers of the state under his command, and would be reelected indefinitely. That phrase merely repeats the Leninist slogan that public ethics, the laws, and the constitution—including the general interest, citizens' votes, and human rights—cannot be above the objectives of a revolutionary project, but such discourse continues to sustain and justify Daniel Ortega's daily outrages and crimes even though his government is no longer revolutionary but rather a caudillo-like, dynastic, dictatorial, corrupt venture.

In dictatorships, particularly those inspired by Marxism, public opinion is controlled by the government, and freedom of expression is limited or nonexistent. Consistent with this repressive policy, Ortega defined the independent press as an "enemy" to be silenced, controlled, or eliminated. With this objective in mind, he co-opted the press through perks; through threats and extortion, got it to censor itself; made paper imports difficult; denied it official information; shut down radio stations, newspapers, and television stations; set up a media conglomerate controlled by his sons; and persecuted journalists judicially and forced them into exile. According to the Superior Council of Private Enterprise (Consejo Superior de la Empresa Privada, COSEP), twenty media outlets have been closed or confiscated by Ortega since 2014 (*El Comercio* 2020c).

In mid-2018, youth protests took place in Managua and other cities, motivated by a social security system reform that established a 5 percent tax on retirement pensions.[5] Suddenly and spontaneously, the citizen indignation that had been building up for years, fueled by disproportionate repression by police forces and civilian groups armed by the government, boiled over. Under the leadership and guidance of the Nicaraguan youth, they launched a massive popular protest against the Ortega–Murillo dictatorship.[6] The moderates hoped that the deteriorated democratic institutions could be reestablished, while the radicals hoped that the authoritarian Daniel Ortega would resign or be removed and that early presidential elections would be held. Everyone was fed up with Ortega's abuses, corruption, electoral frauds, and systematic violations of citizens' freedoms. To recover those very freedoms years before, young Nicaraguans had enlisted in Sandinismo, taken up arms, and offered up their lives.

During these critical days, it seems that Rosario Murillo proactively acted on behalf of the bewildered Ortega, who had not imagined the possibility that his government would have to face a popular revolt. "Let's go all out" was the war cry with which the vice president called on the police and the Sandinista gangs to undertake an "operation cleanup" of demonstrators in the streets and squares of Managua. She also publicly defended the regime and denounced the demonstrators. Before these events took place, she would interject the invocation "God willing" in her public speeches.

After these events, it became clear to citizens that the Nicaraguan government was being led by the second-in-command and that the vice president was the one who did and undid. This influence became evident when she changed Ortega's image, discourse, practices, and strategies so that he could win the 2006 presidential election. It was not in vain that he had called her the "eternally loyal" Rosario. He had plenty of reasons to label her as loyal because she had proclaimed his innocence and recriminated his stepdaughter Zoilamérica Narváez when the latter accused him of having sexually assaulted her when she was a girl and raped her when she was a teenager.

The commotion that these events caused in public opinion led to a breakdown in the ties that Ortega's government had established with the Catholic Church and the business community since his return to the presidency of Nicaragua in 2007. When these influential pressure groups moved to the opposition, the president and the vice president put them in the crosshairs of their persecutions.

The Episcopal Conference, bishops, and clergymen, in formal statements and in their homilies in the pulpits, denounced and condemned the violent attacks on demonstrators and the attacks on human rights carried out by the repressive forces of the government. The most critical voice against these outrages was that of the auxiliary bishop of Managua, Silvio Báez (*El País* 2019a). When Pope Francis called him to Rome with no explanation, the bishop said that he had not requested to leave Nicaragua and that "the Holy Father was responsible" for the decision for him to leave his country. Upon arriving in Rome, the prelate called his exile "painful obedience." Writer Sergio Ramírez called it a "forced exile," and former Sandinista Dora María Téllez, who is now an imprisoned opponent, commented that "the Pope had granted Ortega a fervent wish." Báez now lives in the United States.

Both the church and the business community called for "halting the repression, freeing the youth," reinstating freedom of the press, and "discussing the country's democratization." They also warned that "the powerful who imagine themselves eternal" and believe that "repressing the people forever ensures them the power they possess" were blind. Murillo called them "coup plotters, terrorists, demons with cassocks" and said they had "no respect for God, Christ, or the Virgin." Meanwhile, government troops attacked parishes and churches and evicted those who were hiding in them or who were on hunger strikes to demand the release of detainees.

In addition to joining the protests, COSEP became one of the organizers. Until these protests took place, businessmen had maintained regular dialogues with the Ortega government, which they advised in the economic field and to which they offered their collaboration. They also obtained good contracts. In one of their communiqués, they asked for "an end to police repression, the release of those detained and the guarantee of freedom of the press." Later, when the campaign for the presidential elections began, the president and vice president of COSEP were arrested, accused of money laundering, property and assets laundering, treason, promoting foreign interference, and other crimes included in the aforementioned persecutory laws.

The political parties, which had been losing ascendancy in public opinion, played a diminished role in the protests, due to their fragmentation, disputes, and the absence of prominent leaders. Although they came together to strengthen their presence in the Civic Alliance (Alianza Cívica, AC) and the National Blue and White Unity (Unidad Nacional Azul y Blanco, UNAB), an important role was played by the participation of civil society and of many Sandinista leaders and militants who had become disenchanted with Ortega's caudillo authoritarianism and had been abandoning him since the end of the twentieth century.

The international community severely scrutinized the Ortega government. The Inter-American Commission on Human Rights (IACHR) reported that, in the three months of protests, 325 participants were killed and hundreds of Nicaraguans imprisoned and tortured by police and paramilitary gangs armed by the government (2018). More than two thousand were injured, and more than fifty thousand left the country and marched into exile to escape imprisonment and torture and to save their lives. Many of them were young people, students, and inhabitants of the rebellious city of Masaya, which together with Managua and Leon was a stronghold for the popular protests. The international press agreed that the attack on Masaya and its Indigenous neighborhood by hooded government troops was brutal. This was compounded by the destruction, burning, and looting of places where the protests were being held or broadcast, such as Radio Darío and student centers.

An OAS report stated that the police "systematically opened fire against the population and set in motion a repressive wave that included torture and sexual assaults in prisons."[7] It also stated that the violence unleashed was not the result of individual or police excesses but "of a policy of repression promoted and endorsed by the highest State authority." The report issued by the Inter-American Commission on Human Rights (IACHR 2018) maintained that police and parapolice groups, under the command of President Ortega, carried out a lethal repression; that attention to the wounded was denied in public hospitals; and that doctors who agreed to treat them were fired. For a group of independent experts, "most of the murders and serious injuries were the responsibility of the National Police," which acted "in coordination with armed paramilitary groups."

A high-level commission created by the United Nations concluded that the human rights violations "led to an alteration of the constitutional order that seriously affects the democratic order," and a UN High Commissioner for Human Rights denounced that in Nicaragua "violence and repression have led to a systematic erosion of human rights and exposed the general fragility of institutions and the rule of law" (OAS 2019e).

The OAS called the attention of public opinion and the governments of the American continent to the outrages suffered by democracy and human rights because of the Nicaraguan government. The United States imposed economic sanctions, which were tightened in the following years and extended to officials and companies of the Sandinista government and family members of Daniel Ortega. They included freezing capital deposited abroad and prohibiting U.S. companies from doing business with those companies. When announcing them, U.S. Treasury Secretary Steven Mnuchin stressed that the economic sanctions imposed by the Trump administration affected companies used "to launder money and prop up the Ortega regime at the expense of the Nicaraguan people."

Among the dozens of officials sanctioned were Vice President Rosario Murillo, as well as three of her children, the presidents of the National Assembly and the electoral authority, the heads of the police and the army, the attorney general, several ministers, FSLN leaders, the president's private secretary, financial institutions, and an oil company.

For their part, the European Union, the United Kingdom, and even the usually impassive Switzerland also ordered the freezing of assets of Ortega's relatives, police chiefs, public enterprises, and dozens of officials close to the president, for "their responsibility in the deterioration of human rights, democracy, and the rule of law." With 90 percent of the votes of its members, the European Parliament approved the application of economic sanctions against the president and vice president of Nicaragua. It warned all of them that if laws being processed in the National Assembly aimed at repressing and electorally disqualifying opponents, pursuing cybercrimes, and controlling the international financing of civil society were approved, it would suspend the trade agreement that Europe maintains with Nicaragua.[8]

In 2020, the OAS General Assembly passed a resolution calling on the Nicaraguan government to "reestablish democratic institutions and respect for human rights through free and fair elections." It also called for forming an "independent, transparent and respectable" Supreme Electoral Council to allow the reestablishment of the exercise of civil and political rights.

This firm reaction of the international community, in defense of democracy and freedom, did not yield results. In late 2020, the Nicaraguan government, rather than reversing its repressive policy, made it harsher by issuing the very laws that the United States and the European Union had questioned. Thus, to the bloody repression in the "streets," the Ortega dictatorship added control over the daily life of Nicaraguans, by restricting, prohibiting, and penalizing freedom of expression, the rights of the opposition, and the activities of civil society.

The docile Sandinista assembly enacted three repressive laws: on cybercrimes, foreign agents, and sovereignty. Later on, the General Law for the Regulation and Oversight of Non-Profit Organizations was also issued.

The first, which was called the Gag Law, typifies a long and varied list of crimes committed through "information and communication technologies," that is, the so-called social networks, referring to posting opinions and obtaining and disseminating information. Guilty parties may be punished with fines and imprisonment of up to ten years.

The second obliges citizens working in companies, foundations, or other organizations that receive funds from abroad to register as foreign agents and to report their financing and activities to the government, in order to avoid external interference. To monitor their activities and punish those who do not comply with the law, it provides for the application of the Anti–Asset Laundering Law.

The third punishes those who threaten the rights of the people, organize protests with external financing, incite foreign interference, call for military interventions, propose economic blockades, demand or applaud the imposition of sanctions, and harm the greater interests of the nation. Punishments are up to twenty years in prison, loss of eligibility to hold public office, and the stigma of being considered a traitor to the homeland.

The fourth is of a markedly persecutory nature because it gives the government the power to oversee NGOs' activities and to limit their external funding and also gives congress the power to dissolve them summarily.

The newspaper *La Prensa*, the oldest in Nicaragua (founded in 1926), was effectively closed down. The government deprived it of paper and electricity; imprisoned its manager; intervened in its bank accounts; and forced its director, Carlos Fernando Chamorro,[9] into exile by accusing him of customs fraud and laundering of money, goods, and assets and by issuing an arrest warrant. Other media outlets were also raided, such as Televisión Digital, owned by the brother of presidential candidate Cristiana Chamorro. Its equipment was confiscated, and its director, Pedro Joaquín Chamorro, was arrested. Meanwhile, audiovisual media controlled by the children of dictator Ortega or by businessmen close to the government operated freely.

The Sandinista constitution limited the reelection of the president of the republic to one term (he had already been president between 1985 and 1990), which is why Ortega could not run again in 2011. Two years before the end of his government, with the argument that the prohibition in Article 147 of the constitution affected a human right and the equality of citizens before the law, he got a chamber of the Supreme Court of Justice, illegally formed, to declare the inapplicability of that provision. Subsequently, the National Assembly, with an absolute Sandinista majority achieved through one of the many electoral frauds, reformed the constitution, established the indefinite reelection of the president of the republic, and eliminated the second round of voting to facilitate the triumph of the candidate-dictator (Icaza Gallard 2016, 88–89, 103).

With the approval of the indefinite reelection of Daniel Ortega, which would make it possible for him to govern Nicaragua in perpetuity, the siege with which the dictator had been cornering Nicaraguan democracy, to turn it into a corrupt and tyrannical autocracy, ended.

Before that, Ortega had already placed all the powers of the state under his control and command, de facto or de jure: the justice system, the National Assembly, the Attorney General's Office, the Comptroller's Office, the Electoral Council, the armed forces, the police, even the autonomous municipalities. Now, according to the Inter-American Commission on Human Rights, the justice system and other public powers "are subject to the Government's will and control," the doors to democratic participation closed, opposition political movements deprived of their legal status, the media shut down, and social and civil-society organizations persecuted.

Meanwhile, Ortega had also subordinated the Sandinista Party to his absolute authority. After stripping it of its ideals, he turned it into an instrument of his ambition to return to power and remain in power indefinitely. He eliminated internal democracy to prevent the free election of leadership and debate on the political decisions of candidates and those in office. In its place, he imposed his vertical authority, which leaders and members had to accept submissively. Those who did not agree to be obsequious servants were removed from their functions and from the party and replaced by those who agreed. For these reasons and Ortega's dictatorial exercise of power, many have been leaving the party ranks voluntarily since the beginning of the twenty-first century.

Fifteen Nicaraguan human rights organizations, in a report endorsed by the Inter-American Commission on Human Rights, denounced that Ortega has committed "crimes against humanity in the framework of State terrorism" by criminalizing social protests; imprisoning, kidnapping, and torturing opponents; setting up clandestine prisons; firing teachers and health professionals; and killing children and adolescents in the 2018 protests.

The 2016 and 2021 presidential elections were held under these undemocratic conditions. In this case, the dictator did not observe protocol and did not even wait for the voting to take place before committing the customary electoral fraud. In the first, in which he was elected for a third term, he nominated his wife for the vice-presidency, and the CSE, made up solely of Ortega supporters, eliminated opposition candidate Luis Callejas from the race. In the second, he obtained a fourth consecutive term using similar means, which became draconian. He had the opposition's seven presidential pre-candidates arrested since they were preparing to challenge him for the presidency. So that nothing would be missing in the buffoonery he had staged, he was accompanied by "bit players in his show" (*candidatos comparsa*) whose campaign expenses were paid for with public money.

As stated in the first pages of this book, one of the innovations of the twenty-first-century dictators is having electoral frauds begin before the citizens even turn out to vote.

The European Union called these elections "fake," the OAS said they were "a parody," the IACHR warned that they were seeking to "perpetuate Ortega in power," and the United States called them "dictatorial." The electoral process and the results were rejected by thirty-six European[10] and American countries, and only five Latin American countries accepted them, with Bolivia, Cuba, and Venezuela even applauding the fraudulent results.

As the virtual sole candidate, Ortega supposedly triumphed with 76 percent of the votes cast and managed to win seventy-five of the ninety-one legislative seats available, an absolute majority. According to a poll conducted by CID-Gallup, if any opposition candidate had managed to intervene, he would have obtained 65 percent of the votes, against 19 percent for Daniel Ortega. According to the NGO Urnas Abiertas, 81 percent of the electorate abstained from voting.

The calls made by the Episcopal Conference to Catholic couple Ortega–Murillo to release political prisoners, to respect "the vote of the people," and to guarantee "credible, fair and transparent" elections were in vain. So were those made by the OAS General Assembly, the UN Human Rights Council, and the Inter-American Court of Human Rights.

According to human rights organizations, at mid-2022 Nicaragua had more than 190 political prisoners,[11] of which only ten predated the revolt of 2018, the year that Ortega resolved to exterminate the opposition. The political prisoners include politicians, businessmen, journalists, feminists, activists, artists, students, and even Sandinista comrades such as Dora María Téllez, Víctor Hugo Tinoco, and Hugo Torres,[12] as well as the presidential candidates who tried to participate in the elections won fraudulently by the Ortega–Murillo slate. In the Sandinista dungeon of Chipote, they have been subjected to different forms of torture, the most benign of these being permanent light or darkness in their cells. To escape from the persecution of the dictatorship, one hundred thousand Nicaraguans have voluntarily gone into exile, mainly in Costa Rica, to save their lives and to ensure their own and their families' freedom.

Some of the approximately forty political prisoners detained during the electoral process have now been judged and convicted with sentences of up to fifteen years for the "crimes" of conspiracy, effects on national integrity, and dissemination of fake news. The hearings are held in secret, in the jails where the prisoners are being held, not publicly as stipulated by the penal code. The accused are questioned by prosecutors and convicted by judges acting as though they were political commissioners of the dictatorship, on the basis of testimonies given mostly by police officers.

The twenty-seven sentenced individuals include Dora María Téllez, a former Sandinista guerrilla member, and Lesther Alemán, the young student who challenged Ortega verbally during the 2018 popular uprising and asked him to resign in order to save Nicaraguan democracy. Also included is Cristiana Chamorro, the most popular of the presidential candidates who aspired to run against Ortega; she has been accused of the crime of asset laundering through the NGO that she headed. For twenty-five years she had worked to defend freedom of speech and to promote independent journalism. Chamorro was sentenced to eight years in prison and charged a sizeable fine. During the trial, the prosecutor did not call any expert witness to demonstrate that the crime of which she was accused had actually been committed, and the police officers that testified against her said that they were acting under instructions from their superiors.

Civil society was not exempt from the Sandinista government's persecution by the police and in the courts either. It was targeted after Ortega and Murillo managed to thwart the popular uprising of 2018. In subsequent years, especially between 2021 and 2022, the couple began a campaign to eradicate the NGOs with ties to opposition political leaders. Organizations with no political alignment were no exception, even some that had been founded by the Sandinistas themselves, as well as some U.S. and European organizations that had been implementing social programs in Nicaragua for many years. In 2022, a group of United Nations experts established that more than seven hundred NGOs had been shut down. These organizations had been defending human rights; promoting equality for women; fighting for the conservation of nature; training, aiding, and advising Indigenous communities and marginalized social sectors; and providing education and health care services to the neediest. The dictatorship made twelve private universities subject to state control and, according to Reporters without Borders, shut down some twenty media outlets, including Catholic radio stations. More than one hundred journalists had to seek exile in order to protect their freedom.

The once ostensibly very Catholic Ortega and Murillo used to put expressions of their religious faith regularly on display. However, they suddenly left it aside and began persecuting Catholic bishops, priests, and nuns, accusing them of "subversive activities." The Missionaries of Charity (a religious order founded by Mother Teresa of Calcutta) were politically harassed, judicially persecuted, and expelled from the country. Some priests and bishop Rolando Álvarez, a critic of the human rights abuses committed by the Sandinista government, were arbitrarily arrested. Places of worship were attacked by law enforcement; the papal nuncio was expelled from the country; and a number of priests were tried in criminal courts, in some cases using fraudulent accusations of sexual misconduct.

The authoritarian political process analyzed in the preceding pages has led to the replacement of Nicaraguan democracy by a dictatorial regime, similar to the one installed by the Somoza family overthrown forty years earlier by the revolutionary Sandinista youth and other democratic forces. The ideals of reestablishing democracy, guaranteeing transparent electoral processes, honestly administering public funds, guaranteeing the exercise of civil liberties, respecting human rights, and abolishing political dynasties have been buried by Daniel Ortega's dictatorship.

The Ortega–Murillo children control a variety of businesses and media, some created with funds taken from the economic aid granted by Chávez to Nicaragua (estimated at forty-five billion dollars), for which the government has never been accountable. Those who demand respect for democratic institutions; exercise their rights, liberties, and constitutional guarantees; and carry out protests and demonstrations are repressed by the police and paramilitary groups; many are imprisoned, tortured, exiled, or murdered. The ideal of transforming Nicaragua economically and socially, to turn it into a democratic society at the service of all its inhabitants, has been replaced by the interests, ambitions, businesses, and conveniences of Daniel Ortega, his wife, and his children. The most important of these are to accumulate as much power as possible, to remain in power indefinitely, to exercise power ruthlessly, and to enrich the ruling family and those who faithfully serve it.

In order to have all the traits of the Latin American dictators of the twentieth century, this old-time revolutionary is determined to form a political dynasty that will rule Nicaragua forever. He had his wife, Rosario Murillo, elected vice president and has politically and economically empowered his children, thus forming a dynastic clan that has replaced Sandinismo and the people in governing his country.

None of these absurd events was foreign to the Somoza family. In this regard, it is worth citing the pertinent part of a text written by Edmundo Jarquín, a former presidential and vice presidential candidate:

Almost nothing is possible without access to Ortega, his wife and/or his "little sultans." The enactment of a law, court rulings, concessions, company registrations, identity cards, scholarships, access to social programs, public-sector employment, the legal status of political parties, imprisonments and releases from prison, exports to Venezuela, and even sections of municipal markets or Covid testing are impossible without knocking on Carmen's doors or having access to the "little sultans." (Jarquín 2020)[13]

If you add up the years Daniel Ortega has been in office, including the de facto presidency of 1979–1985 following the triumph of the Sandinista Revolution, he will have governed Nicaragua for thirty-two years if he completes his fifth term, which began in 2022. This period would be equivalent to the total duration of the governments of all three members of the Somoza family: Anastasio and his sons Luis and Anastasio.

The guerrilla who took up arms to put an end to the Somoza family dictatorship, reestablish democracy, and consecrate economic and social equality has reedited the old story of the Latin American caudillos of the nineteenth and twentieth centuries. Once in power, they forgot their democratic declarations; installed dictatorial regimes; enriched themselves compulsively; and repressed, persecuted, and victimized their critics. In addition, they fraudulently got themselves reelected to govern for the rest of their lives, an ambition they could not always fulfill.

Forty-two years after the Sandinistas triumphantly entered Managua to put an end to the Somoza dictatorship, Daniel Ortega governs his country as though the last Somoza had commissioned him to perpetuate the regime Somoza's father had established.

NOTES

1. Interview on Telesur, YouTube.com, July 26, 2009.

2. Quote from the funeral of Tomás Borge (cited in Gioconda Belli, "Ortega y Murillo escriben su epitafio," *El País*, November 4, 2021, https://elpais.com/opinion/2021-11-05/ortega-y-murillo-escriben-su-epitafio.html).

3. The name comes from Augusto Sandino, a Nicaraguan revolutionary from the first third of the twentieth century who, as the head of a guerrilla group, managed to put an end to the U.S. occupation of Nicaragua.

4. Óscar Arias, Napoleón Duarte, Vinicio Cerezo, José Azcona, and Daniel Ortega, respectively.

5. That measure made the young people with grandparents who received it indignant, as did the fires that had occurred on the Indio Maíz ecological reserve and that had been neglected by the government.

6. Previously, there had been minor protests by peasant farmers, originating in the risk of losing lands that were to be used for the construction of an interoceanic canal

negotiated with a Chinese businessman. The government had controlled these situations by preventing the protesters from reaching Managua.

7. After the report was issued, Ortega expelled the OAS mission from Nicaragua.

8. The European Union has not confirmed this European Parliament resolution.

9. His father, Pedro Joaquín Chamorro, was killed during the dictatorship of Anastasio Somoza Debayle.

10. Ortega called the European countries that had condemned the fraudulent Nicaraguan elections "fascists, Franco supporters, and aligned with Hitler."

11. Information from the online resource Mechanism for Recognizing People Held as Political Prisoners (Mecanismo para el reconocimiento de personas presas políticas), an NGO in Nicaragua. Ortega has called them "Yankee imperialism sons of bitches" and said that the international press that reported on those facts were "servants of the CIA."

12. A retired Sandinista army general who died in prison after being convicted.

13. He calls Ortega's children "little sultans," in keeping with Max Weber's concept of "sultanism."

Chapter 7

The Government of Nayib Bukele

I have gone from being the dictator in El Salvador to being the coolest dictator in the world.

—El Salvadoran president Nayib Bukele (2019–)[1]

Unlike the other twenty-first-century dictators, who came from the military, union, peasant, guerrilla, and university worlds, Nayib Bukele came from the business world, somewhat more distant from politics and its eventualities than the others. In his early youth he had abandoned his university law studies to work for his father, a successful Palestinian emigrant. His father's business was involved mainly in the fields of advertising and communication, and for several years those activities linked him to the electoral campaigns of the Farabundo Martí National Liberation Front (Frente Farabundo Martí para la Liberación Nacional, FMLN).[2]

He had not been aligned with the ideas and practices of Marxist social and political organizations, so he had no ideological relationship with the so-called twenty-first-century socialism. Instead, he seemed more akin to capitalism, the market economy, and a smaller state role in development. Despite his background and these differences, the current president of El Salvador shared four defining characteristics with the political regimes established by the twenty-first-century dictatorships: authoritarianism, caudillismo, populism, and messianism. Following Chávez's example, Bukele has also sent signals that he intends to extend the Salvadoran "political model" to other Central American countries.

Even though his ideas did not coincide with the Marxist thinking of the FMLN, he joined that party and not the Nationalist Republican Alliance (Alianza Republicana Nacionalista, ARENA), which did represent his own ideas.[3] The former had ceased to be a revolutionary party since it decided to insert itself into the democratic life of El Salvador. It accepted representative democracy as a form of government and adopted a moderate socialist stance, even social-democratic positions. Nominated by the FMLN, Bukele was first elected mayor of a small town outside San Salvador and then elected mayor of the capital city in 2015. The positive, effective, and innovative management of the two municipalities and the social programs he implemented won Bukele widespread support, which he used to begin to carve out a national leadership role.

He was expelled from the FMLN barely halfway through his second term in office. According to the party's ethics committee, his expulsion was for violating the party's principles and statutes; committing acts of insubordination; promoting division; exhibiting personalistic attitudes; disrespecting women; and insulting, maligning, and slandering leaders and colleagues. A month later Bukele announced that he was forming his own party, which he called New Ideas (Nuevas Ideas). Registered in 2018, the party was ideologically pigeonholed in what came to be called populist conservatism or the populist Right.

The Supreme Electoral Tribunal impeded recognition of Bukele's party and also the sponsorship he received from another small party, the Social Democrats. This victimized him in public opinion, but he finally ran in the 2019 presidential race, supported by the Grand Alliance of National Unity (Gran Alianza de Unidad Nacional, GANA). He was surprisingly elected in the first round of voting, with 53 percent of the votes, something that had never happened before. He became the first president of the current democratic period that had not come from the FMLN–ARENA bipartisanship, which had governed El Salvador for two decades. However, despite his ample national and municipal win, he could not rely on a majority in the parliament.

In the first six months of his term, President Bukele focused his attention on policies of transparency, security, and public health.

With collaboration from the OAS and the participation of the Attorney General's Office, the government promoted the creation of the International Commission against Impunity in El Salvador (CICIES) to investigate and prosecute acts of corruption that had occurred in previous governments and in Bukele's. Its work was independent and harsh, and it was able to establish the responsibility of government officials in office for acts of that nature.

Bukele was personally determined to address the serious issue of personal safety and security from which El Salvador had been suffering for many years and which placed it among the countries with the highest murder rates in the world: 103 murders for every 100,000 inhabitants in the mid-2000s. These crimes occurred throughout almost all the Salvadoran territory and were mostly committed by three groups: Barrio 18 Sureños, Barrio 18 Revolucionarios, and MS-13, known as "the gangs."

Through a Territorial Control Plan, Bukele managed to significantly reduce the daily murder rate from twenty to three between 2019 and 2021 and consequently lower El Salvador's high crime rate. The plan was based on several measures: improving surveillance in prisons, reducing the funds of criminal gangs, bolstering the agencies in charge of safety and security, and incorporating the military into the fight against crime. Such a significant outcome must have benefited from the government's clandestine negotiations with the gangs, which curbed their operations in exchange for certain concessions made for gang members in prison, according to a report from the digital newspaper *El Faro* and confirmed by the U.S. government.[4]

Bukele's leadership and managerial experience—the former due to the widespread influence his opinion has on citizens—have been decisive for the relative success of the COVID pandemic vaccination program in El Salvador. In terms of the percentage of vaccinated people in relation to the total population, El Salvador is in an intermediate position in Latin America, and in Central America it is second only to Costa Rica. This positive result has encouraged the recovery of economic activities and employment.[5]

Because these policies responded to the needs and concerns of the population, they had an enormous impact on public opinion. Three of the four Salvadoran presidents[6] in the twenty-first century had been criminally prosecuted and convicted for serious corruption offenses. The first was deceased, the second in jail, and the third on the run. Nothing was more important to Salvadoran families than staying alive despite the daily murders committed by criminal gangs and escaping the disease, death, poverty, and unemployment caused by the coronavirus pandemic.

Not only the positive results of Bukele's administration can account for the high levels of popularity (over 80 percent) that he has enjoyed during the first half of his term in office. His charismatic youth, communication skills, convincing propaganda, advertising experience, populist discourse and practices,[7] and skillful use of social networks have also played a role, as has the citizens' perception that he was a contradictor of the discredited political system represented by the ARENA–FMLN bipartisanship. In this context, the early manifestations of authoritarianism, rather than harming him, favored him since they conveyed the image that he had the will and the character to do what needed to be done in El Salvador.

In early 2020, Bukele violently burst into the Legislative Assembly's meeting room. He entered accompanied by armed military and police personnel; took a seat in the main chair; and as if he were its president, prepared to lead the session that had been called by the Council of Ministers, as empowered by the constitution to do so in "extraordinary circumstances." The assembly had been reluctant to approve a $109 million loan obtained by the government to improve military and police equipment for their fight against criminal gangs. The session, which he arbitrarily tried to convene, could not begin because the mandatory quorum was not present. After looking at the sky and devoutly invoking divine illumination, he left the room. On the outskirts of the legislative palace, a crowd was waiting for him, part of which had been brought in by the government. He informed them that "God had spoken to him and asked him to be patient," and for that reason he would not occupy the assembly by force. After disparaging the deputies and calling them "scoundrels" and "criminals," he threatened them, saying that if in a week they did not approve the loan from the Central American Bank for Economic Integration, he would call for "popular insurrection." This possibility was foreseen in Article 87 of the constitution, but to reestablish the constitutional order, not to abolish it. He concluded his fiery speech by saying that "it is now clear who is in control of the situation," in other words, that all the powers of the state were at his fingertips.

Before these events occurred, he had already exhibited his authoritarian disposition when the COVID pandemic was unleashed. With the excuse that he needed to take extreme measures to combat it, he issued numerous repressive decrees outside the legal system, several of which were declared unconstitutional by the corresponding chamber of the Supreme Court of Justice. Nonetheless, he continued to apply them as if there had been no pronouncement by the body in charge of overseeing the constitutionality of the government's acts.

After the virtual disappearance of the ARENA and FMLN parties and their leaders, only the media and civil society were left in El Salvador's political sphere. Following the example of the other twenty-first-century dictators, Bukele considered them part of the government's enemy camp. To silence them or make them complacent, he has discredited them and intimidated them with labor inspections and tax audits, withdrawn official advertising, and marginalized them from the distribution of official information. Radio and television stations, as well as social networks, have become instruments of government propaganda and attacks on opponents and on the corruption apparatus and abuses of power. The same thing has occurred with the NGOs, which he is attempting to put under state control through a Law on Foreign Agents fashioned after the one issued by Daniel Ortega's dictatorship.

On Bukele's orders, an investigation into money laundering was started against the prestigious digital newspaper *El Faro*, which had published a report on government officials' clandestine negotiations with the heads of criminal gangs operating in El Salvador. It also reported that the cell phones of journalists, directors, and even some staff members had been tapped through a sophisticated information system that Israel sells only to governments. According to the University of Toronto's Citizen Lab, the phones of thirty-seven journalists and human rights activities were tapped.

In the Republic of El Salvador, the dictatorial drift of President Nayib Bukele, elected by the people to govern their country according to constitutional norms and laws and to reestablish a sound democracy, thus got underway and progressed.

In the parliamentary elections held in February 2021, the New Ideas Party managed to have fifty-six deputies elected, with eight more from its ally GANA. This result allowed the government to have an absolute majority in the Legislative Assembly. This unusual outcome virtually did away with ARENA and the FMLN, the parties that had dominated Salvadoran politics for three decades and whose representation was reduced to ten seats and four seats, respectively.

Bukele's high levels of popularity were a determining factor in the resounding triumph of the government's lists of legislators. His popularity served as the foundation on which the election campaigns of his candidates for the legislature were built. The candidates themselves did not present any proposal to the voters, nor did they exhibit their "new ideas." They even refused to debate with the opposition candidates and to give interviews to the independent press. They did not visit neighborhoods, towns, and cities to meet with voters and refrained from holding popular rallies. They limited themselves to repeating, ad nauseam, that the people should throw out what was the "same as always," represented by the ARENA and FMLN candidates, whom they blamed for all the ills the country was experiencing, including corruption and nepotism. Following the successful formula for Bukele's previous election campaign, they communicated directly with voters through social networks, especially Twitter and TikTok. Undeterred, they also violated all the prohibitions and restrictions established in the election law, such as that of using public resources, goods, personnel, and funds in their campaigns (Zemmouche 2021).

Since President Bukele had obtained a two-thirds majority in the Legislative Assembly, he did not need to call a constituent assembly to tailor a constitution for his authoritarian political project, as Hugo Chávez, Evo Morales, and Rafael Correa had all done. Instead, he followed the path opened up by Daniel Ortega, of overreaching in the use of his power and reforming the constitution with the rhetoric that he was proposing to "found a new country."[8]

When President Bukele's violent incursion into the Legislative Assembly headquarters took place, the constitutional chamber of the Supreme Court of Justice declared that his actions had been contrary to the constitution, reproached the army and the police for their participation in that abuse of power, and called the citizens' attention to the authoritarian danger that was looming over Salvadoran democracy.

The first resolution issued by the new Legislative Assembly at the start of its sessions was to remove the five members of the constitutional chamber. In their place, magistrates with ties to the government and to the New Ideas Party were appointed. Both these actions were in violation of express constitutional provisions, without any previous thoughtful debate on the legal validity and moral justification of such an unusual resolution. The same arbitrary procedure was followed by the assembly to surprisingly dismiss the attorney general and appoint a person trusted by the president to replace him. The attorney general had initiated investigations of high-ranking government officials for their participation in acts of corruption. Simultaneously, police picket lines had taken over the headquarters of the court and the Attorney General's Office. Once these abusive acts had been consummated, Bukele sent the following tweet: "Brave deputies fulfilling the popular mandate. God and the people are with you!"

Once in office, the new attorney general dissolved the commission that the government, together with the OAS, had formed to investigate corruption in public administration (CICIES). To justify his unusual decision, he argued that the regional organization had hired a former Salvadoran official accused of corruption. The OAS General Secretariat denied this assertion and accused the Salvadoran government of having requested that its officials not be investigated unless they were from previous administrations. This request could not be accepted, among other reasons because several investigations were already underway regarding acts of corruption that had occurred during the Bukele administration. Once the commission was dissolved, these investigations were shelved.

In an equally summary manner, the Legislative Assembly reformed the Judicial Career Law, ordering the mandatory retirement of judges and prosecutors who were over sixty years old or had served for more than thirty years. This reform affected approximately one-third of the former and dozens of the latter. Everyone was aware that the new judges and prosecutors would most certainly be appointed by the government, which they would then serve faithfully.

According to the Inter-American Court of Human Rights, "the mass dismissal of judges, particularly at the highest levels, constitutes an attack on the judiciary and against the democratic order." Human Rights Watch accused Bukele of "undermining basic democratic checks and balances" and using the military in public security operations. Similar pronouncements were made by the United Nations, the European Union, and the United States.

At the same time, by means of an ad hoc law, the assembly granted immunity to officials accused of corruption in the purchase of medicines to combat the pandemic. The Supreme Court of Justice was not allowed to investigate the assets of high-level government officials. The Institute for Access to Public Information, the Court of Accountability, and the Human Rights Ombudsman's Office, agencies in charge of overseeing government administration, were weakened, and entities by nature autonomous and independent were made subordinate to presidential authority (Moallic 2021). Furthermore, the investigations carried out by CICIES, including several cases of corruption at high levels of the government, were suspended. Digital media outlet *El Faro* meanwhile disclosed that the government was covertly negotiating a truce with the heads of criminal gangs (MS-13 and Barrio 18) for their criminal operations.

The sum of these facts that went against honesty, transparency, and public morality led the United States to include fourteen officials, seven of them close to President Bukele, on the Engel corruption list. Two of them[9] were sanctioned, according to Secretary of State Antony Blinken, for "facilitating and organizing secret meetings" with gang leaders. In addition, the justice minister's mother and Marta Catalina Recinos, Bukele's cabinet chief, were sanctioned for corruption, for operating "a multimillion-dollar corruption scheme in several ministries."

Meanwhile, the new constitutional chamber of the Supreme Court of Justice issued a ruling that opened up the possibility that incumbent presidents could be reelected immediately after the end of their terms, and it ordered the Supreme Electoral Tribunal to implement that ruling, which was clearly dedicated to President Nayib Bukele. That resolution reversed a 2014 ruling that had prohibited presidential reelection within ten years after the end of the term for which a president was elected. For its part, the constitution prohibits "a person who has held office for six months in the previous term or in the last six months prior to the beginning of the presidential term" from running for president, and the constitution can only be reformed through a favorable vote of two legislatures.

This dizzying amassing of power in the president of the republic has not left aside law enforcement, which Bukele has co-opted with increases in salaries and in the number of personnel in the police and the army. He uses both armed groups to carry out his abuses of power or simply to demonstrate that he has police and military personnel who will back him in imposing and enforcing his orders.

While Daniel Ortega has put his wife and children in charge of the office of public affairs, Bukele has handed over the management of important public affairs, inside and outside the country, to his brothers. Those matters should be the responsibility of ministers and other officials who now find themselves forced to comply with and execute the orders they receive from the Bukele family. These could include loan negotiations, contract awarding, administrative resolutions, government concessions, legal and regulatory reforms, and all kinds of appointments and dismissals. Since they hold no office and receive no salary, his brothers cannot be held accountable for the decisions they make and the instructions they give. Paradoxically, one of Nayib Bukele's presidential campaign banners had been to "End the Nepotism" practiced by ARENA and the FMLN (Moallic 2021).

On September 15, 2021, the bicentennial of the independence of Central America, there was a massive popular demonstration in San Salvador of union members, students, feminists, ex-combatants, professionals, small entrepreneurs, ARENA and FMLN militants, members of civil society, and regular citizens who had come together to protest against the Bukele dictatorship for very diverse reasons. This was the first sign that El Salvador could come to have a democratic core aimed at recovering democracy.

In late March 2022, criminal gangs surprisingly resumed operating and between a Friday and a Sunday killed eighty-seven people, mostly in one day. According to the Salvadoran media, this was the worst slaughter in the last thirty years. Unlike what had happened in the past, a good number of the victims were not individuals previously targeted by gang members but rather everyday citizens walking along the streets, performing their everyday tasks, or going out to enjoy the weekend. Through this bloody massacre, the gangs sent the government the menacing message that they intended to restart and intensify their criminal operations. Speculation has it that it was a response to some unfulfilled commitment Bukele had supposedly made to the gangs so that they would curtail their operations.

Since these bloody events called into question Bukele's greatest political achievement, which had been much appreciated by almost all Salvadorans, he reacted to the gangs' challenge with an equally indiscriminate, relentless, and disproportionate repression. After he declared a state of exception and, without any court order, summarily made the punishments stipulated in the penal code harsher, police and military forces arrested thousands of citizens considered suspicious, including minors, on the orders continuously issued by Bukele through social networks, not through judges and prosecutors. All this was applauded by a wide majority of the citizens, especially the poor and destitute living in shantytowns and working in the countryside.

A government in which the president controls and rules the legislative and judicial branches and other state bodies is not democratic since the central elements of the republican regime have disappeared: the rule of law, the division of power between the executive and legislative functions, and the independence of the justice system.

How right is the Inter-American Court of Human Rights in warning that "the greatest current danger facing the region's democracies is not the abrupt breakdown of the constitutional order, but the gradual erosion of democratic safeguards that can lead to an authoritarian regime, even if it is popularly elected" (IACHR 2021)?

From what has been examined in the preceding pages, it can be concluded that Nayib Bukele was accurate when he changed his title from "President of El Salvador" to "Dictator of El Salvador" in his Twitter profile; he was just as accurate when he uttered the phrase that appears in the epigraph to this chapter.

NOTES

1. Twitter message from September 2021, https://curadas.com/2021/09/21/nayib -bukele-10-frases-polemicas-del-presidente-salvadoreno-videos/.

2. Five socialist and communist groups that, since 1979, had unleashed a bloody civil war against the military dictatorships, during which seventy-five thousand Salvadorans died. They came together to found the FMLN in 1992. This party inserted itself into democratic life, won the presidency seventeen years later, and governed between 2009 and 2019.

3. ARENA was founded in 1981 by an extreme-right military man, Roberto d'Aubuisson, with the aim of offering the country an alternative to the revolutionary political movements. He governed without extremism for four consecutive periods between 1989 and 2009.

4. According to the *New York Times*, the U.S. Department of the Treasury had established that Bukele's government "provided economic incentives to gangs and preferential treatment to jailed gang leaders, such as access to cell phones and prostitutes" (*New York Times*, March 27, 2022).

5. See Our World in Data, https://ourworldindata.org.

6. In the order they governed: Francisco Flores (1999–2004), Antonio Saca (2004–2009), and Mauricio Funes (2009–2014).

7. During the parliamentary election campaign, personal computers were handed out to students in public secondary schools.

8. According to the project drawn up by a commission chaired by Vice President Félix Ulloa and submitted to the president, 215 of the 274 articles of the constitution will be reformed.

9. Justice minister Osiris Luna and the reconstruction director of Social Fabric (Tejido Social), Carlos Marroquín.

PART II

The Government of Rafael Correa

Chapter 8

The Correa-Tailored Constitution of 2008

> Because the president of the republic, listen closely, is not just the head of the executive branch, he is the head of the entire Ecuadorian state, and the Ecuadorian state is the executive, legislative, judicial, electoral, transparency and social control, the superintendencies, the attorney general's office, the comptroller's office. All of that is the Ecuadorian state.
>
> —Ecuadorian president Rafael Correa Delgado (2007–2017)[1]

The government program of candidate Rafael Correa and Alianza PAIS (Patria Altiva y Soberana, loosely Lofty and Sovereign Homeland Alliance), the electoral group that sponsored his candidacy, announced that they would carry out a profound political reform to "refound" Ecuadorian democracy and put an end to the so-called partyocracy.[2] They blamed the parties and the political class for the economic crises, social problems, and almost all the ills suffered by the country in the last quarter of the twentieth century. Therefore, the first step of the "Citizens Revolution" they proposed would be to replace the existing democracy—which they considered was merely formal and excluded the majorities—with a participatory democracy to be defined by a constituent assembly through a new constitution.

In the speech Correa delivered to the National Congress upon taking office, he foreshadowed the authoritarianism with which he intended to govern Ecuador. Contrary to the provisions of the constitution then in place, he announced that his government's first act would be to call for a popular consultation, so that the people could voice their opinion on convening a constituent assembly. He did this immediately by issuing the corresponding executive decree.

I was one of only a few citizens to argue openly for the advisability of voting against convening a constituent assembly. My party, Popular Democracy

(Democracia Popular), also adopted that position and was the only political organization to do so. I was convinced that the constituent assembly would not contribute to improving the quality of Ecuadorian democracy but would instead worsen it, among other reasons because the new constitution would grant Correa control over all the powers of the state. Through multiple public appearances, mainly in the media, I did what I could to make voters realize the serious risk that democracy and liberties would run if a constituent assembly were called and a new constitution were issued.

When I embarked on my solitary campaign for the No position, in an interview done by Martin Pallares and published by the newspaper *El Comercio* (April 1, 2007), I was asked to respond to the question, "What is the real aim of the assembly?" I said, "The only aim is absolute power for the president of the republic, who wants a congress at his service, a Constitutional Court, a Supreme Electoral Tribunal, a Comptroller's Office, a Superintendency of Banks and Companies at his orders." He also wanted to eliminate political pluralism and move toward the hegemony of a single political party: Alianza PAIS. During other interviews, I added that Correa would try to take over the justice system in order to protect himself and those under him and to persecute his adversaries—all with the aim of wielding absolute power indefinitely, through successive reelections, with the argument that making the Citizens Revolution a reality and building a new socialist society would take a long time. I also ended that first interview by predicting that "if Yes wins, all will be lost, just as it was lost when Yes won in Venezuela."

In the popular consultation of April 15, 2007, the government obtained a resounding victory when 82 percent of the voters voted in favor of the constituent assembly. Correa's popularity and high credibility were decisive in this overwhelming result. The abusive use of economic resources, government agencies, and advertising for election purposes, as well as the disgrace into which political parties and leaders had fallen, also played a role. Ecuadorians had placed such trust in the word of the emerging political leader that the deceitful threat that he would resign if the No vote won reinvigorated the Yes campaign after it had reached a low point during the campaign. In fact, all parties and social organizations, including civil society, voted yes, without considering the uncertain future that the constituent assembly might create for Ecuadorian democracy.

In the voting held on September 28, 2007, to elect the members of the Constituent Assembly, Alianza PAIS obtained 61 percent of the vote, that is, 79 seats out of the 130 at stake. This win was obtained in all provinces, social classes, age groups, and levels of education, by a politician who had not been heard of two years before and a party that had appeared only a year earlier.

Some of the proposals of Correa and his party were not novel since they repeated concepts, statements, and institutions already included in the constitutions of 1979 and 1998, such as popular consultations, the recall of certain officials, the citizens' initiative in legislative matters, and the equitable financing of electoral campaigns. In some cases, their proposals were limited to the concepts of the highly criticized representative democracy that had appeared in previous constitutions, including the independence and autonomy of the justice system, the lawmaking and oversight powers of the legislative function, the obligation of oversight agencies to defend general interests and fight corruption, the transparency of public acts, accountability, the independence of the electoral boards, and the candidates' equitable access to advertising and media during election campaigns.

The proposals contributed by Alianza PAIS's "ideologues" were not original either. If they had been fulfilled—but they were not—they could have contributed to improving the representativeness of democratic institutions. One example of this was the call to strengthen the independence and autonomy of the justice system and oversight agencies so that they could effectively monitor and supervise officials' actions and sanction them if appropriate.

Others were simply utopian, such as replacing "formal democracy," to which they attributed all kinds of shortcomings, with "participatory democracy," in which all citizens could take part in "public decision making and monitor the actions of their representatives."

In view of what would happen later and the provisions and institutions that would be introduced into the Montecristi constitution to favor the authoritarian exercise of power and control over all state entities, the proposal to "reduce hyperpresidentialism" is striking. A similar contradiction occurred in the cases of the call for the justice system to be "independent, autonomous, and not managed by political parties" and the call for electoral processes not to be controlled by the parties. During Correa's government, both the body in charge of overseeing the parties and the ordinary and constitutional courts were exclusively composed of Alianza PAIS (AP) members or sympathizers, so that they would serve the political interests of the regime.

The Constituent Assembly members from Alianza PAIS were lavish in the articles on citizens' rights, freedoms, and guarantees, into which they poured their ideals, hopes, and dreams. They called the new society that they proposed to build "good living," and it would be the ultimate aim of the government of the Citizens Revolution: *sumak kawsay*, according to the ancestral vision of the Quechua culture. They incorporated into the dogmatic part of the constitution almost all the demands that student groups, environmentalist movements, Indigenous organizations, protesting sectors, and ideological groups had expressed for decades. In these matters, the influence of the Constituent Assembly members coming from nongovernmental organizations (NGOs), of which there were many, was significant.

Based on the criticisms that Correa would later make of the "excesses of the Montecristi guarantees," it can be concluded that he did not support the proposals of his fellow party members in terms of individual freedoms, rights, and guarantees. However, he was forced to accept them in order to avoid conflicts, but above all not to appear moderate, and even conservative, in the eyes of the revolutionary members of the Constituent Assembly. Given what would happen later in his government, he probably thought that these articles would actually be applied according to his own opinions and wishes.

Correa's interest was focused on the institutions and articles of the organic part of the constitution since he was aware that he had to take care that its provisions would leave him breadth for exercising his presidential authority at the expense of the scope of the state's other functions and bodies. As will be seen in the following chapters and as confirmed in his government, this was the purpose for which the Constituent Assembly had been convened.

The poor political education and weak democratic conviction of many Constituent Assembly members from Alianza PAIS, their lack of knowledge about the principles and institutions of the rule of law, and the widespread belief that no legal norm could hinder the realization of the Citizens Revolution's goals contributed to achieving that purpose. These limitations of the Alianza PAIS delegates and the authoritarian leadership of Correa created the conditions for a constitution to be tailor-made for him in Montecristi. The president and his legal secretary participated in the drafting of conceptual definitions and certain provisions, through instructions given to the members of the Constituent Assembly from his party. Since there was no previous democratic and participatory discussion of the draft constitution within Alianza PAIS, most of the party's members were not in a position to contribute to the debates. Furthermore, since they held an absolute majority in the Constituent Assembly, with the ability to approve whatever they could think of, they did not care what the other political forces represented in the Constituent Assembly thought and proposed.

The assembly members from Alianza PAIS arrived in Montecristi[3] for the naive purpose of refounding Ecuador. They were convinced that little or nothing could be rescued from what had been previously thought and written in the field of constitutional law, without having thought about the political institutions they had to create or modify in order to achieve such an ambitious goal. They had not even thought about the constitutional provisions that would help to materialize their proposals to achieve social equality and end Ecuador's economic dependence, and even less about the need to raise the quality of politics, promote the formation of a new party system, and improve democracy. This was probably because they were conditioned by ideological dogmas, an impetuous voluntarism, a superficial and biased knowledge of national reality, and an obsessive quest for originality.

Their eagerness to draw up a constitution that did not resemble the previous ones and to deny everything that had been done to broaden liberties, improve democracy, and address its governance problems led them to underestimate the contributions of the last constitutions, especially those of 1979 and 1998. They also suffered from a widespread ignorance of constitutional law and lacked political experience, legislative practice, legal training, and the skills needed to draft legal texts. These weaknesses caused them to fall victim to novelties, lyricism, extravagance, nonsense, obscurity, confusion, repetition, and contradictions in the drafting of the constitutional texts.

President Correa, on the other hand, besides having similar shortcomings, was not interested in correcting the ills of Ecuadorian democracy and in improving the quality of political institutions, but rather in ensuring his control of power and his ability to remain in power beyond the period for which he had been elected. He lacked inspiring ideas and specific proposals regarding the main guidelines for the most important political project of his government. His speeches during his presidential campaign, the one he made on the day he took office, and those he repeated during the campaign for the popular consultation and during the work of the Constituent Assembly did not help to fill such gaps. If the head of state was not in a position to define the content of the political reforms whereby the participatory democracy he had offered would be born, the members of a heterogeneous party formed only a few months before without a definite ideology—and operating as an election committee, not as a political organization—were not going to be in a position to do so. For these reasons, instead of promoting a visionary constitutional reform that would shape the future of Ecuadorian democracy, Correa was interested in strengthening the executive branch, weakening the legislative branch, opening the doors to immediate presidential reelection, and controlling the judicial branch.

Multiple factors contributed to the fact that the president's will was imposed in the Constituent Assembly and the government party proceeded as if it were defining its own doctrine and program and not the institutions of Ecuadorian democracy. These factors included Correa's vertical leadership, the AP's absolute majority, the approval of the constitutional articles by a simple majority, widespread dogmatism, the conviction that they were the embodiment of political wisdom, and the fact that they monopolized the highest positions in the Constituent Assembly and on the different commissions. This denial of political pluralism prevented them from writing a constitution that would cover all Ecuadorians regardless of their political stance. The constitution produced in Montecristi was only for the members of the Citizens Revolution—for them and not for "everyone" as one of the slogans of Correa's government used to say.

The articles of the dogmatic part were more extensive than in previous constitutions because, in addition to reproducing guarantees and freedoms contained in the 1998 constitution, the new text included new rights and established procedures to implement them—which is not appropriate in a constitution—and they were written in a lyrical, pompous, and repetitive way.

As for economic and social rights, which came to be called the rights "of good living," the new text did not make substantive contributions, but rather introduced novelties and curiosities. These included rights to healthy and nutritious food, to water, to rural–urban migration, to recreation, to exercise and sports, to a healthy environment, to public space, and to free time. It recognized nature as having rights and approved elective suffrage for Ecuadorians living abroad, for young people over sixteen years of age, for foreigners residing in Ecuador, and for members of the military and police. Recognized in the previous constitution, the collective rights of Indigenous communities and Afro-Ecuadorians were extended to the coastal peasants known as "montubios." Meanwhile, the opposition's and minorities' right to representation in plurinominal elections was eliminated.

The articles of the organic part, in general terms, corresponded to those of the 1998 constitution, some of whose provisions were repeated, expanded, modified, or confused. However, new articles were incorporated to create numerous public institutions, the most novel of which was the Council for Citizen Participation and Social Control (Consejo de Participación Ciudadana y Control Social, CPCCS), which was given the status of the fourth branch of government. This was a cause for concern since it was not a customary body and did not appear in Ecuadorian constitutional law, but above all because it did not originate from a vote of the citizens yet was to be in charge of appointing the highest-ranking state officials. Its members had to be nominated by individuals or social organizations and selected through merit-based competitions. As will be seen in the following chapter, President Correa would use this body to control the most important institutions and submit them to his will.

The Montecristi constitution is strongly presidentialist due to how many powers it granted to the head of state and how it undermined other functions, especially the legislative function. Although it repeated provisions from previous constitutions, the article on the powers of the president of the republic granted other powers that excessively strengthened presidential authority. For example, he could dissolve the National Assembly if it took on other functions or obstructed the implementation of the National Development Plan or if a serious political crisis or domestic unrest occurred. Once the assembly was dissolved, legislative and presidential elections would have to be called, in which the president could run again. In the meantime, for a period that could last for months, he was empowered to pass laws of economic urgency.

In both cases an opinion of the Constitutional Court was required. He could be reelected immediately only once, but a special privilege was added so that Correa's first reelection would not be taken into account.

Despite this accumulation of hyperpresidentialist provisions, in his speech at the closing session of the Constituent Assembly, Correa asked the attendees, "Where is the accumulation of powers in the president of the republic?"

Although the possibility of revoking the mandate of the president of the republic was extended and fewer signatures were required to proceed (10 percent instead of 15 percent of those in the voter registry), an absolute majority of voters and the prior approval of the Constitutional Court were necessary. He could be impeached at the request of one-third of the members of the National Assembly for crimes against the security of the state, public administration, genocide, and crimes against humanity, provided that the proposal had been previously approved by the Constitutional Court. Curiously, another article stated that the National Assembly could also remove the president from office for the seizure of functions, a serious political crisis, and domestic unrest. This is one of the many examples of confusing and contradictory texts in the Montecristi constitution. A two-thirds vote of the National Assembly was required for his censure and dismissal, in which case the vice president would temporarily assume the presidency and early legislative and presidential elections would be called immediately.

The legislative function remained in one chamber composed of 124 legislators, twenty-four more than in the previous constitution: 104 provincial, fifteen national, and six from abroad. The National Assembly was deprived of powers it had had under previous constitutions and which should be inherent to it, such as the powers to interpret the constitution; to appoint judges to the National Court of Justice and the Constitutional Court; and to name the National Electoral Council, comptroller, attorney general, public prosecutor, ombudsman, superintendents, and Central Bank directors. Other restrictions on its powers under the previous constitution were maintained, such as the prohibition for legislators to take initiative in laws that created public expenditures or established or suppressed taxes, as well as the restriction that censuring a government minister might cause his or her dismissal.

Above the National Court of Justice is the Constitutional Court, which the new constitution granted powers improper for a body of this nature, among others to decide on the constitutionality of a call for popular consultations, the impeachment of the president of the republic, the dissolution of the National Assembly, and a call for new elections. It may also issue laws if the National Assembly commits omissions and may review the sentences, orders, and resolutions of courts and judges, including the National Court of Justice, even if the rulings have been executed. By granting it this power, the new constitution created a fourth judicial instance that would delay proceedings, worsen legal uncertainty, and politicize the justice system.

On July 25, 2008, the constitution was approved by ninety-four Constituent Assembly members from Alianza PAIS and its allies; thirty-two voted against and four abstained. In his proclamation, whereby the Citizens Revolution's masterpiece was to begin to rule the destiny of Ecuador, the president of the republic did not refer to its basic content, nor to how it would contribute to the country's development or even to how democracy would stop being exclusive and become participatory. As on previous occasions, he resorted to rhetorical digressions. He said that the new constitution was "unparalleled in republican history" because "every word, every concept, every one of its articles had been developed and written as a pluralistic, collective, democratic, and participatory song." He said that its provisions "contained thousands of voices, hearts, feelings, reasons, [and] thoughts, conceived with the deepest love," supposedly love for the homeland. He must have been so convinced of how good the new constitutional text was that he would later say that it was "his government's most important work" and the "best constitution in the world," for which reason "it would last three hundred years." Hugo Chávez had said something similar some time earlier.

In the constitutional referendum of September 28, 2008, the constitution was approved by nearly two-thirds of the voters (64 percent) in almost all cities. One exception was Guayaquil, where the No vote had a narrow win despite influential Mayor Nebot's advocacy for it. A good number of the Yes voters cast their ballots as a show of support for the president rather than for the benefits of a constitution that, according to the polls, they were not interested in learning about. Some voted yes motivated by the social benefits that had been magnified in the government's huge publicity campaign.

In Ecuador's prodigious constitutional history, the 2008 constitution, with its 444 articles, surpassed them all and became the second longest in the world, after the constitution of India.

The 2008 constitution must be the only Ecuadorian constitution whose discussion and drafting did not involve jurists knowledgeable in constitutional law but rather people from other professions or without university degrees. Those who drafted it did not reflect on the experiences left by the nineteen constitutions the country had had previously, texts written by politicians who wanted to change public life, just like those of 2008 did. In addition to being regulatory—which is why it is so long—it contains articles preceded by invocations that express aspirations, point out objectives, lay out means, and make proclamations.

Unlike previous, carefully written texts, the Montecristi constitution has poor legal wording and grammar. It contains numerous syntax, punctuation, and agreement errors and unnecessarily uses both masculine and feminine references to individuals, professions, and functions. The "clumsy, need-less use of [both] masculine and feminine genders" and the pomposity of the constitutional text were criticized by language scholar Susana Cordero (*El Comercio* 2010). In addition to detracting from the foremost law of the state, all this impedes understanding it fully and gives rise to different interpretations. Some articles were even written by foreigners recruited for that purpose.[4]

The constitution was not the result of a democratic debate, nor did it reflect the pluralism of the political society.[5] So, unlike what had happened with the other two constitutions of the present democratic period (from 1979 and 1998), it expressed only the thinking of Alianza PAIS. Those who conceived and drafted it did not consider the possibility that political forces from ideological groups of the opposition could take power. Since they were convinced that they would remain in power indefinitely—they spoke of hun-dreds of years—they drafted a constitution for Rafael Correa and the Citizens Revolution, not for a pluralistic democratic society. It did not even take into account economic and social changes in Ecuador, the worldwide collapse of real socialism, and the adoption of the market economy worldwide—as though it had not been adopted in China and India, countries that account for more than a third of the world's population.

The new constitution not only did not correct the weaknesses and imperfec-tions of certain political institutions, but it also made them worse. It did not ensure the rule of law, democratic checks and balances, the independence of the justice system and oversight bodies, the representativeness and transpar-ency of the electoral system, political pluralism, transparency among authori-ties, and accountability. Instead, it established a political system that would fatally lead to having the president of the republic end up as the sole holder of power and be able to commit all sorts of excesses and abuses with impunity.

The Constituent Assembly members from Alianza PAIS, convinced that they had drafted a memorable constitution, took measures so that it could not be changed, would remain intact, and would forever guide the path of Ecuadorian democracy and national development. (This illusion had also been harbored by many of those who had drafted the previous nineteen con-stitutions.) So that their provisions could never be changed, they established a "mega-padlock."[6] The president of the republic, the National Assembly, and the Constitutional Court had to agree to the changes. The proposals could not alter the "fundamental structure" of the constitution and the "nature and con-stituent elements of the State," establish "restrictions on the rights and guar-antees" of citizens, or modify "the reform procedure." If the Constitutional Court deemed that these requirements had been met, the proposal could finally be voted on by the citizens in a referendum. The constitution could also be reformed by convening a constituent assembly.

As seen in previous paragraphs, the new constitution lacked the virtues attributed to it by the president. Moreover, in the conceptual, legal, and grammatical spheres, nothing worse had ever been written in the prolific constitutional history of Ecuador. For this reason, many thought that at some point it would be reformed, at least to clarify arcane phrasing, eliminate contradictions and repetitions, and repeal inadvisable norms. They also thought that the reform would come once the president and the leaders of Alianza PAIS had become more enlightened on public affairs and as they faced the difficulties posed by national and international realities. No one expected, however, that the first reform would be proposed by the very person who had praised it so much, and worse yet that the proposal would be accompanied by a criticism of the "nonsense" that Constituent Assembly members from his party had enshrined, specifically the "hyperguarantees" provided by some articles. With this pronouncement, Correa contradicted and disavowed the Constituent Assembly members of the Citizens Revolution, for whom the core of the constitution they had written was the expansion of guarantees, freedoms, and constitutional rights.

In early 2011, two and a half years after the new constitution was issued, Correa announced that he had decided to call for a popular consultation and a referendum in which he would ask the people to voice their opinion on ten questions. Some were aimed at learning the citizens' opinions on certain issues, and others at reforming institutions and limiting individual rights and freedoms. These questions had been previously reviewed by Correa. They contained a broad legal and constitutional reform since they modified a dozen constitutional articles referring to the justice system and personal guarantees, as well as a dozen laws. In view of the president's disregard for the law and his authoritarian style, it was not surprising that the call for the consultation and referendum did not abide by the constitutional norms that regulated the procedure.[7]

Article 104 of the constitution empowered the president of the republic to order the National Electoral Council to call for a popular consultation on issues he considered advisable. He was therefore empowered to ask the citizens to voice their opinion on the prohibition of gambling, bullfighting, and cockfighting. However, he was not empowered to ask the people to criminalize "unjustified private enrichment" and the "failure to affiliate workers to the Social Security system." Nor could he ask them to restrict guarantees in legal proceedings involving those who committed crimes, a demand made by broad sectors of the population. According to the official propaganda, this reform would allow the government to address delinquency, reduce crime, and protect people's safety and security. According to the constitution, all these matters fell within the jurisdiction of the National Assembly. By virtue of his popularity, what Correa was really seeking with these ten questions was to obtain votes in favor of justice system reform, not so that he could improve it but so that he could control it.

The question asking voters to authorize a communication law was also unconstitutional since it entailed a limitation on the "right to free communication" and on the "right to seek, receive, exchange, disseminate, and produce information without prior censorship." Furthermore, the constitution prohibited the restriction of constitutional rights and guarantees and declared unconstitutional "any action or omission of a regressive nature that unjustifiably diminishes, hinders, or voids the exercise of a right."

The call for a referendum was also unconstitutional. According to the constitution, an amendment that implied a change "in the nature and constituent elements of the State, that altered the fundamental structure of the constitution and established restrictions to rights and guarantees" was not possible. This prohibition was ignored in the question asking voters to approve the replacement of the Judicial Council with a Transitory Judicial Council (CJT). The same was true for the questions referring to a longer period before preventive detention expired and the prohibition that other precautionary measures could be substituted for detention.

The question that reduced the number of members of the Judicial Council and modified its composition should have been previously reviewed by the National Assembly and then submitted to a popular vote in a referendum. This should also have been done because, in the appendix that accompanied the text, twenty-nine articles of the Organic Code of the Judicial Branch and other laws were modified. Such modifications are solely the power of the legislative function.

In both the consultation and the referendum, there were also problems of form that affected the transparency of the voting. The ten questions were cunningly written with wording that enticed voters to vote yes, since the questions were preceded by statements pondering their advisability, usefulness, and virtues.[8] In addition, they were accompanied by numerous and extensive appendices with eighteen pages of rubbish that were impossible to read and were not understood by many voters.

Since it was not in the government's interest to inform citizens about the real content of the consultation and referendum questions, it was not interested in disseminating and explaining them. It limited itself to flooding radio and television with a focused publicity campaign referring to problems and concerns felt by the citizens. Then, as plebiscitary caudillos usually do, Correa asked them to vote yes as an act of faith and loyalty to their leader: "Trust me," he repeated a thousand times.

The Constitutional Court rejected the report submitted by the representative of the Indigenous movement, Nina Pacari, in which she proposed that four of the five referendum questions be eliminated and suggested that the remaining referendum and consultation questions be modified. In the report, she alleged that the questions that restricted rights and altered the structure of the state should be submitted to a constituent assembly, in accordance with Articles 441 and 444 of the constitution. Instead, an ad hoc report, supposedly drafted by court advisors—but in reality drafted by government officials— was issued, recommending the approval and modification of the first (preventive detention) and second (alternative measures to detention) questions, so that their text would not ostensibly violate the constitutional prohibition to restrict rights and liberties.[9] In both the consultation questions and the referendum questions, the Constitutional Court eliminated the lead-ins since they induced voters to give affirmative answers. Even though that court was not constitutionally empowered to modify the texts of the questions and the president had said that he would not accept any change, he agreed to the modifications it had introduced.

The favorable opinion of the Constitutional Court came as a surprise to no one in view of the obsequious relationship that most of the members of the Constitutional Court maintained with the president. The violation of the constitution was so blatant that National Assembly President Fernando Cordero, who was also Correa's crony, publicly admitted that some questions were unconstitutional. The presidential initiative to place the justice system under his authority motivated the split of the political movement Ruptura de los 25 from the government ranks.[10]

When the president proposed the consultation and the referendum, the opposition thought that his victory would be overwhelming, and all the polling firms agreed. However, this was not the only cause of the prevailing pessimism. It was considered impossible for citizens to vote against questions with which it was difficult to disagree since they included problems felt by broad sectors of society. Such was the atmosphere of victory that reigned in Alianza PAIS that Correa even boasted that he would win the consultation and the referendum "ten to one."

The widespread belief that the government would obtain a resounding victory disconcerted the opposition. One sector fell silent, and another called for voters to protest by annulling their votes. It was in this defeatist political environment that the civic forum Cauce Democrático was born, an initiative that I promoted with well-known people from the political, economic, artistic, military, and literary spheres. In its first manifesto, it asked citizens to vote with a "resounding no" on all the questions of the referendum and the popular consultation in order to censure the government's authoritarian and unconstitutional actions, to prevent it from taking over the justice system, and "to avoid the formation of a dictatorial regime."[11] This approach, which brought the opposition out of its immobilized state, was gradually gaining followers, the numbers of which increased steadily when the polls registered a consistent rise in the negative vote. Given his influence among his city's electorate, if Guayaquil mayor Jaime Nebot's late support for the No vote had been timelier, he would have contributed to the rejection of at least those questions that were going to allow the government to control the justice system and restrict freedom of expression.

In the popular consultation and the constitutional referendum of May 7, 2011, the ten questions received an average of 47 percent of the votes. Only the first one exceeded 50 percent, probably because it referred to the sensitive issue of citizen safety and security. This would have been the only question approved if the "participatory" 2008 constitution had not modified the rule that the Yes votes had to exceed the total of No votes plus the number of null votes and blank votes in referendums and consultations, as had happened in the 2007 popular consultation and in the 2008 referendum. In the controversial questions on justice and the media, about which the government had been so keen, the difference between Yes votes and No votes was barely 3 percent. Overall, as compared to the results of the 2008 referendum, Correa's numbers fell again, this time by another seventeen percentage points.

Four years later, in 2015, Correa proposed new constitutional reforms. However, ignoring the premises of participatory democracy, he did not submit them to popular opinion through a consultation or a referendum, but rather to the review and resolution of the National Assembly, and he called them amendments. He went this route because of the risk that they might not be approved by the voters, given the narrow margin with which the changes he had proposed in 2011 had been approved (*El Universo* 2017d). Above all, he chose this approach because the reform of his particular interest—which would allow him to be reelected as many times as he wanted, that is, for life—was unpopular according to the polls. In the assembly, on the other hand, he would not face any difficulty because he had a large majority ready to please him. The other reforms were politically unimportant, except for the one that turned the media into a public service.

The sixteen amendments, including the indefinite reelection of the president of the republic, were approved by three-quarters of the members of the National Assembly, almost all of whom were Alianza PAIS militants. To general surprise, at the last minute and at Correa's request, a transitory provision was introduced, whereby the indefinite reelection would apply as of the presidential elections of 2021. Apparently, Correa considered it advisable to postpone his reelection due to the risk that he could be defeated in 2017 and to let the economic crisis be dealt with by another president.

NOTES

1. *Enlace ciudadano* (Citizen Broadcast), no. 111, held at the Abel Jiménez Parra Coliseum in Guayaquil on March 7, 2009, https://www.youtube.com/watch?v =3RnJRGmK0Wg.

2. This became a pejorative expression used to refer to the parties that had governed Ecuador in the 1980s and 1990s.

3. The Constituent Assembly met in the small, remote town of Montecristi, located in the coastal province of Manabí, due to Correa's interest in connecting the Citizens Revolution to the Liberal Revolution of the late nineteenth century, whose caudillo, Eloy Alfaro, had been born there.

4. Spaniards Roberto Viciano and Albert Noguera, in a report submitted to the Office of the President of the Republic, stated that they had prepared consultation documents, drafts of mandates, constitutional texts, and guidelines for the presentations of the Constituent Assembly members from Alianza PAIS (*El Universo* 2008d). If that was true, those advisors did not write better Spanish than the party members did.

5. Illustrative of this is the book in which the author narrates his day-to-day experience as a member of the Constituent Assembly (Lucio-Paredes 2008).

6. When the 1998 constitution was approved, the Social Christian Party leader and National Congress president, Heinz Moeller, had said that it had been given a "padlock" to impede its reform. Article 282 called for two debates, a year apart, and then sanction by the president of the republic.

7. Among others, the organic laws for constitutional guarantees, citizen participation, the legislative function, the judicial function; the laws for financial institutions, companies, and communication; and reforms to the penal and penal procedures codes.

8. The following phrases preceded some of the questions: "In order to improve citizen security, do you agree that . . . ?"; "In order to avoid the excesses of the media, do you agree that . . . ?"; "In order to avoid labor exploitation, do you agree that . . . ?; "In order to combat corruption, do you agree that . . . ?"

9. Most of the ones it approved were led by the president of the Constitutional Court, Patricio Pazmiño, the frontman for rulings in the interests of the government.

10. Formed by a group of rebellious young people who criticized the parties and their leaders, whom they accused of having "screwed Ecuador." During Correa's government, they held secondary positions, but their foremost leader, María Paula Romo, formed part of the Political Bureau, which was occasionally consulted on decision making. In their four years there, they laid the groundwork for Correa's dictatorial project.

11. It was formed to defend democracy and the freedoms trampled on by Correa's government. It was composed of Pedro Pinto, former vice president; Wilfrido Lucero, former president of the National Congress; José Ayala Lasso, former foreign minister and former United Nations High Commissioner for Human Rights; Guillermo Landázuri, former president of the National Congress; Ernesto Albán Gómez, former education minister; José Gallardo Román, former defense minister; Pablo Better, former finance minister; Medardo Oleas, former president of the Supreme Electoral

Tribunal; Abelardo Pachano, former president of the Central Bank; artists Osvaldo Viteri and Milton Barragán; Elsa de Mena, former director of the Internal Revenue Service; and writers Patricio Moncayo, Simón Espinosa, Julio Echeverría, and Juan Andrade Heymann.

Chapter 9

The Process of Concentrating Power

With the approval of the 1979 constitution through a referendum and, in the same year, the inauguration of the government of President Jaime Roldós, the longest democratic period that Ecuador has had in its history got underway.

However, over the next twenty-eight years, until the beginning of Rafael Correa's government, the rule of law, the separation of powers, and the independence of the justice system were not always respected.

Authoritarian President León Febres Cordero (1984–1988) ignored decisions made by the National Congress and the Constitutional Court and by an act of force prevented the Supreme Court of Justice appointed by the legislature from taking office.[1] President Lucio Gutiérrez (2002–2005), in order to avoid the impeachment that his opponents were plotting in the National Congress, formed a majority that exchanged political protection for the replacement of the Supreme Court of Justice.

Presidents Abdalá Bucaram, Jamil Mahuad, and Lucio Gutiérrez were deposed by congress after popular protests left them defenseless. When the first of these was ousted, Vice President Rosalía Arteaga did not assume the presidency, as called for under the constitution; instead, Congress President Fabián Alarcón did. Before Vice President Gustavo Noboa assumed the presidency, to replace the ousted Mahuad, an ephemeral dictatorship was put in place by former Supreme Court of Justice President Carlos Solórzano; Lieutenant Colonel Lucio Gutiérrez, who was in active service; and Antonio Vargas, the president of the Indigenous movement.

When President-Elect Rafael Correa was sworn in before the National Congress on January 15, 2007, he refused to swear that he would submit his actions to the constitution, just as Hugo Chávez had done in Venezuela. When the president of the congress administered the respective oath, Correa responded, "Before God and before the Ecuadorian people, I swear to fulfill the mandate given to me by the Ecuadorian people last November 16th." His refusal to comply with a traditional political formality was an early sign of his disconnection from democratic practices. However, the National Congress overlooked his omission, as did the parties, the media, and public opinion.

During his election campaign in the first round of voting, candidate Rafael Correa had announced his intention to call for a constituent assembly as soon as he assumed the presidency. However, he did not continue doing so in the second: he buried the proposal due to the misgivings it raised. According to his discourse, he wanted to put an end to a "failed democracy" and open the doors to a "socialist" and "participatory democracy."

The idea of convening this kind of assembly had been present in the national debate since the early 1990s, among parties, political leaders, and social organizations from both the Right and the Left. Some considered it necessary to correct the governance problems that prevented the proper operation of the democratic system, and they tried to do this in the constitutions of 1979 and 1998. Others believed that it was necessary to replace institutions and norms that hindered national development or the socialist revolution that the people supposedly wanted. There was no lack of people who blamed the constitution for all the ills suffered by the country, without having a clear idea about what reforms should be introduced to correct them or being aware of the fact that political practices had weighed more than constitutional norms in the history of Ecuador.

The first to propose the convening of a constituent assembly (in 1994) was former president León Febres Cordero. That initiative was later endorsed by former president Rodrigo Borja, center-left presidential candidate Freddy Ehlers, and almost all the leaders of the political and social movements of the Left, with more emphasis on the Indigenous organization Conaie.[2] When Fabián Alarcón assumed the presidency in 1997 after the collapse of Abdalá Bucaram's government, he committed himself to convening a constituent assembly under the name National Assembly, in order to avert the danger that it might declare itself the depository of popular sovereignty and decide to replace him. In the popular consultation held for that purpose, 65 percent of Ecuadorians supported convening it. Although the National Assembly declared itself a constituent assembly when it undertook its functions, it limited itself to reforming the 1979 constitution, and its task resulted in the 1998 constitution. It focused its attention on improving political system governance and on updating certain economic concepts as a function of the changes that occurred worldwide after the collapse of real socialism in the Soviet Union and its European satellites.

The 1998 constitution had been in force for only eight years when President Correa announced that he would call for a constituent assembly. It had been discussed and approved by a broad consensus among the eleven political forces represented in the respective constituent assembly, including some that would later become part of the political coalition that supported his presidential candidacy: the Socialist Party, Pachakutik, the Democratic Left, and the MPD. However, most provisions had been approved unanimously, many with a two-thirds majority, and only a few by a simple majority.

For the new president of Ecuador, the 1998 constitution posed an obstacle for his government to carry out the revolution he had promised the Ecuadorian people. If it was not replaced, it would be impossible for him to solve economic problems, put an end to social injustices, confront the powers that be, and refound the country.

These proposals were alien to the socioeconomic reality of those years. The country had overcome a serious crisis at the end of the century, the economy had begun to grow again, inflation disappeared, real wages were improving, and poverty was being reduced. This was in part due to the monetary and foreign-exchange stability achieved by adopting the U.S. dollar as the national currency rather than to the economic reforms incorporated in the 1998 constitution, and this is evidence of how little constitutional texts have mattered in the country's economic and social development.

It did not require political acumen to suspect that the motives behind the presidential proposal were different. First, Correa felt the need to replace a legislative body in which the government did not have a single legislator with another in which Alianza PAIS would have a parliamentary representation equivalent to the outcome of the presidential election. Candidate Correa had not registered slates of National Congress candidates for his political organization, in order to earn the support of citizens critical of that legislative body and its deputies. Second, he saw the advisability of having a constitution tailored to his authoritarian inclinations and his ambition to remain in power indefinitely. Third, he believed that laws and republican institutions, instead of expressing the pluralism of democratic society, should be shaped by the ideas of the Citizens Revolution. Consequently, the new constitution should not reflect the diversity and pluralism of democratic society, in which different ideologies and parties coexist and alternate, but rather the unique thinking of the Citizens Revolution. In line with this discourse, Correa had said that in the voting to elect members to the constituent assembly, "60, 70, 80, 90 percent should be from Alianza PAIS" (*Página 12* 2007; repeated in his inauguration address on January 15, 2007).

The 1998 constitution did not include the legal figure of a constituent assembly and, consequently, did not include any authority's power to convene it to draft a new constitution. According to Article 280 of the constitution, it could only be reformed "by the National Congress or by means of a popular consultation."

Ignoring these constitutional provisions, the president argued that Article 104 of the constitution authorized him to call for popular consultations "in matters of transcendental importance for the country." However, he paid no attention to the second part of that article, which limited such power to matters other than reforming the constitution. According to Article 283, if he wanted to convene a constituent assembly for this purpose, he could only do so in urgent cases previously approved by the National Congress, or if the latter had not "reviewed [and then] approved or denied the constitutional reforms proposed to the legislative body in the term of one hundred and twenty days."

Disregarding these explicit constitutional limitations and taking legislative powers from the National Congress by means of an executive decree, he issued a statute (actually a law) in which he called a constituent assembly with "full powers," established the way its members would be elected, and regulated its operation. This was exactly what had been done in Venezuela by President Hugo Chávez years before. Besides being unconstitutional, this call contained gaps, errors, inconsistencies, and even nonsense, some of which he was forced to correct—for example, the absurd and discriminatory provision that the candidates to participate in it could not be older than forty-five.

From that moment on, the 1998 constitution remained in force only in matters that were not contrary to President Correa's political objectives, which were not at all democratic and were clearly authoritarian. This is what military dictatorships would do in the nineteenth and twentieth centuries when they overthrew constitutional presidents by means of a coup and assumed power.

The statute was sent to the Supreme Electoral Tribunal, with the peremptory request to immediately call for the unconstitutional popular consultation. Noticing the hesitant attitude of its members and aware of the arbitrariness with which the head of state was asking them to act, he abusively threatened them with their dismissal and replacement (*El Universo* 2007a). Pressure also came from violent sympathizers from MPD, Alianza PAIS, and other progovernment groups, who surrounded and attacked the headquarters of the electoral body, without the police being able to prevent them.[3] Instead of denying the presidential request and calling attention to his iniquitous behavior, the frightened TSE agreed to send the request to the National Congress to examine its legal applicability.

A majority formed by parties claiming to be of the Left—Sociedad Patriótica (PSP), Roldosista Ecuatoriano (PRE), Izquierda Democrática (ID), Pachakutik, Movimiento Popular Democrático (MPD), and Red Ética y Democracia (RED)—along with some independents and two dissidents from Democracia Popular approved the call for a referendum one month after President Rafael Correa's government began.[4] They did so under the threat that he would ignore congress's decision and call the constituent assembly on his own.[5] On the day of the vote, congress was surrounded by aggressive demonstrators from peasant and social organizations. In this way, by means of manifest arbitrariness, violent actions, and a string of insults, he managed to get the National Congress to submit to his plan and authorize calling the unlawful referendum.

The authoritarian president had said that the first thing the Constituent Assembly should do with its full powers was to dismantle the National Congress because it was an institution that "did not represent anyone." To neutralize this danger, the political groups that approved the call for a constituent assembly introduced a provision that prohibited it from affecting the terms of office of the state officials elected in the most recent elections. Because this resolution limited his powers and prevented their dismissal, Correa pressured the TSE to call the popular consultation without taking into account the restriction established by the legislators, an order with which the TSE complied.[6]

Instead of initiating a political proceeding against the TSE for having modified the resolution of the legislative body, the National Congress, with the votes of the PRIAN, PSP, and PSC parties, agreed to remove the TSE president. This body, already turned into the executor of the mandates of the quasi-dictator, dismissed the fifty-seven deputies who had voted for that measure, with the argument that Article 155, letter e, of the Election Law empowered it to dismiss and suspend for one year the political rights of the "public employee, official, or authority outside the electoral organization who interferes in the functioning of the electoral bodies." This provision could not be applied to deputies since they were not public officials but rather were elected by the citizens to perform a government function, and they had the privilege of the jurisdiction of the Supreme Court, according to the provisions of Article 143 of the aforementioned law.

So irreverent was the submission of the TSE to the orders received from the President's Office that it dismissed deputies who were not present at the session in which said resolution was voted on or who had abstained. Meanwhile, it "pardoned" some congressmen who had voted in favor, such as National Congress President Jorge Cevallos and Congressman Pedro Almeida, author of the motion whereby the TSE president was removed.

By means of these abusive, unconstitutional, arbitrary, and violent means, Correa managed to remove all the opposition deputies from the National Congress just two months after assuming the presidency and to form a majority among the remaining ones.

The dismissal of such a large number of deputies resulted in a standstill in the National Congress since there was not the quorum required for it to be able to meet. The impasse was resolved by incorporating the alternate deputies, and the motion for them to assume the functions of the regular deputies was presented by Congressman Andrés Páez of the Democratic Left (Izquierda Democrática, ID). The newcomers were called "tablecloth deputies" because, ashamed of their disloyalty to the parties that had nominated them, they covered their faces with tablecloths when they were discovered by keen journalists in the venue where they had been gathered by the government.

The coup with which President Correa put the TSE and the National Congress at his service was conceived, directed, and executed by the minister of government, Gustavo Larrea, a former militant of the Ecuadorian Left. He formed the government majorities in the electoral and legislative bodies and recruited the alternate deputies, hid them in an inn near Quito, took them into the Legislative Palace in the wee hours of the morning, and used the national police to keep the regular deputies from entering. He also encouraged the violent gangs that carried out fascist assaults on the Supreme Electoral Tribunal, the National Congress, and the legitimate deputies.[7]

When Correa was approached by journalists, he justified the aggressions against the dismissed deputies by saying that they had received "a dose of their own medicine," even though their conduct had been peaceful and democratic. In addition, he downplayed the physical aggressions they had suffered with the exclamation "Bienhechito!" (Well done!).

The president and his supporters, by seizing the other powers of the state, acted as the Fascist blackshirts and Nazi brownshirts had acted when attacking and eradicating the Italian and German democracies. By means of these unconstitutional, arbitrary, violent, and criminal means, Correa managed to form a progovernment legislative majority, composed of deputies from the ID, MPD, Pachakutik, RED (of former vice president León Roldós), PRE, PSE, and dissidents from the UDC (formerly Democracia Popular, DP). Public opinion was astonished that the alternate deputies, made regular deputies, called themselves the National Dignity Bloc (Bloque de la Dignidad Nacional). The new majority reorganized the legislative commissions and rewarded the tablecloth deputies by appointing a first vice president from their ranks: Miguel Castro.

In order to intimidate the dismissed deputies, Correa sought to bring legal proceedings against them. His threat to prosecute and imprison them was followed by a request to that effect from an obliging prosecutor and a criminal proceeding initiated by a cooperative judge. To avoid ending up in jail, some of them sought political asylum in Colombia and were only able to return to Ecuador after the government consolidated control of the National Congress. For the prosecutor and the judge to suspend the criminal proceedings, it was sufficient for the president to say that he found the deputies' imprisonment "untimely."

The legal controversy about the legality with which the TSE had proceeded in dismissing fifty deputies was settled by the Constitutional Court. After examining the facts, it ordered they be reinstated in their functions. Correa did not care about this resolution and ruled that the deputies "remained dismissed" (*El Mundo.es* 2007). For their part, the same MPD-led groups of assailants who had attacked the TSE and the opposition deputies violently evicted the magistrates from their courts without the police doing anything to protect them. The government majority in the National Congress ignored the attack suffered by the constitutional justice system of the state and, instead of defending it and protesting against the outrage, dismissed the members of the Constitutional Court. The latter had warned that, if such a resolution were approved, "a very serious and irreparable violation of the precarious institutional stability existing in the Republic" would be committed.

This was indeed what happened, with the aggravating circumstance that, with the dismissal of the Constitutional Court, the dictatorial political project initiated on the day the popular consultation was called—with the aim of placing all the powers of the state under the tutelage of the president of the republic—had culminated almost in its entirety.

Subsequently, the congress formed a new Constitutional Court with people linked to the government and the allied parties of the Left, and it acted as though it were an office under the Presidency of the Republic.

In this way, in the span of only five and a half months, Correa had managed to place the National Congress, the Supreme Electoral Tribunal, and the Constitutional Court under his authority, and he had eliminated the division of power between the executive and legislative functions, as well as the independence of the bodies in charge of constitutional and electoral oversight. Months later, the Constituent Assembly would replace the heads of other entities with government-aligned officials, including the independent Supreme Court of Justice.

In the popular consultation of April 2007, despite the opprobrious events described above, an overwhelming majority of four out of every five voters approved the call to convene a constituent assembly. Hence, it was the citizens themselves who opened the doors to Correa's dictatorship. The massive yes vote meanwhile produced the perverse effect of "legitimizing" the abuses of power, the gross arbitrariness, and the barbaric outrages committed against the constitutional order by the president of the republic.

Political parties, social groups, business sectors, civil-society organizations, and private media were not exempt from blame,[8] some for supporting the authoritarian process and others for remaining silent.

Affected by the epidemic of naivete that had contaminated political society, many joined the Correa stampede. Those on the left identified ideologically with the revolutionary project, those in the center sympathized with the progressive president, and those on the right supported him so as not to be out of tune with the majority feeling of the population. The position taken by the influential mayor of Guayaquil, Jaime Nebot, illustrates this. So that there would be no doubt of his support for the constituent assembly, at the moment he voted in the popular consultation, he showed the public and the television cameras his yes vote. Few stopped to think about the danger that the constituent assembly would become the legal instrument that Correa would use to lay the foundation of a long-term dictatorial regime.

One of the first acts of the Constituent Assembly was to issue Mandate 1[9] to give itself "full powers." In that context, it resolved that its decisions were "hierarchically superior to any other rule of law," warned that it would not be "subject to control or challenge by any of the constituted powers," threatened sanctions against those who failed to comply with this provision, and ordered a recess of the National Congress, whose functions it assumed. It could not make such decisions since there was a constitution in force (the one from 1998) and there were constituted powers that it had to respect. Later, through Mandate 12, the elections of mayors, prefects, and city council members were suspended, and the terms of those in office were extended.

Then, gradually and selectively, officials who had demonstrated a certain independence were removed from office: the comptroller, the attorney general, the federal prosecutor, superintendents, members of the Banking Board, and directors of the autonomous Central Bank. The vacancies were filled by people that the president trusted, people with whom he had had a personal or university relationship and who were willing to show deference to him and obey his orders. In this way he extended his presidential power to almost all state institutions, except for the justice system. In order to force and justify these changes, President Correa and Vice President Moreno hastened to submit their resignations to the Constituent Assembly. These were accepted, but both of them were immediately reinstated.

Later, once the Constituent Assembly was dissolved, the government would take the first step to bring the judicial system under its control. Though not very apparent, the Montecristi constitution had to be approved by the citizens in a referendum so that its norms could take effect. Without this having occurred, it created a "Congresillo" (little congress) composed of members of the National Congress that it selected. Then it applied a transitory provision that was not in force, ordering a reduction in the number of members of the Supreme Court of Justice by drawing lots. In protest against this arbitrariness, its members resigned, and the vacancies were handled by congress by promoting associate justices to magistrates. With this new abuse of power, the government got rid of a politically independent court since it had been formed by means of a merit-based competition conducted under the supervision of the United Nations and the OAS.[10] In view of so many arbitrary measures, the newspaper *El Comercio* dared to say that a "virtual dictatorship" was taking shape in Ecuador.

With the approval of the constitution by two-thirds of the voters in the 2008 referendum, Correa achieved his government's most desired political objective, one that he had been pursuing since he took office: to eliminate the rule of law, without that unfortunate event being seen as abolishing the democratic system, either at home or abroad. Thanks to the new constitution, the following circumstances acquired constitutional status: concentration of power in the Presidency of the Republic, diminishment of the National Assembly's attributions, and loss of independence for the Constitutional Court and the National Electoral Council. In addition, thanks to the subordinate role that Correa gave the Council of Citizen Participation and Social Control (CPCCS), he was able to designate oversight authorities. Ecuadorians had no memory of a "constitutional" president with such excessive power.

The establishment of Correa's autocratic regime had much to do with the CPCCS, this strange body composed of seven members proposed by citizens or social organizations and selected through fraudulent merit-based competitions. Its excessive attributions were to be vigilant of the transparency of the acts of authorities, to fight corruption, to educate Ecuadorians in civic values, to demand accountability, to promote citizen participation, and to appoint the highest-ranking state officials, with the exception of the president, the vice president, and legislators—a very important task. Consequently, the appointment of the attorney general and superintendents fell under its responsibility. They were to be chosen from the short lists presented by the president of the republic, while the federal prosecutor, comptroller, ombudsman, National Electoral Council, and Judicial Council were to be chosen through merit-based competitions. With the participation of other agencies, the CPCCS was also to appoint the members of the National Court of Justice, the National Electoral Council, and the Constitutional Court.

Correa used the CPCCS so that the highest-level officials and magistrates of the state, by their nature independent from the government, would not only have ties to him but also be dependent on him. He justified this undemocratic procedure by saying that it would put an end to the intervention of the highly questioned partyocracy in such appointments and that the assignment of this responsibility to persons nominated by the "uncontaminated" social organizations would guarantee that their decisions would be based on the merits, experience, morality, and capacity of the nominees. Few realized that this unusual body had been designed so that the president would be the one to select the appointees.

Once this methodical process of empowerment was completed, violations of the constitution and laws became selective and less conspicuous. In order to achieve his objectives, it was enough for Correa to use the broad powers granted to him by the constitution or to make use of the state bodies that depended on his authority and responded to presidential demands. It was no longer possible for the National Assembly, the Constitutional Court, and the oversight bodies to monitor, object to, disapprove, control, and render ineffective arbitrary or dishonest acts that the president and members of his government might commit. In order to impose his authority, Correa no longer needed to disregard their decisions or bend their will using the violence of the Correa crowds. The broad scope of authority granted by the new constitution placed him in the privileged position of obtaining whatever he wanted from the National Assembly, the Constitutional Court, the National Court of Justice, the National Electoral Council, the Attorney General's Office, the Comptroller's Office, the Federal Prosecutor's Office, the Central Bank, and the Superintendency of Banks and Companies, and the Superintendency of Insurance Companies. The members and officials of these agencies knew that, if they wanted to keep their positions, they had to react positively to presidential requests, sometimes made publicly.

The 2008 constitution, despite having responded to Correa's wishes and received his excessive praise, ended up bothering him, so it did not cause him any embarrassment to disregard it or interpret it according to his interests. He did so through laws, regulations, decrees, or simple administrative decisions, as will be seen in part III, chapter 11. However, there were still areas out of reach of the long and powerful presidential arm, at least out of reach of his absolute control, such as the justice system and certain freedoms, especially freedom of expression. To overcome these limitations, he proposed several constitutional reforms, to be voted on in the popular consultation and in the referendum he called, a matter examined in the last pages of the previous chapter.

In order to weaken certain economic sectors considered enemies of the government, the directors and main shareholders of financial and communication companies were prohibited from owning shares in other economic activities.[11]

Even though the media had been favorable to him in the electoral campaign that earned him the presidency, he could not tolerate the fact that they became critics of his administration once he had been elected because of the authoritarian excesses examined in this chapter. Since he was not in a position to submit them to his designs as he had done with the powers of the state, he chose to create a legal instrument that would allow him to control them. For that there was nothing better than a regulatory council, approval for which he requested from the voters in a referendum. Later, a new legislature approved the Communication Law, which gave the government powers that would enable it to achieve the goal of controlling private media: press, radio, and television. It was necessary to prevent them from disseminating news, information, editorial opinions, and journalistic investigations on the administration, particularly on the thorny issue of corruption. This law was passed in a summary manner and without debate.

The Superintendency of Communication created by this law was in charge of scrutinizing the content disseminated by the media and of establishing the ultimate responsibility of journalists and the companies for which they worked. This and other provisions were used to fine them and force them to publish corrections in the formats provided by government officials. In addition, there were criminal lawsuits in which Correa sued for millions of dollars in compensation for the alleged moral damages that some publications had caused him to suffer. Meanwhile, official advertising was used to reward the "friendly" press and to bargain with the "enemy" press. At the same time, Correa set up a network of state-owned media, a subject that will be analyzed in part III, chapter 14.

One of the many consequences of these abuses of power, of the punitive Communication Law, and of the creation of the Superintendency of Communication was the appearance of self-censorship among journalists, newspaper and magazine owners and editors, and privately owned television and radio stations. Fearing administrative or judicial prosecution and onerous fines, they moderated their editorial opinions, stopped conducting and publishing investigations on acts of corruption, and suppressed information that could provoke the president's anger.

Of all the questions submitted to the voters, the most important, and the main reason for calling the referendum, was the one referring to the justice system. As mentioned above, the question proposed the creation of a Transitory Judicial Council to be in charge of restructuring the judicial function. Since its three members were to be appointed by entities controlled by the president, opinion leaders, political leaders, and editorialists expressed their concern about the danger that the judicial function would lose the relative freedom it still had and become dependent on the executive function. They rightly pointed out that Correa's proposal entailed the intention to replace professional and career judges with politicized judges dependent on his will. This is what happened. Judges he trusted completely were appointed and used according to his interests. This had not happened even during the military dictatorships, as will be analyzed in greater detail in part III, chapter 13.

Along the same lines of persecution, Correa took actions against civil society and the programs of the so-called nongovernmental organizations (NGOs), in which some leaders of Alianza PAIS had been involved and through which they had fought against previous governments. To this end, Correa issued two decrees, regulating their activities and authorizing oversight by a government agency, the Secretariat of the People. They were obliged to report to the government on their activities, their funding sources, and the programs they carried out, as well as to allow government inspectors to verify the information provided. International organizations were required to submit their work programs in the country to government approval. This led NGOs to self-censor and led some international cooperation organizations to leave the country.[12]

In the presidential and legislative elections of March 17, 2012, the government obtained a wide victory. In the case of the legislative elections, the sizeable win was due to a system of seat allocation that excessively rewarded the list with the most votes. Thanks to that system, Alianza PAIS managed to seat 100 of the 123 members of the National Assembly, despite having obtained only 57 percent of the votes cast. Correa used this absolute majority to neutralize any hint of opposition control and to have the National Assembly pass laws and make constitutional reforms in his interest, such as the indefinite reelection of the president of the republic.

The coup examined in this chapter, which allowed the constitutional president to put all the functions and institutions of the state under his command, was of a different nature than those that had taken place in Ecuador in previous centuries. It was executed in a cunning manner by a president elected by the people, with the discourse that he was proposing to found a new democracy, when what he was actually proposing was to establish a dictatorship. It began with disregarding the 1998 constitution; continued with issuing a tailor-made text, pushed through on the basis of maliciously held popular consultations and referendums and consolidated through the manipulation of electoral and plebiscitary processes; and concluded with the exercise of absolute power.

In the twentieth century there had never been a president, or a dictator, who had managed to accumulate such inordinate power. This surprising and pernicious anomaly occurred in the modern Ecuador of the twenty-first century, during the longest democratic period ever experienced by the country, at a time when the country and the people had made significant progress and most citizens were in a position to be informed about public affairs.

NOTES

1. Congress had terminated the terms of the ministers on the Supreme Court of Justice and designated new magistrates (Hurtado 1998).

2. I was one of only a few who spoke out against convening a constituent assembly. I considered it unnecessary because the problems that were affecting Ecuador's democracy and development could have been solved through a constitutional reform made by the National Congress. Once voters approved a constituent assembly, my party (Democracia Popular) asked me to represent it and to head the list of its

candidates for the province of Pichincha. I was elected and then designated its president when it was inaugurated.

3. Forty people were trying to assault them, so they had to leave the building and meet elsewhere; they complained about the police's "passive attitude" in the face of the assault (CLACSO 2007).

4. Later on, a video circulated in which National Congress President Jorge Cevallos (PRIAN), Finance Minister Ricardo Patiño, and UDC congressman Jaime Estrada agreed to change the next day's agenda in order to approve the call for the popular consultation. Aware of the conspiracy they were plotting against the democratic order, they agreed to deny publicly that they had met and to say that they did not even know each other.

5. He also verbally abused the members of congress, calling them "cavemen, caciques, conspirators, traitors, and snakes."

6. Those who voted that way were Elsa Bucaram (PRE), René Mauge (ID), Hernán Rivadeneira (Socialist Party), and TSE President Jorge Acosta.

7. Congressmen Oswaldo Flores, Henry Carrascal, and Carlos Larreátegui were physically assaulted (*El Universo* 2007b). Congresswomen Gloria Gallardo and Sylka Sánchez were about to be lynched when they "were fleeing from a group of people that would have killed them . . . if they had caught them" (*La Hora* 2007).

8. As indicated in the previous chapter, my party (Popular Democracy) and I were among a very few that launched a political battle against convening a constituent assembly.

9. A sui generis legal principle, a mix of constitutional norms and legal norms, unprecedented in Ecuador's legal order. The list of approved mandates can be seen in Basabe-Serrano (2009).

10. The malicious and arbitrary government operation was facilitated by the surprising dissidence of magistrate José Vicente Troya, who agreed to be named president of the Supreme Court's associate justices.

11. The main targets of those prohibitions were the newspaper *El Universo* and the bank Banco Pichincha, firms against which Correa held grudges. Once this matter had been approved, banks and media were forced to sell companies that formed part of their regular lines of business—in the case of the former, money exchanges and insurance companies.

12. Early on, in late 2007, Correa had made the following threat: "We'll do that in January. We're going to eliminate all those foundations" (*El Universo* 2007f).

Chapter 10

The Ruse of Citizen Participation

First as a candidate and then as president, Correa, alongside the leaders of Alianza PAIS and those elected to represent the governing party in the Constituent Assembly, made citizen participation the cornerstone of the political reform they proposed to carry out. Throughout the electoral campaign, they systematically criticized "formal democracy" and the institutions that composed it, as contained in the 1998 constitution. They challenged it for having been merely electoral, favoring the intervention of few, excluding many, and for being an instrument used by the parties to legislate, appoint authorities (which is precisely what all democratic countries do), and decide the fate of Ecuador behind closed doors.

In the virtuous participatory democracy that the Citizens Revolution offered to build, the opinions of the citizens would always be taken into account. They would participate directly in debating public affairs, approving programs, solving society's problems, appointing the highest authorities of the state, providing input for government decisions, and drafting the constitution. The program of Alianza PAIS stated that "a mobilized society" should "closely monitor the deliberations" of the Constituent Assembly and seek "a broad social agreement" to be "drawn up by all the inhabitants of Ecuador" and stated that, while the new constitution was being discussed, the government and the assembly would carry out daily "democratic pedagogy" through a "national dialogue."

It is worth quoting Alberto Acosta, a Citizens Revolution ideologue, president of the Constituent Assembly, and the most determined advocate for citizens' participation in public affairs: "The project for a life in common," which Alianza PAIS proposed to draw up in the Montecristi constitution, would be participatory, unlike other constitutions drawn up "behind the people's backs." "Every citizen needed to be a member of the Constituent Assembly, needed to debate, discuss, propose, and participate" on an ongoing basis. In order for the Constituent Assembly to have "a mobilized society, participating in its decisions," he and his party colleagues would be willing to

135

"devote half their time to dialogue with the grassroots, with different sectors, with unions, businessmen, students."

Instead, the Constituent Assembly took a different path and created legal conditions for the president of the republic to set himself up as the be-all and end-all of participation. It did not promote a "process of reflection and analysis of the needs of society," which should precede the discussion of constitutional articles. Nor did it favor the broad participation of the "mobilized society" so that the latter could not only participate in the election of assembly members but also "closely monitor the Constituent Assembly's deliberations in order to appropriate the constitution and then pressure for compliance." Moreover, a good number of the Constituent Assembly members from Alianza PAIS limited themselves to voting for articles in whose conception, discussion, and approval they did not participate, some of them written by individuals and institutions outside the assembly, including foreigners.

The officers of the Constituent Assembly's plenary and commissions came solely from among members of Alianza PAIS. Before the proposed constitution was presented, laws and mandates were approved in discussions in which very few assembly members took part. Such legal texts, which were submitted by a legislation commission, were voted on in the plenary without discussion since the members of the assembly could not make observations or propose changes. Thus, laws and mandates were approved by the eight members of the government party who formed the majority of that commission and not by the 130 members of the Constituent Assembly. Several texts, especially those of interest to the government, were not even written by the assembly but rather in the Office of the President of the Republic.

The essence of this discriminatory and nonparticipatory position of the Constituent Assembly did not change, but its form in debating constitutional reforms did. Although the articles were discussed and voted on in the commissions and in the plenary, Alianza PAIS's way of thinking always ended up imposing itself. Any articles, texts, and proposals put forward by members of other parties, no matter how reasonable and advisable they were, were not taken into account.[1] The positions adopted by the members of the government party were always adamant since voting was previously determined and sometimes peremptorily ordered by government officials or assembly authorities. Before being submitted to the plenary, the articles were approved in reserved sessions of members of Alianza PAIS. When they could not reach an agreement or when opposing positions appeared, President Correa traveled to Montecristi to settle the disputes. This was what happened when discussing whether an invocation to God should head the constitution. Civil-society organizations, business associations, social groups, and, in general, sectors that could be affected by certain constitutional provisions or had something to contribute were ignored or listened to selectively.

If the members of the Constituent Assembly belonging to other political organizations could not influence the approval of the constitutional texts, the possibility that the people would be heard was much more remote—much less that "all Ecuadorians" would be heard, as the leaders of the government of the Citizens Revolution had rhetorically promised.

Those who did participate, even to a greater extent than many assembly members from Alianza PAIS, were people outside the Constituent Assembly, even though they had not been elected by the people to legislate on their behalf. Many articles that were discussed in the working groups were drafted in the government's planning office (Senplades) or in the office of the legal counsel for the president of the republic. They were also the sources for speeches read by assembly members from Alianza PAIS during the debates. Spanish professionals who served as advisors, especially Roberto Viciano, even drafted some articles of the constitution. In short, these individuals participated more than the Ecuadorian people, more than assembly members from the opposition, and even more than assembly members from Alianza PAIS, in conceiving and drafting the constitution of a country that was not theirs and that they did not know and understand.

The Constituent Assembly was also a resounding deception in terms of Alianza PAIS's offer to democratize Ecuadorian politics and transform a democracy of the few into a democracy of all.

Restrictions on the exchange of ideas, such as those that took place in Montecristi, had not occurred in any of the legislatures in the present democratic period, and not in the Constituent Assembly of 1998 or even in the commissions formed by the last military dictatorship to prepare the draft constitution submitted to the referendum of 1978. To find a parallel with what happened with the discussion of the 2008 constitution, one would have to go back to the Conservative domination of the nineteenth century and the Liberal domination at the end of that century and the beginning of the twentieth century.

Yet, when closing the campaign for yes votes in the referendum called to approve the constitution, Correa went so far as to say that it had been "the result of years of social struggles of workers, teachers, Indigenous people, women, environmentalists, youth, the disabled, [and] emigrants."

Constituent Assembly President Alberto Acosta had been interested in having the social sectors voice their opinion on the text of the constitution and in having a broad debate on its content, at least by the assembly members from Alianza PAIS and the allied parties. He went so far as to say that the Montecristi constitution was going to distinguish itself from the previous ones for being participatory since it would be the result of a "frank and pluralistic debate" because democracy "could not be pressed by time." President Correa was so opposed to these participatory mechanisms that he complained that Acosta was being "too democratic," devoting too much time to debates, and "consulting everyone all the time."

Pressured by the need to be able to rely on the power that the new constitution would grant him, the approval of which was being delayed by the dialoguing Acosta, Correa requested the resignation of the man who had been the mentor of his political rise and one of the cornerstone ideologues of the Citizens Revolution and the Ecuadorian Left. Those who had elected Acosta did not take part in his dismissal: the members of Alianza PAIS, the allied parties Pachakutik and MPD, and socialist sectors. He was replaced by Assembly Vice President Fernando Cordero, whose first decision was to eliminate the already diminished citizen participation in one fell swoop. During his presidency, debates were so restricted, even for his party colleagues, that the cumbersome articles that had not yet been approved were dispatched in a little more than thirty days, and two hundred articles were passed in a summary manner in barely a week.

Diminishing of the Constituent Assembly members' right to participate in drafting the new constitution—and of the right of the Ecuadorian people, whose opinion, it had been said, was going to be consulted daily and reflected in the provisions of the constitution—did not end there. At the last minute, articles not reviewed by the commissions or approved by the plenary were incorporated. When errors and omissions were discovered, the executive board, with participation by the president's legal advisor, Alexis Mera, made conceptual and legal corrections and introduced new articles. These were then approved by the docile government majority, even though they had not been seen or discussed.

There was also no participation within the government since ministers and other officials at that level did not usually take part in defining the policies and programs of their own institutions. Nor did they take part in discussing decisions made by President Correa, which they sometimes learned about through information provided by the press. Correa's authoritarian ways and practices—and his belief that knowledge, wisdom, enlightenment, and intelligence were his and no one else's—led him to underestimate the opinions of his collaborators. The modest education and limited knowledge of many of them, who had been chosen for their party militancy rather than for their competence, were contributing factors. One example of this was the fact that they did not react, protest, or resign[2] when they were verbally and publicly mistreated by the president.

The ministers' access to the president's office to discuss decisions or the progress of the programs they were in charge of was limited, partly because their large number (some forty) prevented them from being received by the president except occasionally. They were also fearful of being harassed by the despotic leader and knew that he was not very open to receiving comments, listening to criticism, and tolerating discrepancies. In order to keep their jobs, it was better for them to be discreet, praise his positions, laugh at his jokes, and comply with his orders without complaining. With this submissive behavior, in addition to avoiding rude reprimands, they won his goodwill, kept their positions, and even received promotions. Correa's egocentricity led him to the extreme of making others' successes and triumphs his own and to blaming his collaborators for any mistakes, failures, and fiascos.[3]

There was similar subordination among officials who were not obliged to obey him because they were not part of the executive function and did not depend on presidential authority, such as superintendents, prosecutors, comptrollers, attorneys general, even judges on the National Court of Justice and the Constitutional Court and members of the National Electoral Council. They were also aware that they had reached such high positions because of presidential protection, not because of their merits, and that they could be forced to leave.[4]

Finally, government officials, legislators, heads of other state functions, members of oversight bodies, and all those who wanted to keep their positions and move up politically were convinced that "whoever did not go along was out of the picture,"[5] that is, politically helpless. If they were also getting richer, they feared that once they left the presidential umbrella, not only would they lose their lucrative positions but so would the relatives for whom they had also found positions in the government.

Since the government party controlled almost all the National Assembly commissions during Correa's decade in office and had also held an absolute majority since the 2012 elections, the members of Alianza PAIS were the ones who legislated without caring about the opinions of the representatives of other political organizations. The latter were also denied participation by the procedure established for the approval of laws.

Legislators' participation in parliamentary debates, which is inherent to deliberative bodies, was subject to restrictions. Most legislators, even those from Alianza PAIS, could not participate in the discussion of the legal norms submitted to the assembly because a commission, not the plenary, determined their final content. The observations made by the legislators in the first debate were taken into consideration at the discretion of the respective commission. In the second debate, the assembly did not discuss or vote on each article separately but rather on the report prepared by the corresponding commission, which sometimes went so far as to incorporate articles that had not been seen by the plenary.

Once the laws reached the president's office, the National Assembly's participation in defining and drafting their content was reduced. The president did not limit himself to vetoing the provisions with which he disagreed, as prescribed by the constitution; he introduced articles that had not been included in the original draft and had not been seen by the assembly. By proceeding in this way, in addition to usurping the power to legislate, he violated the citizens' participation as expressed through assembly members elected by the people to represent them. He even vetoed some laws that had been presented by his fellow party members and approved by the National Assembly, after contemptuously describing those laws as bulky mumbo jumbo ("mamotretos").[6]

The president held no meetings or consultations with the Alianza PAIS legislative bloc in order to share opinions and reach a consensus, unless there were conflicts that could jeopardize their unity or prevent the approval of a law of interest to the government. Correa's poor opinion of his party's legislators had to do with this and led him to say publicly that they could pass the laws they wanted because he could then override them with his veto.

This is what happened when one of the assembly's commissions introduced modifications to the penal code proposal submitted by the executive branch. Even though it had not yet been approved by the assembly, Correa announced that, because he did not agree with the changes introduced, he would "veto it totally instead of wasting time" in discussions since the assembly members from his party approved "any nonsense."

Even more contrary to citizen participation was Correa's response to the intention of a third of Alianza PAIS's assembly members to reform a provision of the penal code related to abortion. Led by their most prominent legislators, they proposed that women who had been raped, not only those who had mental deficiencies, could have an abortion without being incriminated. After accusing them of "treason" and saying they had "stabbed him in the back," Correa threatened to resign. He claimed that they had agreed not to touch the issue, even though there was no record that he had met with his party bloc for that purpose. Fearing that the threat could be carried out, beleaguered assembly members Paola Pabón and Gina Godoy, promoters of the initiative, withdrew it. Correa was not satisfied and announced that they would be kicked out of the National Assembly through the revocation of their mandates. So that there would be no doubt that the only one who could impose his ideas in the participatory democracy of the Citizens Revolution was Rafael Correa, he added the threat that he would withdraw from Alianza PAIS. Faced with the annoyance that such despotic behavior produced among assembly members and other government officials, Correa accepted a compromise solution: the legislators would retract their proposal, and the party's disciplinary body would sanction them benignly, with a one-month suspension in the exercise of their parliamentary duties. They were also forbidden to make statements to the press.

With such extortion through threats, blackmail, and punishment, Correa restricted the right of the assembly members from his party to have their own convictions and to promote them in the National Assembly through the exercise of the participatory democracy enshrined in the constitution and advocated by the Citizens Revolution. No one dared to contradict Correa, and Assemblywomen Pabón and Godoy submissively accepted and complied with the sanctions imposed by him, including that of keeping a humiliating silence (*ICN* 2012).

President Correa's political party, Alianza PAIS, did not favor the political participation of the citizens who joined its ranks either. It was not born out of a congress or assembly of members; for several years, it lacked a governing body to represent it; and when it had one, its directors were merely figure-heads because they did not meet or decide anything. The party did not approve the principles of its doctrines or the government program of candidate Rafael Correa, nor did it nominate its candidates for its first electoral campaign or subsequent ones. In the decade that it governed Ecuador, the party's activi-ties were reduced to the tasks of an election organization: recruiting voters, getting them to rallies, and supporting the proselytizing activities of the can-didates. Meanwhile, the activities typical of party members were absent: pre-senting their points of view to the president, discussing his major decisions, and participating in the selection of candidates for various positions. All this continued during the Citizens Revolution's subsequent terms in office.

One illustration of this is what happened at the national convention in which the party was founded, held belatedly in mid-2010, four years after it was formed as an electoral organization. During its meetings there was no debate on its doctrines and program or on the results of the government's administration. Most of the time was devoted to listening to speeches and musical performances by artists hired to entertain the attendees. One of the few debates was whether Alianza PAIS should be called a party or a move-ment, a matter that concluded with the adoption of the latter because the former was considered unpopular.

Rafael Correa, who was at the same time president of Ecuador and presi-dent of Alianza PAIS, did not render accounts to his party regarding his gov-ernment or his party management, and his party's leaders and militants did not request them either. None of them thought of complaining about such omissions, which went against the participatory democracy proposed by that political organization.

On the few occasions that AP's governing bodies met, their decisions were not approved by individual votes by each member but rather by a show of hands, that is, by acclamation. The governing bodies were made up of gov-ernment officials and assembly members because they were more prone to discipline, obedience, and slogans than those who did not hold public-sector positions.

Once Correa was elected president and took office, Alianza PAIS disappeared from the political scene and only returned when popular consultations or electoral campaigns were involved. Despite being the official party, it did not have an institutional relationship with the president that would allow it to participate in defining the government's economic, social, and international policies and to express its concerns. These functions were assumed by a political bureau not even incorporated in the statutes of Alianza PAIS. It was composed of people that Correa trusted, and its members came and went as a function of their loyalty and the president's mood. This bureau in fact exercised functions that should have belonged to the governing bodies of AP, such as responding to government inquiries and voicing opinions on matters of some importance.

Such was the dependence of Alianza PAIS on presidential authority that its governing bodies did not choose candidates for the assembly and other popularly elected positions. In the 2013 elections, when it had to choose candidates for the National Assembly, Correa said that he would choose them, taking into account loyalties and poll numbers. This procedure led him to include soccer players, professional drivers, and show business personalities on the list, all of them outside his party.

In the 2011 referendum and popular consultation called to reform the constitution and several laws, the nonexistence of Alianza PAIS as a government party and its nonparticipation in government decisions was confirmed. Party leaders and assembly members learned about the call through news issued by the media. When approached by journalists to explain the contempt they had suffered from the president, the head of their party, they answered that since they were "organic" (i.e., disciplined, obedient, obsequious), they had no comments for him. This is not what usually happens in democratic societies, in which even opposition parties are informed or consulted about important government decisions.

The assembly members from Alianza PAIS incorporated into the 2008 constitution the statement that citizens would participate "at all levels of government" and in the "preparation of national, local and sectorial plans and policies." For that purpose, the Constituent Assembly created the Council for Citizen Participation and Social Control, which was charged with promoting the people's direct involvement in public affairs. However, during Correa's decade, there was no evidence, not even a hint, that the CPCCS had undertaken any action whatsoever to promote citizens' participation in designing government programs and authorities' decision making.

The procedure followed for forming the CPCCS was restrictive and exclusive and in no way participatory since the selection of its members did not involve the universe of citizens, even indirectly. Minuscule social organizations, even individuals, who did not represent anyone, nominated candidates.

Through a merit-based competition, ad hoc commissions supposedly selected the "best" candidates. In this singular meritocratic process, by which the heads of the justice system, the Attorney General's Office, the Comptroller's Office, and the Federal Prosecutor's Office, among other important institutions, were appointed, a handful of people took part, and not the universe of voters, either directly or indirectly. It also created conditions for the government to manipulate the selection so that those faithful to the government would be chosen and not the most well prepared.

The process in the National Congress, which had traditionally been in charge of appointing the heads of such institutions, was much more democratic and participatory. The legislators had been elected by millions of voters, came from all provinces of Ecuador, and represented the ideological and political diversity of national society. This mechanism was generally conducive to the election of honest, well-prepared, and experienced officials, independent of government, whose moral and professional integrity citizens could trust.

In democratic societies, the most important and complete form of participation is the direct participation of the people through their votes in the election of presidents, vice presidents, legislators, and local authorities; in the recall of their mandates; in popular consultations on matters of general interest; and in referendums to approve constitutions or reform them. The 1979 constitution was the first to establish some of these forms of direct citizen participation, which were expanded in the 1998 constitution and maintained in the 2008 constitution.

Because two consultations and two referendums (examined in other chapters) were called during the decade in which Rafael Correa governed, it could be said that the participatory democracy proclaimed by the Citizens Revolution was indeed expressed and practiced in this regard. However, some clarifications are in order. The people were not called upon to contribute to perfecting democracy, but rather to distort it, later abolish it, and then replace it with a dictatorial regime. In the 2007 referendum, President Correa disregarded the 1998 constitution and violated the constitutional order then in place; in the 2008 referendum an autocratic constitution was approved, which would allow him to take over all the powers of the state; and in the 2011 referendum, he got the citizens to give him control over the justice system and communication. The use of illegal and dishonest unconstitutional procedures, the manipulation of public opinion through massive official propaganda, the use of public resources, and the absence of independent electoral authorities prevented voters from expressing themselves freely and prevented electoral campaigns from being fair and results from being reliable. The same could be said of Correa's repeated reelections.

The president, his ministers, administrators, and other high-ranking officials did not favor the participation of citizens and the organizations that represented them in the debates of public affairs, including those in the National Assembly and in the media. These officials were not accountable for their actions by granting interviews and providing information, partly because the president ordered them not to do so. They avoided attending forums and debates and were reluctant to receive business associations, social groups, and civil-society organizations to let them express their concerns or voice their opinions on any policy or measure that the government was about to adopt.[7] When he received observations and criticisms about his administration, Correa did not discuss them or refute them by providing reasons and evidence, as usually occurs in democratic debate. He preferred to discredit their sources by making malicious accusations, showering insults,[8] mocking them, and laughing at them on his Saturday broadcasts, sometimes accompanied by clowns. On television screens, he tore up newspapers after referring to news stories and comments that had displeased him. He challenged his opponents to settle disagreements with fisticuffs, to "punch each other," as he said. His verbal aggressions were frequently followed by defamatory television and radio broadcasts and by comments and reports with the same tone, and these were disseminated by the public media. With these actions, rather than encouraging democratic participation, he stifled it.

The other form of citizen participation in the debates on public affairs is usually revoking the mandates of certain authorities for not having fulfilled the responsibilities entrusted to them by the voters. This institution, which appeared for the first time in the 1998 constitution, was also included in the 2008 constitution and extended to the president of the republic. Since reducing the percentage of petitioners encouraged recalls, the National Assembly introduced more requirements to make recalls or impeachments more difficult, thereby contradicting the popular participation preached by Alianza PAIS.

As seen in the previous chapter, citizen participation in public life became a mockery in the 2013 and 2017 legislative elections. Months before, through a legal reform, the access of opposition candidates to the National Assembly was restricted by a seats allocation system that disproportionately favored the majority party of the government—forgetting that, in the program offered during the 2006 presidential campaign, the AP had committed itself to building "a participatory model" that would allow "all citizens . . . to exercise power, be part of public decision making, and monitor the actions of their political representatives."

The government and the Alianza PAIS party claimed that the itinerant ministerial cabinets periodically sent to different provincial capitals were a model of popular participation. Previous paragraphs have noted Correa listened to himself and not to others and that the ministers refrained from expressing their opinions because of their reverential fear of him. There were even more reasons for similar distrust among those attending the provincial cabinets, besides the fact that they were conceived of as demonstrations that the government was present in all the provinces of Ecuador and not to discuss the specific problems and felt needs of the different localities.

As we have seen, once Rafael Correa and his followers were installed in power, the people's participation in public affairs was restricted or eliminated rather than promoted. The Constituent Assembly was not participatory in its discussion and approval of the 2008 constitution. Ministers and high-ranking government officials did not even participate in defining the most important public policies. The legislative powers of the National Assembly were reduced through unconstitutional vetoes. The directors and militants of Alianza PAIS did not participate in key decisions made by Rafael Correa, first as president and later as dictator. Opposition political and social organizations and their leaders were excluded from the debates on public affairs and, moreover, were demeaned or persecuted when they voiced opinions. Any person who criticized any of Correa's actions was disparaged, slandered, and sometimes prosecuted and convicted. With few exceptions, the president-dictator did not dialogue with representatives of unions and civil-society organizations. For its part, the CPCCS did nothing to prevent these limitations to popular participation and certainly did not promote it as provided for in the constitution.

So who participated in debating and addressing national problems during the government of the Citizens Revolution? Actually, only one citizen, only one authority, only one Alianza PAIS militant: Rafael Correa.

NOTES

1. In a book in which the author recounts his experience in Constituent Assembly sessions, he said, "There are almost no examples in which the majority has agreed to move beyond his ideological view . . . to accept proposals from others" (Lucio-Paredes 2008, 271).

2. Officials from that era have said that there were female ministers who were so affected by the president's unrestrained reproaches that they could not hold back their tears.

3. Former government minister Gustavo Larrea, in an interview with the newspaper *Hoy* (February 27, 2011), said that when one of Correa's initiatives failed, he blamed his collaborators, but if it was successful, the victory was his, even though he would never even have imagined it.

4. This is what happened with the first superintendent of banks, Alfredo Vergara, and even with Constituent Assembly President Alberto Acosta, both of whom were removed from their functions.

5. Said about the Mexican policy attributed to the leaders of the hegemonic PRI, the party that governed Mexico for decades during the twentieth century.

6. Laws or reforms were totally vetoed in the following bodies of law: Organic Law for the Legislative Function, Law for the Defense of Retailers, Organic Law for the Judicial Function, Law for Border Development, and the Law for Statistics, among others.

7. Correa exceptionally met with businessmen, but with those the government chose and not with business leaders, more as a media show than to discuss issues and policies of interest to the production sectors.

8. Among other adjectives and nouns: brutes, buzzard, cavemen, childish, clowns, constipation face, cocktail mummies, corrupt, corrupt press, cowards, crazy, delinquents, despots, dog, fat cats, fools, f***ing worthless, good-for-nothings, gravediggers, half man–half woman, horrible fatty, idiot, ignoramus, imbeciles, immoral, loan sharks, midget, crab louse (referring to Indigenous leader Lourdes Tibán), limited (referring to Nobel Prize winner Mario Vargas Llosa), mafiosos, mercenary, miserable, nefarious woman, neighborhood thug, poor devils, golden ponchos (referring to Indigenous leaders), ink mercenaries, morons, the most idiotic of idiots, a pig (referring to assembly member Cléver Jiménez), poor little man, pouty face, rags (demeaning term for newspapers), riffraff, rogue, rotten, rubbish, scoundrels, sewer with antennas, sick, stupid, thieves, traitors to their country, turncoat (referring to Alberto Acosta, his ideologue and mentor prior to their rift), trash, twerp, unburied corpse (referring to the author of this book), unburied corpses (referring to three ex-presidents), unhinged, vultures, wild beasts (referring to journalists), and wretched human.

PART III

Democratic Institutions in an Autocratic Regime

Chapter 11

The Rule of Law

The rule of law, the legal expression of democracy, is based on the constitution and the laws that govern the life of political society and on mandatory compliance with them by authorities, citizens, and the different organizations they tend to form. Those who exercise power must necessarily frame their actions within legal precepts, with no excuse that can justify noncompliance, not even the merit of the goals that a government intends to achieve: economic, social, political, patriotic, or revolutionary. The precedence of a ruler's will and authority over law is typical of dictatorial, autocratic, or totalitarian regimes. In countries run by democratic regimes, all inhabitants are equal before the law, regardless of race, social status, religion, ideas, gender, age, wealth, sexual orientation, political militancy, or power. When the acts of the members of a political society are subject to legal norms, it is said that the rule of law exists.

As we have seen in previous chapters and will examine below, the rule of law did not exist during the decade in which Rafael Correa governed, but rather it was the rule of the will of the state's highest authority. Thus, the president failed to comply with, violated, and ignored the norms contained in the constitution and in the laws, even those he issued, with the excuse that "nothing and nobody" could hinder the progress of the "revolutionary project" and that his arbitrary actions were legitimized by the people in elections, consultations, and referendums. The vagueness of the 2008 constitution, the predominant presidential authority enshrined therein, and his inclination to interpret legal norms according to his own convenience contributed to this stance.

As previously indicated, in the solemn ceremony in which he took office before the National Congress, he refused to swear that he would govern subject to the constitution and the law, even though under their provisions he had registered his candidacy, participated in the election campaign, won the presidential election, and that day assumed the presidency.

Not many hours passed before he committed the serious unconstitutional act of calling for a popular consultation so that the people could voice their opinion on convening a constituent assembly and issuing a new constitution, a matter examined in part II, chapter 9. The 1998 constitution did not contemplate the possibility of a constituent assembly, and its Article 282 provided that constitutional reforms were to be made by the National Congress. Later, a law was issued to convene a constituent assembly although doing so should have been solely in the power of the legislative body. A series of abuses of power and violent outrages ensued, with which he subjected the Supreme Electoral Tribunal and the National Congress to his authority and later dissolved the Constitutional Court.

Years later, in the call for the consultation and referendum of 2011, he again violated the constitution, this time the 2008 constitution, despite the fact that it was his and his party's work. He made the call ignoring Article 441, which prohibited constitutional amendments that would change "the nature and constituent elements of the State" and "alter the fundamental structure of the Constitution." This is precisely what he did by proposing that the Judicial Council be replaced by a transitory council and modifying its composition as established in the constitution. This was not the only unconstitutional act he committed with the call for the consultation and referendum.

During Correa's administration, the constitution was reformed de facto through lower-level legal norms such as laws, regulations, executive decrees, ministerial agreements, contracts, or simple administrative decisions. Of the many examples that could be cited, I will examine the most relevant ones.

Article 422 of the constitution prohibited entering into treaties in which the state ceded jurisdiction to international arbitration bodies in contracts signed with foreign legal entities. In keeping with this norm and at the request of the government, the National Assembly denounced the investment protection treaties that Ecuador had signed with many countries. Nonetheless, in the contracts entered into with the China Development Bank, the government agreed to submit disputes to the London Court of International Arbitration and to Chinese courts. Moreover, in the Planning and Public Finance Code approved by the National Assembly, there was a provision that gave the attorney general the power to authorize those jurisdictions.

The second paragraph of Article 11 and the first paragraph of Article 40 of the constitution established that foreigners visiting the country would not be discriminated against, nor would their stay be considered illegal if they did not have a visa. In compliance with this constitutional norm, the government extended the visa exemption to all countries. However, it later reinstituted visa requirements, warning that "open borders" and "universal citizenship" were causing the massive entry of all kinds of individuals, some of whom were linked to organized crime or sought by the justice systems of other countries,[1] or were using Ecuadorian territory to immigrate to the United States.

Article 105 of the constitution provided that the mandate of popularly elected authorities could be revoked. The stampede of recalls unleashed led the National Electoral Council to issue a regulation that modified the constitution by adding other requirements.

Article 120 of the constitution attributed to the National Assembly the power to enact laws, and Article 137 stated that the legislators had to approve them in two debates. These provisions were modified by the Organic Law of the Legislative Function, by providing that the discussion and approval of the articles of a bill should not take place in the plenary but in the respective commission, composed of only a dozen legislators. After approving articles, the commission had to prepare a report for the review and vote of the National Assembly. The National Assembly did not discuss the articles or approve the law but only the report, a procedure that implied the exclusion of the legislators as a whole in the enactment of laws.

Paragraph 17 of Article 57 of the constitution established the Indigenous communities' right to be consulted before the adoption of a legislative measure that could affect their rights. However, the National Assembly approved the Territorial Organization Code without such prior consultation, despite the fact that it contained provisions that affected how Indigenous people could organize themselves and how natural resources in regions inhabited by them could be managed and exploited.

The constitution stated that the president of the republic could decree a state of emergency for sixty days, extendable for up to thirty more. Following the police uprising of September 30, 2010, Correa issued a decree of this nature, transferring the security of the legislative precinct from the police to the armed forces. From that date on, he extended the state of emergency as many times as he wished, regardless of the aforementioned constitutional limitation, as if two years after that event the internal unrest was still active. The same thing happened with the numerous decrees in which he declared the country, or part of it, in emergency,[2] many of them issued without providing any justification.

Through an obsequious Supreme Electoral Tribunal, President Correa dismissed more than fifty deputies from the National Congress. By means of abuses of power, deceit, and street violence, they were replaced by alternates, as seen in part II, chapter 9.

In violation of the constitutional provision that the power to legislate belongs solely to the legislative branch of government, Correa reformed laws through lower-level legal mechanisms such as decrees and regulations. By means of this arbitrariness, he usurped the legislative function's power to legislate, first the power of the National Congress and later that of the National

Assembly, by issuing the statute whereby he called for a popular consultation in 2007 to convene a constituent assembly. He also legislated on his own, by incorporating into the laws approved by the National Assembly articles that had not been included in them and by inappropriately using his right to veto.

Despite the fact that the constitution provided that the bills should refer to "only one matter," the president sent the National Assembly texts containing different matters, sometimes in transitory provisions added to the bill under review.

The constitution empowered the president to submit projects of economic urgency, a status that obliged the assembly to approve them within a certain period of time. He made use of this power to submit bills that did not meet the urgency requirement but that he was particularly interested in having enacted. In order to prevent their discussion, assembly officials and members of the government resorted to all kinds of tricks. Thanks to them, he managed to have bills enacted without the required analysis, debate, and consideration. Some of these referred to the creation of taxes.

It is true that Ecuador, for cultural reasons, has been a country in which the day-to-day behavior of citizens, social groups, businessmen, and authorities has not been modeled on its constitution and laws but rather on the systematic, malicious, and blatant violation of the legal order, as occurred during Rafael Correa's three terms. Perhaps with the exception of the despised dictatorship of Ignacio de Veintemilla 140 years ago, Ecuador seemed to have no memory. This arbitrary presidential practice permeated ministries, public enterprises, and even independent and autonomous institutions in charge of ensuring compliance with the constitution and the law: the National Assembly, the National Court of Justice, the Constitutional Court, the Attorney General's Office, the Comptroller's Office, and the Federal Prosecutor's Office.

As has been noted, during the long government of Rafael Correa there was no rule of law but rather the rule of his omnipotent will. He did not subject his actions to the provisions of the constitution and the laws; he interpreted them according to his interests and ambitions; he reformed them through lower-level recourses or simply ignored them. He displayed systematic disregard for the constitutional order, both the one he inherited and the one he imposed on the country. This is only possible in a dictatorial regime and in no way in a democratic government in which the rule of law prevails.

By ignoring the constitution and the laws on a daily basis and making arbitrariness a common practice, President Rafael Correa generated the perverse effect of strengthening the culture of illegality that has been present in the lives of many Ecuadorians for centuries.

NOTES

1. Some foreigners were extradited to the United States because they were on Interpol lists.

2. From the start of his mandate in 2007 until October 2010, he issued 114 decrees declaring a state of exception (*Gestión* 2019).

Chapter 12

The Division of Power

In a democratic system, power is not concentrated in a single institution and the person who represents it. Instead, it is divided among the various bodies that make up the state. Constitutional law arrived at this political definition to avoid the disappearance of the republican regime and the establishment of an autocracy for life and to avoid affecting citizens' rights and freedoms with the existence of a single holder of power. This risk was particularly real in presidential systems of government since the head of state was elected for a fixed term, could possibly be reelected, had broad powers, administered considerable economic resources, commanded the armed forces and the police, and exerted influence in all areas of national life.

In order to prevent the president from monopolizing power beyond the limits established in the constitution, those who envisioned the republican form of government gave separate powers to the various state bodies and created a system of checks and balances among the executive, legislative, and judicial functions. This set of independent and autonomous institutions was responsible for monitoring the actions of officials, preventing their excesses, sanctioning wrongdoings, settling conflicts, and protecting citizens' freedoms.

This presidentialist political model was included in Ecuador's 1979 and 1998 constitutions, and it served as the basis for the exercise of power by the eleven governments that succeeded each other until 2007, when Rafael Correa assumed the presidency.

Limited, shared, and controlled presidential power was not appropriate for a politician without democratic principles and with marked authoritarian inclinations. It did not require clairvoyance to conclude that such a leader, once elected, would undermine the democratic system of government—even more so if he was bent on refounding Ecuador by convening a constituent assembly. Thus, it was not unreasonable to conjecture that the new constitution Correa would issue would be used to free himself from democratic constraints and extend his authority beyond the limits established in the constitution, as Venezuelan president Hugo Chávez had done years earlier.

Curiously, the exact opposite was stated in the government program of the Citizens Revolution, which proposed to reduce the "hyperpresidentialism" supposedly contained in the 1998 constitution. However, the Constituent Assembly members from Alianza PAIS ignored this party position and in the 2008 constitution disproportionately strengthened the authority of the president of the republic. Nothing similar had been included in the two constitutions of the current democratic period or in the twentieth century.

The methodical process of eliminating the separation of powers began by disregarding the 1998 constitution, which remained in force only formally, in all matters that did not oppose the president's authoritarian designs. It continued with the convening of an unconstitutional and nonpluralistic constituent assembly dependent on the government, and it concluded with the issuing of a new constitution tailor-made for President Correa and his ambitions. Besides granting him broad powers, the constitution created an institution that would allow him to expand them: the Council of Citizen Participation and Social Control (CPCCS for its acronym in Spanish).

Just as important as the institutionalization of presidential authoritarianism in the 2008 constitution were the measures taken by President Rafael Correa to expand his power through the antidemocratic control of all state functions and institutions. These were so expeditious that in the two months following the inauguration of his government, he had already placed the Supreme Electoral Tribunal, the National Congress, and the Constitutional Court at his service.

This voracious process of concentrating power was consolidated and expanded with the inauguration of the constituent assembly. Through the "mandates" it issued (a legal figure that does not exist in the current constitution and is alien to the Ecuadorian legal tradition), the Constituent Assembly declared the National Congress to be in recess and assumed its functions. Correa then appointed the comptroller, the attorney general, the federal prosecutor, superintendents, members of the Banking Board, and directors of the autonomous Central Bank. Thus, before the new constitution was even approved by the Constituent Assembly and voted on by the Ecuadorian people, the president had already gained control of all public powers, with the sole exception of the judicial system.

The 2008 constitution eliminated the republican regime of the separation of powers and democratic controls and instead created an autocratic state. In it, the executive branch expanded its powers, the legislative branch lost powers, and the judicial branch lost its independence. Something similar happened simultaneously with other autonomous state bodies.

When the Constituent Assembly was adjourned, it replaced the National Congress elected by the people with a mini legislative body called the "Congresillo" and composed of some of its own members. Since the new constitution was not yet in force because a referendum had not yet been held to approve it, the assembly applied the transitory provision that authorized the restructuring of the Supreme Court of Justice by reducing the number of its members and then replacing them with associate judges. It was said that this was done to free the court from political tutelage, deliberately ignoring that it had not been formed by the parties represented in the National Congress but rather by means of a merit-based competition audited by representatives of the OAS and the United Nations.

Nonetheless, this relative control of the justice system seemed insufficient to the president since the new magistrates—although they were condescending to him—did not come from the ranks of the Citizens Revolution, maintained a certain independence, and could not fully earn his trust. With the aim of taking over this last institution, which still escaped absolute control by the government, he called for a referendum in 2011. In it, the people were consulted on the creation of a Transitory Judicial Council (TJC), which would be in charge of restructuring the judicial function. (This issue was discussed above and will be studied in depth in the following chapter.) In effect, the TJC undertook restructuring not to improve the competence of the magistrates and guarantee their independence but rather to place them in the chains with which the president would lock away the democratic institutions.

This rapid rise of presidential power was formalized with the creation of the CPCCS. It was said that this brand-new body would be composed of people with no political affiliation, chosen through merit-based competitions whose "quality" and procedures would guarantee independence, integrity, and professionalism in the appointment of the most important state officials. Such competitions were manipulated so that the citizens who were chosen, without having any particular merits, would fulfill the requirement of being recommended by Alianza PAIS leaders and at the same time would commit themselves to diligently executing the instructions given by the president's collaborators, as seen in part II, chapter 9. Citizens who had been taken out of anonymity to hold offices they had never imagined they would perform were predisposed to repay the immense honor they had received.

When all the state powers had been placed under presidential authority, the president of Ecuador ceased to be a president and became a dictator.

The following facts illustrate the magnitude of the subordination of the National Assembly, even though it was more independent than other institutions and carried greater political weight.

In the second term of the legislature, which began in 2009, the Alianza PAIS movement had not managed to earn a majority representation, so, in order to get its bills approved, the government needed to add votes from other political groups. Just like the highly criticized partyocracy, it did so by handing out favors, by using unconstitutional vetoes, or by declaring approval decisions valid despite not having been made within the legally determined period.

In order to vindicate the legislative and oversight powers of the National Assembly, which had been trampled on by the president, legislators from the opposition and Alianza PAIS reformed the Organic Law of the Legislative Function. The most important changes were as follows: it could be convened with half the votes of its members plus one; the auditing commission should be limited to supporting political proceedings, and the others to reporting on bills; and the assembly regained the power to approve laws after their articles had been discussed by the plenary and to indict or impeach ministers and officials of similar rank.

These legal reforms, though limited to the functions of a legislative body, displeased Correa. In order to prevent their enactment, he prohibited their publication in the Official Record. He alleged that they had to be submitted beforehand for their review even though Article 63 of the Organic Law stated the contrary and through a previous reform the assembly could send them directly to be recorded. None of this was respected by the president or by the Constitutional Court to which he appealed. The latter, in a clear violation of the law, declared such power unconstitutional, "temporarily" suspended the aforementioned article, and prohibited the president of the assembly from sending the reforms to the Official Record and the latter's director from publishing them. In this illegal and abusive manner, with the connivance of a court that set aside its obligation to defend the constitution, the government truncated the National Assembly's legislative and oversight powers.

Violating the constitutional provision that the armed forces are not deliberative in political matters, the government tried to involve them in order to turn them into the armed wing of the Citizens Revolution. This was revealed by Defense Minister María Fernanda Espinosa in the speech she made upon assuming her functions. She introduced herself as the defense minister "of the Citizens Revolution" and not of the state, she addressed the members of the military as comrades ("compañeros and compañeras") and not by their ranks, and she told them that "the country was living through a more profound revolution than Alfaro's." By virtue of this, she said "they were called to defend" the government at a time when it was "the target of possible conspirators." For his part, Correa, in the speeches he delivered at military ceremonies, aired personal and political grievances, challenged his critics, and belittled his opponents.[1]

Such pronouncements were not echoed by the armed forces. As they remained outside the political controversies and showed no interest in getting involved in the Citizens Revolution, the president was determined to weaken and divide them. To this end, he manipulated laws and regulations to remove the commanders of the army, navy, and air force as often as he wished. One day he appointed the members of the high command and another day he dismissed them, in order to circumvent the military regulation that obliged him to form it with the most senior officers. He affected the viability of the Armed Forces Social Security Institute by reducing its funding and transferred military enterprises that were not related to the military's specific functions to the state. He even went further by taking the class struggle to the barracks, with a discourse that promoted confrontation between officers and soldiers, saying that the former were immersed in privileges while the latter suffered from shortages and marginalization.

Correa sent the National Assembly a bill aimed at restructuring the armed forces, which reduced the number of military personnel; created a special security corps for the protection of the president; gave them responsibilities of the national police; and created militarized bodies to care for national parks, prisons, and customs, where those affected by the reduction in military personnel could be employed. The project displeased commanders, officers, and soldiers because they had not been consulted and deemed that the bill distorted their function of protecting the country's external security. This claim halted the bill.

Unlike what had happened in Venezuela and Nicaragua, the Ecuadorian military did not get involved in political conflicts and did not submit to the government. Complying with the constitutional definition that they were not deliberative, they acted as mere observers of the political disputes.

Despite the aforementioned facts and the fact that the 2008 constitution eliminated the armed forces' attributions of guaranteeing the validity of the democratic system and collaborating in internal security, in the police uprising of September 30, 2010, they made a public statement defending the constitutional order. In addition, the high command complied with the presidential order for a military squad to release him from the police kidnapping to which he said he was subjected.

This is how the armed forces ended up being the only state institution that escaped the political control of the president of the republic. The institutional strength of the Ecuadorian military bodies was grounded in not becoming an instrument of his political project.

From this analysis, it can be concluded that the division of power among the executive, legislative, and judicial functions and the independence of the oversight bodies did not exist during the decade in which Rafael Correa governed Ecuador. He confirmed it himself in the statement quoted at the beginning of the second part of this book, in which he categorically affirmed to be "the head of the entire state," not only of the executive function but also of the "legislative, judicial, electoral" functions, and other institutions that compose the state.[2]

It was not what he had thought four years earlier, in the days when he participated in the conspiracy that ended in the overthrow of President Gutiérrez, as can be seen in the following statement:

What we are living through is unbelievable and let's not beat around the bush. The situation does not call for patches or rectifications. We have to go all or nothing to mend democracy and punish those who broke it. At this moment we have a de facto dictatorial government that controls the Constitutional Court, the Supreme Electoral Tribunal, the Supreme Court of Justice, [and] probably the National Congress. Where are individual guarantees to be found? Where is that elementary division of powers that Montesquieu so wisely proposed for a healthy government to be found?[3]

NOTES

1. Correa also expressed his annoyance in a letter sent to National Assembly President Fernando Cordero, in which he said that the assembly members had approved a "legal monstrosity" that issued resolutions that, due to their "poor semantics" or wording (from which the letter also suffered), led to "huge grins" and "embarrassment for others"; had "wasted time in petty arguments"; had traveled too much; and had intended to "disrespectively interfere" in the executive function.

2. The video in which this statement is made can be viewed at https://www.youtube.com/watch?v=3RnJRGmK0Wg.

3. Interview conducted by Gonzalo Rosero on Radio Democracia on January 4, 2005.

Chapter 13

The Independence of
the Justice System

According to the simple definition that Plato and Greek philosophy offered more than two thousand years ago, justice has the responsibility of "giving each his [or her] due." Individuals, public institutions, and private organizations turn to it to have their disputes settled by judges and courts through the examination of the procedural facts and the rights of the litigants. Nothing outside what is recorded in the judicial files, however important, can be taken into account by the magistrate who hears a proceeding, least of all the opinions, requests, and pressures of political authorities or economic powers.

In order for citizens to be equal before the law, for due process to be respected in litigation, and for rulings and sentences to be just, the justice system must be autonomous and judges must be independent. By virtue of the vast territories in which governments exercise their power and the many means they can use to impose their will, they are in an especially privileged position to condition the rulings of judges and magistrates in matters of their interest.

In light of these principles, it is worth studying what happened with the justice system during the decade of Correa's time in power.[1]

The governments of the current democratic period generally respected the independence of the justice system, with the exception of those presided over by León Febres Cordero and Lucio Gutiérrez. On the other hand, in the National Congress, there were majorities that upon the inauguration of a new legislature dismissed the Supreme Court of Justice (CSJ, for its acronym in Spanish) and replaced it with an agreement between parties. In order to prevent the CSJ appointed by the National Congress from taking office, Febres Cordero surrounded its headquarters with small tanks in an abuse of power whereby, working together with the legislative branch, he forced the appointment of a consensus court. Later, after leaving the presidency, he used the sizeable representation of his party (PSC) in the congress to have judges he

161

trusted appointed, mainly on the CSJ and in the judicial district of the province of Guayas.

This worrisome politicization of the justice system and the need for the country to have independent and honest judges and magistrates led voters in the 1997 referendum to voice their opinion forcefully in favor of the creation of a justice system free from the influence of political parties. For this purpose, taking into account the nominations made by centers of learning and the Catholic Church, the National Congress elected a consensus-based Supreme Court of Justice composed of jurists, academics, and magistrates with distinguished professional careers. The 1998 Constituent Assembly respected and reinforced this transcendental process by consecrating magistrates' tenure for life and establishing a system of co-optation for future renewal.

Barely seven years passed before passionate and volatile Ecuadorian politics kept this notable democratic advancement from lasting.

In order to avoid being removed from office as proposed by former presidents León Febres Cordero and Rodrigo Borja,[2] President Gutiérrez formed a majority in the National Congress by aligning with populist and socialist parties,[3] under the costly condition that the CSJ would be dismissed and another would be appointed with his recommendations, as in fact happened. Once in office, the president of the new court, Guillermo Castro, annulled the criminal proceedings for embezzlement against Abdalá Bucaram. This ruling triggered popular protests and demonstrations that ended with the removal of Gutiérrez by the National Congress. The recently appointed CSJ was immediately dismissed and remained without a president for almost a year.

A third CSJ was formed through a merit-based competition conducted under the supervision of an international oversight team made up of representatives of the United Nations and the OAS. The findings were submitted to the National Congress for its review and decision. The congress was not empowered to appoint the members of the court since that 1998 constitutional attribution had been eliminated by the Constituent Assembly when it declared that members of the court would serve for life. However, that void was filled with an ad hoc law issued for that purpose, without a constitutional basis.

Even though the CSJ was formed without political interests and influences—the magistrates having been chosen for their abilities and moral virtues and having the endorsement of international organizations—Ecuador's unpredictable and conflict-ridden politics caused the new court to suffer the same fate as the previous one. Barely two years later, President Correa not only repeated what the partyocracy and Presidents Febres Cordero and Gutiérrez had done but also took government intervention in the justice system to extremes that made the painful events described above pale in comparison.

Perhaps because these events were too fresh and Alianza PAIS leaders had vehemently condemned them, motions to replace the Supreme Court of Justice for the fourth time in just ten years were denied in the Constituent Assembly. As this was not the perspective of the president, in whose authoritarian project a justice system independent from his political interests did not fit, the democratic scruples of the assembly members were shelved. Once the articles of the new constitution had been approved, a transitory provision was surprisingly introduced, opening a door for the government to besiege the independent and professional justice system then existing.

That provision maliciously ordered that ten days after the results of the referendum were proclaimed, the thirty-one members of the CSJ would cease to serve, and twenty-one would be chosen by lot to remain until a new National Court of Justice was elected, as provided for in the new constitution. Such was the president's haste in consummating the takeover of the judicial function that he did not even wait for the constitution to be approved in the referendum.

Even though the referendum had not yet been held and the new constitution and the transitory provision therefore did not legally exist, the Little Congress resolved to apply it. When the magistrates resigned in protest against the arbitrary and abusive procedure, the government set up a new court with the associate justices of the magistrates that had resigned, overlooking the fact that eight of them had been sanctioned or questioned for various offenses.

This scandalous abuse of power would foreshadow what was to come: the absolute subordination of the justice system to presidential authority. The government's smooth-talking behavior silenced the "progressives" and "revolutionaries," who justified Correa's authoritarian excesses with the subterfuge that he was creating a new Ecuador. It was unacceptable that a professional, independent, and honorable Supreme Court of Justice should be arbitrarily dismissed by means of procedures used by the so harshly criticized partyocracy.

Authoritarian Rafael Correa was not enthusiastic about the Supreme Court of Justice he had forged because, although it was compliant with him, it was not entirely subject to his will. Lower-level judges, some of them career judges, were meanwhile reluctant to accept the government's requests. Moreover, even though the constitution had been approved by the people in the referendum, the convoluted procedure established to shape the new court delayed its formation.

These were the circumstances that led Correa to call a second referendum, in which he proposed the creation of a Transitory Judicial Council (CJT, also known in English as the Transitional Council of the Judiciary), to be composed of one representative of the president of the republic, who would preside; another one appointed by the National Assembly; and a third one named by the Citizens Participation Council. Ultimately, the three would be appointed by the president, with the second and the third also being subject to his will. This ad hoc body, due to both its origin and its composition, was to be given the powers of the Judicial Council as determined in the constitution, in addition to the power to "restructure the judicial function," sanction judges and magistrates, and replace them.

Those who were appointed to the CJT lacked the suitability required to perform such a complex task. They were personally, administratively, and politically linked to the head of state: two of them had been secondary government officials, and the third had presided over an electoral body.[4] They were not prominent jurists, prestigious academics, or magistrates with judicial experience. The person who was to preside over the CJT had nothing to do with law and justice because he had a degree in systems engineering. People of little professional merit, with no knowledge of the problems of the judicial function and politically committed to the government, were incapable of assuming and fulfilling the responsibility of reforming the justice system.

A first sign that the members of the CJT would perform their duties subject to presidential authority was that Correa chaired its initial sessions. Publicly admitting their subordinate status, the members limited themselves to executing the orders they received. They replaced judges who did not meet the demands of the government and conducted fraudulent merit-based competitions that would allow them to choose judges they trusted. So Correa was not actually interested in improving the professional competence of judges and magistrates, shortening judicial proceedings, ensuring the reliability of rulings, eliminating political interference, and moralizing the justice system— the objectives offered to citizens in the referendum campaign when asking them to vote yes.

Rafael Correa was not the appropriate person to lead a judicial reform that would increase the morality, independence, and quality of the justice system: in a lawsuit he filed against a banking institution, he had used his office to obtain a favorable verdict that unduly enriched him.[5] At the end of the last century, a bank had sued him for not having paid a credit card bill. Ten years after being declared in default, and four days before assuming the presidency, he filed a lawsuit for moral damages against Banco Pichincha (which had acquired the portfolio in which said obligation was recorded),[6] arguing that it had tarnished his reputation by placing him on the lists of the national financial risk center as a delinquent debtor. The career judge who was about to issue the ruling (Alfredo Grijalva) was untimely replaced by a temporary judge (Fabricio Segovia), who ordered payment of the five million dollars claimed. Once the ruling was issued, he left the court and the former judge was replaced. This large compensation was reduced to US$300,000 by a higher (second-instance) court but later raised to US$600,000 in the appeal heard by the National Court of Justice.

The irregularities involved in this judicial process were serious, blatant, and scandalous. Correa did not sue the bank when the alleged tort occurred but rather waited until he was elected president to do so. He had accepted the validity of the unpaid debt since he voluntarily paid it to the creditor bank, years after being notified of the default. To justify the spontaneous payment, he alleged that it had been paid by his secretary without his consent, an argument that he was unable to prove in the proceedings. Even though the hearings were related to his personal affairs, he attended them accompanied by the Presidency's legal advisor, aides, policemen, and bodyguards, for the evident purpose of intimidating the judges. Judge Segovia, who granted him the first multimillion-dollar indemnity, was used by the government in other proceedings so that he would take similar actions.

The judges of the third instance, the National Court of Justice, doubled the compensation and changed the appealed ruling, even though in an appeal hearing the judge cannot modify the ruling and must only rule on its legality.[7] One of the key players (Carlos Ramírez) was selected to be a member of the new National Court of Justice and later appointed its president. The US$600,000 compensation awarded to Correa was much higher than those awarded in similar cases. The lawyer who represented Correa in the judicial process (Galo Chiriboga) was later appointed attorney general.

The incumbent president did not pay income tax (an estimated US$200,000) on the US$600,000 compensation received, arguing that he had been exempted from doing so by the director of the Internal Revenue Service, Carlos Marx Carrasco. When that official was asked for the substantiating documents, he said that the decision had been made verbally, even though the tax code stipulated that both inquiries and official responses must be in writing. In order to benefit the president, his superior, Carrasco thus violated the Tax Regime Law, Article 2 of which states that income tax must be paid on "Ecuadorian-sourced income obtained free of charge or as payment." The income exempted from income tax, as listed in Article 9, did not include any exemption for any compensation that taxpayers might receive for moral damages.

Asked by journalists about how he would use the large sum received immorally, Correa said, "We'll see if we give it to the poor or buy headquarters for Alianza PAIS." He did neither. He used the money to purchase an apartment in Brussels at a cost of US$331,000. The balance was initially deposited in a national bank but later transferred to a foreign bank.[8] Correa had previously said that those who sent national capital abroad were "antipatriots" because by doing so they were "contributing to the development of the [countries that are] exploiters."

Since he had manipulated the justice system in order to win a lawsuit of personal interest; pressured officials, judges, and magistrates; and obtained decisions and rulings that enriched him, it would have been naive to expect different actions in judicial proceedings of interest to the government. Moreover, through the referendum, millions of voters had implicitly authorized him to interfere in the justice system by voting in favor of a constitutional reform that created the Transitory Judicial Council. He himself announced it in a speech delivered in the Amazon (Baeza, January 8, 2011). Referring to concerns expressed by jurists, opponents, and journalists that he could use the council to get his hands on the justice system, he affirmed "of course I'm going to" and later added "[but] to improve that court with which nobody can be satisfied." "That court" was "his court," the one whose judges he had chosen in violation of the Montecristi constitution.

The certainty that the proposed justice system reform would not yield positive results began to become evident as the merit competitions for the selection of the members of the National Court progressed. The court was largely made up of relatively young lawyers who did not include outstanding jurists, distinguished academics, prestigious magistrates, or judges with vast experience. The main "merit" of some applicants was that they were sympathizers or members of Alianza PAIS, government officials, or judges who had served the government diligently. Those who fulfilled this requirement received high marks in the final subjective confidential interview, displacing candidates who had obtained better scores on the experience and knowledge assessments.[9]

As feared by opponents, jurists, journalists, and editorialists, the CJT became the judicial instrument that, through the rulings and decisions it issued, the government would use to control the justice system, persecute government adversaries, and protect public officials. The targets were politicians, journalists, Indigenous leaders, social leaders, and civil-society activists who criticized abuses of power, denounced acts of corruption, carried out protests and demonstrations, or challenged presidential authoritarianism. Judges and magistrates who heeded requests and complied with orders issued personally or through officials close to the President's Office kept their positions or received promotions, while those who disobeyed were dismissed by the CJT or by the Judicial Council established in the constitution that was later approved. These bodies acted on the basis of a provision introduced into the Organic Code of the Judicial Function; the provision referred to an "inexcusable error," which was imputed to any judge who did not comply with the president's requests.

Such was his lack of restraint that Correa, now a dictator, in his Saturday broadcasts[10] and his speeches often announced legal proceedings to be initiated, the person to be accused, and the sentence to be issued, or he cited a court decision he disliked and gave a peremptory order for it to be rectified immediately.[11]

The legal secretary of the President's Office left a written record of this interference in the justice system by sending a circular to ministers and other senior officials, in which he ordered them to file lawsuits for damages against judges who accepted constitutional protection claims to the detriment of the state. In a second communication, addressed to the Provincial Court of Manabí, he threatened the judges of that district should they rule against the state. Lawyers who litigated in courts and tribunals were right to say that political interference in the decisions of magistrates and judges exceeded what had happened before, even in the worst of times.

When the CJT concluded its work after an eighteen-month term, there was widespread commentary in the lawyers' forums that the atavistic shortcomings of the justice system had become worse instead of better: the judges were less independent, and the government's political interference in their decisions was greater. Regarding the new National Court of Justice, it was said that the professional and judicial level of the magistrates had declined and that many of them lacked legal knowledge and procedural experience, for which reasons the quality of reasoning in rulings and sentencing had worsened, thus delaying proceedings and multiplying errors. Referring to judges in general, it was pointed out that, despite not having been pressured, the subordination of some judges was so extreme that they issued sentences thinking about what might please or displease the government or a certain official. There was no shortage of those who had concluded that their "loyalty" to the regime was the surest path to a successful judicial career.[12]

According to Human Rights Watch, the CJT in the eighteen months of its administration suspended 182 judges and dismissed 244, and in 2013 the permanent Judicial Council (also known in English as the Council of the Judiciary) suspended 91 and dismissed 136. The removal of 380 judges in under three years, that is, more than 20 percent of the total number, cannot be explained in any other way than due to government intervention. In this regard, the aforementioned international organization, in a letter dated January 29, 2014, addressed to Judicial Council President Gustavo Jalkh, expressed its concern about the high number of dismissals and noted that the composition of the justice system had been modified substantially through "highly questionable mechanisms that we believe severely undermine judicial independence in the country."

The regular Judicial Council that succeeded the Transitory Judicial Council was no different because it replicated the behaviors and practices of its predecessor, including the tutelage of the president of the republic. Not in vain, its five members had worked for the government for some years and two of them came from the former CJT. Gustavo Jalkh, Correa's then private secretary and former minister of government and justice, was elected to preside over the council. In order to disguise his actions and conceal the reproachable fact that he had entrusted his assistant with leading the "judicial reform," Correa had him nominated for the National Court of Justice.

The president publicly ordered that dozens of judicial proceedings be brought against those he maligned, and all of them ended with convictions. Of these, two stood out due to the interest they aroused in public opinion and the number of irregularities the judges committed to please Correa.

On September 30, 2010, there was a protest in Quito by the city's main police force because of a presidential decree that had reduced economic benefits for lower-ranking members of the military and the police. Disregarding the advice of his collaborators, Correa went to the barracks and entered by force, to reproach the police force's insubordination from a balcony and challenge them to kill him. He even unbuttoned his shirt and bared his chest. Chased by a crowd of unruly policemen, he took refuge in an adjacent hospital and asked the army to rescue him, arguing that he had been kidnapped. His request left a toll of five deaths.

As soon as he returned to his office, Correa alleged that he had been kidnapped and that the police and other conspirators had attempted a coup and a presidential assassination. However, days later he admitted that "it was a mistake to have gone to the regiment." He added, "Many say it was irresponsibility, recklessness; probably, that is my style and I never imagined what was going to happen" (*El Universo* 2010a). Interviewed in the afternoon by the press, Policy Minister-Coordinator Doris Soliz clarified that the police uprising "was not a coup" but rather "an obviously serious insubordination, due to a matter of an economic and administrative nature in one sector of the troops" (*El Universo* 2010b).

Interviewed by international television network CNN, hospital director Colonel César Carrión contradicted President Correa's statements. Carrión immediately received a harsh public reprimand from the angry president, who accused the director of having prevented him from taking refuge in the police hospital and then ordered Carrión to be criminally prosecuted.[13] In that interview, the colonel stated that he had opened the door of the hospital so that Correa could take refuge, had put him in a room for patients, and had provided him with medical attention and care. He also said that Correa had never been detained and, moreover, had expressed his gratitude when he left.

A prosecutor and a judge hurriedly executed the presidential order; the former issued an arrest warrant for the hospital director and the latter sentenced him. That sentence was later overturned by a higher court when its judges found no evidence to incriminate Carrión, even though they were pressured by Government and Justice Minister José Serrano to confirm the first-instance (lower-court) conviction. They were immediately dismissed.[14] After a lengthy judicial process and time in jail, Carrión was declared innocent.

Rafael Correa as an individual, not as president, filed a lawsuit for moral damages against the newspaper *El Universo*, its directors and owners (Carlos, César, and Nicolás Pérez), and its editor (journalist Emilio Palacio). The latter was taken to court for having written an article that Correa considered libelous and the others for having published it. The article, which appeared four months after the events that led to the prosecution of Colonel Carrión, was titled "No to Lies."[15] In it Palacio said that the dictator "should remember that, in the future, a new president could take him to a criminal court for having ordered firing at will and without warning against a hospital full of innocent people" since "crimes against humanity [are] not subject to a statute of limitations." To compensate for the moral damages allegedly suffered, President Correa sought the colossal sum of US$80 million in his lawsuit.

As though it were a lawsuit he were attending on behalf of the state, Correa showed up at the hearings accompanied by an entourage of ministers, aides, and bodyguards. He intimidatingly interrupted as often as he wanted, gave instructions to the judges, announced his decisions in advance, and made the proceedings fit his agenda. The judicial precincts were cordoned off by police and military, and government and Alianza PAIS mobs verbally and physically attacked the defendants and their lawyers. In a self-interested lawsuit that was going to make him a millionaire, Correa used state media to discredit the newspaper *El Universo*, its directors, and journalist Palacio and to defend his own financial ambitions.

In the course of the proceedings, the career judges who did not comply with his requirements were forced to excuse themselves or were replaced by temporary judges. In the first and second instances, the judges sentenced the defendants to three years in prison and payment of the hefty sum of US$40 million to Correa. To benefit the head of state, the Supreme Court of Justice dismissed the appeal filed by *El Universo* despite the abundant irregularities and violations of the lower-court proceedings.

The lawsuit was handled in a very summary manner: all three judicial instances ruled within four short months. Almost all the evidence requested by the defendants was denied, and their witnesses were threatened. The judge in charge of the first instance was dismissed for having said that in his court the president and the defendants were equal before the law. In ruling against the newspaper *El Universo*, the judges acted against express norms since legal entities do not commit crimes of libel. The compensation of US$40 million, instead of the US$80 million that Correa had initially sought, was no small amount. For the sake of comparison, the parents of the Restrepo brothers, two teenagers who disappeared in 1988 after being apprehended by the police and surely victimized,[16] received a compensation of US$2 million from the state for this tragic and heartbreaking crime.

The ruling against *El Universo* led to an international scandal of such magnitude that a group of ex-presidents, headed by former U.S. president Jimmy Carter, published a statement impugning the legality of the judicial proceedings and calling for a review. In light of the avalanche of criticism, Correa found himself forced to "pardon" those convicted and to say that he would not collect the US$40 million indemnity granted to him.

There were multiple pieces of evidence that shocking judicial fraud had been committed in the trial against the newspaper *El Universo*, its editor, and its directors and owners—judicial fraud unprecedented in the recent history of Ecuador and conceived of and executed by the president of the republic and his lawyer, Gutemberg Vera.

The judge in charge of the first-instance verdict, Juan Paredes, in just over twenty-four hours supposedly studied more than five thousand pages of the proceedings, conducted the trial hearing, and wrote a 156-page sentence, a sham that he himself later confirmed. In a video recording he accepted having received the draft sentence on a flash drive and said that he had only printed it and signed it after changing the amount of the compensation. He also confessed that Correa's lawyer had offered him a position in the judicial function "when an opportunity is opened up to competition," as in fact happened. According to *El Universo*'s lawyer, Joffre Campaña, Correa knew that the decision was not written by Judge Paredes (*El Universo* 2012e). Commenting on these facts, the civic forum Cauce Democrático criticized the process and said that "the only thing missing was for the president of the republic to sign it."

Despite the existence of this and other evidence of judicial fraud, prosecutor Antonio Gagliardo refrained from accusing those responsible for the crime of ideological falsehood in a claim brought by *El Universo*. This culpable omission in fulfilling his duty to seek rightful public retribution was not sanctioned by the CJT. On the contrary, as used to happen with those who served the interests of the government, Gagliardo was rewarded with a seat on the Constitutional Court.[17]

Years later, in late 2021, the Inter-American Court of Human Rights ordered the Ecuadorian justice system to annul the guilty verdict and sentence for libel against the newspaper *El Universo*, its directors, and journalist Emilio Palacio, on the grounds that it was disproportionate and "a violation of the right to freedom of expression." The regional court stated that the article that was published by Palacio and that led to the court proceedings was "an opinion article about a matter of public interest" and as such should be "granted special protection because of the importance this type of speech has in a democratic society." In view of these resolutions, it ordered the state to compensate the injured parties and to publish the sentence in the Official Record.

In these and other proceedings, once a conviction was obtained, the president of the republic informed those involved that he would pardon them if they publicly admitted their guilt and asked for forgiveness for having committed a crime. Anguishing over the possibility of a long and unjust incarceration, some people accepted this extortion. Not so four policemen sentenced to twelve years in prison for allegedly having tried to kill him in the police uprising of September 30, 2010. One of them, Geovanny Laso, in an interview for the newspaper *El Universo* (November 27, 2021), said that they were visited in prison by emissaries of the president to ask them to plead guilty in exchange for a presidential pardon. Another, Nelson Puentastar, was invited to the Carondelet Palace and received the same proposal from Correa. However, in his case, if he declared that the policemen had fired the shots, in addition to the pardon he would receive a house in the state's housing programs and a job at a police station. None of the four policemen accepted the president's blackmail. After suffering seven years of unjust imprisonment, they were declared innocent in late 2021, in an appeal to have their case reviewed by the National Court of Justice.

The government set up an international commission, chaired by former Spanish judge Baltazar Garzón, to assess judicial reform. According to the final report it presented, its work was limited to the following areas: human resources, management models, civil and technological infrastructure, budget distribution, and inter-institutional cooperation. These secondary issues comprised four-fifths of the report. Meanwhile, the independence of judges, the guarantees of due process for litigants, and the impartiality of the Judicial Council were not examined, and Garzón and his colleagues did not express opinions on these matters, as though in a judicial reform only the provision of means, instruments, resources, buildings, offices, and technologies were important.

In the last part of the report, they avoided issues that could bother the government. In fact, the only two they touched on were dealt with in cryptic language. Instead of judging or at least mentioning the CJT's manipulation of merit competitions to favor friends of the government, they went astray in obscure digressions. In response to complaints that the government had criminalized social protest, they merely suggested that legal distinctions be made between social protest and terrorism or sabotage.

As the report was issued in late 2012, the commission members had the opportunity to see the political subordination to which the justice system had been subjected. At least one of them must have heard the president publicly ask prosecutors and judges to initiate criminal proceedings against citizens who had dared to denounce acts of corruption and abuses of power. Even if the work they were hired to do was done from their home countries, some assistant must have informed them that the Transitory Judicial Council had dismissed numerous judges for not having complied with presidential orders.

As intuitive citizens had suspected, the dictator and his propaganda apparatus turned the international commission's report into irrefutable proof of how transcendental the reform devised by the Citizens Revolution had been in improving the quality of the Ecuadorian justice system.

When former judge Garzón was asked about the fees paid to him by the Ecuadorian government, as well as to his colleagues on the commission, he refused to reveal the amount.

The assessment done by jurist Luis Pásara, from FLACSO-Spain, was different.[18] After examining court rulings, Judiciary Council resolutions, and statements by President Correa, he reached the following conclusions: that "the problem facing judicial independence was not legal but political" and that it originated in actions "aimed at controlling court decisions in matters of government interest." To this contributed the "severe weakening of the division of powers that characterizes a democratic regime" so that the government could use "the judicial apparatus to support some of its policies and to punish those who were against it." He also concluded that the Judicial Council was the "executing arm" of the president's designs in the "dismissal of magistrates who ruled against the State" and that "the main actor in these pressures was President Rafael Correa," through his "public statements and reproaches" to judges (DPLF 2014).

The Constitutional Court became subordinate to the government just weeks after its inauguration, following the assault carried out by hordes of Correa supporters on its headquarters, the dismissal of its members, and their replacement by those chosen by the conspirators. These events are reviewed in part II, chapter 9, of this book. This political control was maintained when the Constitutional Court was formed according to the new constitution.[19] In both cases it was a body that facilitated the plebiscite initiatives of the president, overlooked abuses of power, interpreted the constitution as it pleased, and rejected or shelved cases brought by citizens and civil-society organizations regarding the unconstitutionality of government acts and the restriction of guarantees, rights, and individual freedoms. This institution, whose first and foremost responsibility was to safeguard the rule of law, actually aided the transition from a democratic regime to a dictatorial one.

The low moral quality and meager legal training of its members contributed to this, as did the submissiveness of its president, Patricio Pazmiño. Correa kept him in this position for two terms, even though he had been accused of corruption and a tax-related investigation was conducted against him for not having justified a bank deposit of US$220,000 in payment for services he had rendered to the government. Investigation of this crime was closed by the Attorney General's Office, and Pazmiño garnered a position as a judge on the Inter-American Court of Human Rights. One illustration of the low moral quality of the Constitutional Court was an atrocious ruling with which it absolved Citizens Revolution militant Floresmilo Villalta, who had been convicted in three judicial proceedings for raping a young girl.

The loss of independence was even greater in other state control and oversight bodies, as was the government's intervention in their resolutions; the heads of these entities behaved as if they were subordinates of the president. This was what happened with the Comptroller's Office, the Attorney General's Office, the Superintendencies, the Banking Board, and other institutions.

Even the international justice system made the Ecuadorian president uncomfortable. With the help of three other twenty-first-century dictators (Chávez, Ortega, and Morales), he unleashed a campaign to discredit the Inter-American Commission on Human Rights. He claimed that it limited the legal and judicial sovereignty of states, that it was conditioned by the Anglo-Saxon legal culture, and that it was dependent on the U.S. government. They demanded that the headquarters be moved to Buenos Aires, that it be prohibited from issuing precautionary measures, and that it only receive funding from countries that had signed the Human Rights Convention. With this restriction, they sought to sink it economically by eliminating funding from the United States. The Ecuadorian government's proposal was considered at a session of the OAS General Assembly but was rejected by all the countries in the region except for Venezuela, Bolivia, and Nicaragua.

In societies in which magistrates and judges support those in power in washing away blame, sheltering their protégés, protecting corruption, silencing critics, convicting innocent people, imprisoning opponents, exacting revenge, and implanting fear, the justice system ends up becoming a despicable institution. This is what happened to the Ecuadorian justice system during the government of dictator President Rafael Correa.

NOTES

1. Detailed analyses can be found in Human Rights Watch (2014, 2018a) and Pásara (2014).

2. The first alleged that he was "traveling a lot" and the second that "he had received foreign economic cooperation in his election campaign," consisting of propaganda posters provided by a Mexican political party, a contribution prohibited under the Election Law.

3. It was comprised by his party, the Patriotic Society (Sociedad Patriótica); the PRIAN of former presidential candidate Álvaro Noboa; the PRE of former president

Abdalá Bucaram; the Marxist-Leninist party MPD; the Socialist Party; and dissident deputies from other parties.

4. Fernando Yávar had been the temporary director of the Guayas Judiciary Council, CJT President Paulo Rodríguez had been the Civil Registry director, and Tania Arias had chaired the Contentious Election Court.

5. The documents for this thorny lawsuit reside in a file in the records of the First Civil Court of Pichincha.

6. The initial debt was with the bank Banco La Previsora (*El Universo* 2008e).

7. In light of an appeal filed by the newspaper *El Universo* in a legal proceeding initiated by Correa, the latter himself said—with proper legal grounds—that the CNJ court that heard the case could not modify the ruling of the lower court.

8. Berenberg Bank, headquartered in Germany (*El Universo* 2008b; *El Comercio* 2011c).

9. An attorney who took part in those competitions, Xavier Zavala Egas, said they were a farce because the president wanted them to be won by people who "in addition to being loyal would be unconditional" (*Hoy*, August 12, 2012). Emails between President Correa, his legal secretary, and the president of the Judicial Council, seeking to intervene in judges' decisions, can be found in a broad analysis of some judicial proceedings performed by the portal *Plan V* in two parts (2017e, 2017f), under the title "Así metió el gobierno de Correa la mano en la Justicia" ("This Is How Correa's Government Meddled in the Justice System").

10. Every Saturday morning, through radio and TV stations, he pondered his projects, policies, programs, and accomplishments; insulted, denounced, and humiliated journalists, Indigenous people, and adversaries; and displayed photographs so that the images would be available to public opinion.

11. At an institutional meeting, several judges complained about the pressure exerted by government officials. One of the judges, Hugo Sierra, reported that, when he was about to sentence Police Hospital Director César Carrión, he received a visit from Interior Minister José Serrano, who was the justice minister at the time and who asked him for a conviction. When submitting his resignation, Judge Miguel Antonio Arias, in Cuenca, denounced "that political power had imposed its own agenda on the administration of justice, the function that it directs and controls through the Judiciary Council" (*Portal 4 Pelagatos*, January 27, 2017).

12. A penalist cited the following statements from some judges: "The request comes from above," and "What can we do? They'll remove us if we don't obey" (Ramiro García Falconí, in an article titled "Reflections and Proposals") ("Reflexiones y propuestas"), *El Universo*, May 13, 2013.

13. Addressing him with the informal *you*, he disparagingly called him a conspirator, a moron, a fool, a subordinate, a bad cop, and a caveman.

14. Jurist Jorge Zavala Egas, in an interview with *El Universo* (August 5, 2012), affirmed that "the judges that judged the police officers from September 30th were rewarded with promotions and ratifications."

15. *El Universo*, February 6, 2011.

16. That event occurred in January 1988.

17. In an interview, jurist Jorge Zavala Egas said that the judges involved in the proceedings against *El Universo* were rewarded with promotions and ratifications of their positions (*El Universo*, August 5, 2012).

18. The study was requested by the Due Process of Law Foundation of the Center for Studies in Law, Justice and Society and the Legal Defense Institute (Pásara 2014).

19. Assembly member Abdalá ("Dalo") Bucaram Pulley declared that, at meetings held at the Presidential Palace in 2007 and 2009, President Correa offered to "order the Constitutional Court to end the political persecution" against his father (*La Hora Loja* 2012).

Chapter 14

Freedoms, Guarantees, and Rights

At least formally, Ecuadorians had access to certain freedoms or liberties, guarantees, and rights before other peoples of Latin America did—including some that even some people in today's developed world do not have—thanks to the Liberal Revolution that, in the late nineteenth and early twentieth centuries, put an end to the stifling dogmatism in which the country had lived since the founding of the republic in 1830.

The 1897 constitution recognized equality before the law, freedom of thought, the absolute guarantee to life, and freedom of worship, and it abolished the death penalty for political crimes. The 1906 constitution consecrated the secular state and freedom of conscience, in addition to prohibiting imprisonment for debt and eliminating certain economic burdens on Indigenous people.

In the following five constitutions (1929, 1945, 1946, 1967, and 1979), individual liberties were expanded and economic, social, and political rights were incorporated, as well as women's right to vote (1929). This forward-thinking inclusion of what are now called human rights culminated in the 1998 constitution, which incorporated Indigenous peoples' collective rights to their culture, people's right to live in a healthy environment, and consumers' right to be protected. These rights were also included in the 2008 constitution.

Throughout the twentieth century, since the Revolution of 1925 put an end to the sectarian dominance of the Liberal Party, public life was characterized by an atmosphere of freedom, pluralism, and tolerance, which allowed citizens to openly express their ideas, voice their concerns, and make multiple demands. They did so initially through flyers, pamphlets, newspapers, magazines, books, meetings, assemblies, street protests and demonstrations, and as of the second half of the twentieth century, through radio and television. In the twenty-first century, those media outlets would be joined by digital media, thanks to the invention of the Internet and mobile telephone services.

177

This open nature of political society meant that not only democratic governments were respectful of citizens' rights and freedoms but also military dictatorships, whose relative tolerance led some of them to be called benevolent or "soft" versions of dictatorships, using a play on words in Spanish. The restrictions that sometimes existed on public freedoms were exceptional and rather short-lived, so in the twentieth century Ecuador did not suffer from the oppressive and tyrannical authoritarianism experienced by other countries in Latin America and the Caribbean.

The media were not out of sync with this tolerant and pluralistic culture, as they were open to the ideological and political diversity of the time, typical of a free society. They generally published the manifestos of Marxist sectors, expressed by the socialist and communist parties and by student and labor organizations with the same ideological inclinations. Although the media belonged to family-owned and -operated companies, they did not identify with specific economic interests and tried to represent the public interest, except for a few that clearly identified with private interests in the late twentieth century.[1] The press, radio, and television freely criticized presidents, ministers, legislators, and judges, even during military dictatorships, which is why their relations with different administrations were difficult and sometimes marked by conflicts. During his third term, President José María Velasco Ibarra shut down the newspaper *El Comercio*, a measure that was soon lifted under pressure from public opinion. Radio stations were also shut down occasionally and temporarily in times of strikes and walkouts.

Many of those who participated in the constituent assembly that drafted the 2008 constitution did not share this national way of being. They had fought in streets and squares and organized strikes, work stoppages, protests, and demonstrations aimed at overthrowing dictatorial and democratic governments alike, in order to implant revolutionary policies and programs of a socialist nature. Some used violent means and lethal weapons and carried out attacks and kidnappings, the fleeting guerrilla group Alfaro Vive being the most visible example. Repressed by law enforcement, a few were imprisoned, tortured, or even killed. There were also assembly members who came from the academic field and from NGOs related to human rights and the environment or who had worked with social organizations and the Indigenous movement.

This group of revolutionaries coming from different political backgrounds enlisted in the Citizens Revolution and saw in the Constituent Assembly of Montecristi a golden opportunity to have the constitution enshrine every right, freedom, or guarantee they could think of.

In the constitution they drafted, they maintained the individual and collective rights of the progressive 1998 constitution and added others that are examined in part II, chapter 9. In Article 1 they stipulated that Ecuador "is a State of rights and social justice" and in Article 11, paragraph 9, that "the highest duty of the State is to respect, and ensure respect for, the rights enshrined in the Constitution." Article 98 created the "right to resist" against "actions or omissions of public power" or against individuals that "may violate" constitutional rights, as well as citizens' right to "demand the recognition of new rights." By virtue of the novel content of these provisions, the Constituent Assembly members from Alianza PAIS praised the "guaranteeing" nature of the 2008 constitution and claimed it as their foremost political contribution to the Citizens Revolution.

A constitution that offered guarantees, like any constitution that places human rights at the center of democracy, was vulnerable to colliding with the authoritarian exercise of power, which by nature would be prone to violate such guarantees. This was corroborated by a review of nineteenth-century Ecuadorian history and of some Latin American countries' last decades in the twentieth century, as well as by what was happening in the government of Hugo Chávez in Venezuela and was beginning to occur in the governments of Evo Morales in Bolivia, Daniel Ortega in Nicaragua, and Rafael Correa in Ecuador during the twenty-first century.

Unlike what the Constituent Assembly members from Alianza PAIS thought, the new leader of the Ecuadorian Left believed that the interests of the state, the government, and the president of the republic were above individuals' and society's rights—as though the French Revolution had not put an end to absolutism more than two centuries ago and implemented the Rights of Man, which the United Nations made a universal doctrine in 1948, to protect individuals against the abuses of public power. Due to his position, during the decade that Correa would govern Ecuador, violations of freedoms, rights, and constitutional guarantees would become commonplace. One warning sign of this was his early-on reproach of fellow party members for having conceived and issued a constitution with "hyper" guarantees.

Freedom of expression was the first right to be limited by Ecuador's new president. Almost all the media had viewed Rafael Correa's presidential candidacy favorably since he was a politician who came from university campuses, outside the so highly criticized political class, and he represented a new, young generation. This positive outlook made them overlook the breakdown of the constitutional order caused by the call for a popular consultation and the call for a constituent assembly. However, they did not ignore the abuses and excesses used to achieve those objectives, such as the removal of fifty opposition deputies and the dismissal of the Constitutional Court, both imposed by means of outrages against constitutional order and violence from the throngs of government supporters.

As soon as Correa won the presidential election, he who had courted the media for political backing and clout in order to win then turned the media into antagonists. From one day to the next, in his own words, "the press that

shamelessly played politics" became the "main adversary" of the government following the "collapse of the political parties."[2] From this it could be
concluded that the media that had supported his electoral campaign—and
almost all of them had—had not been playing politics then but were doing so
once they began to observe his conduct. This double standard would mark the
discourse and actions of all the members of the government of the Citizens
Revolution. During Correa's decade in office, the constitution, laws, rights,
liberties, and public morals would be interpreted and applied according to
political convenience.

The definition of information as a public good and the declaration that the
private media did not serve society and the country, but rather the private
interests of their owners and economic groups, were the premises on which
Correa began to wage his battle against freedom of expression. He said that
"information should be a function of the state, just like justice." This statement implied the decision to place both these areas under government control
just as he had done with independent and autonomous public institutions,
with the rhetoric that he was placing them at the service of the citizens.

Control over public opinion and the media that guide and shape it has
been inherent to fascist dictatorships, Marxist totalitarianism, and Latin
American caudillo-centered autocratic regimes. This is not so much due to
considerations of doctrine but rather to the utilitarian advisability of preventing citizens from knowing about a government's abuses, mistakes, and corruption. These were the motivations that played a role in the obsessive battle
that the president waged against the independent press from the outset of his
government.

Through coercive and intimidating measures, Correa hoped that newspapers, television and radio stations, journalists, and editorialists would not
criticize the government, or at least would do so innocuously. He also hoped
that the investigative journalism that gave rise to allegations of corruption
would disappear and that news, reports, and opinions that might displease
him would not be published. He thought that private media should limit
themselves to reporting and expressing opinions that were beneficial to the
government.

Initially, the private media were not subject to any kind of censorship.
Instead, the president, together with the government's propaganda staff,
launched a campaign aimed at undermining the private media's credibility
and, consequently, the numbers of their readers, listeners, and viewers. Correa
probably thought that, once this objective was achieved, what they published
or said would not matter because their information and criticism would reach
very few or would not be taken into account by the citizens. He described
the independent media as "the greatest de facto power in our America" and
journalism as "the most complete web of lies ever invented."

In speeches and interviews and even in the once-solemn annual presidential messages to the nation, he maliciously, insultingly, and slanderously belittled them. The directors of a newspaper association and of a foundation defending freedom of the press were accused of "treason" for having gone to the Inter-American Commission on Human Rights to present a report on the harassment suffered by freedom of expression in Ecuador.[3] During the broadcasting of the 2010 Soccer World Cup, there was an advertisement in which, without exception, these directors were portrayed as "liars," "thieves," promoters of "violence," and beneficiaries of "illegal and illicit" profits.

The main battleground of the war he waged against the media was his Saturday broadcasts. In these programs, he introduced a segment titled "Freedom of Expression Belongs to Everyone," in which he denied news reports, discredited comments, made accusations, and insulted journalists, calling them "ink hitmen," "stupid reporters," and "wild beasts." He went even further when he made jokes about their physical features, insulting them with epithets such as "dwarfs," "red-faced," "bonsai Tarzan," "horrible fatty," and "smurfs." Without mentioning the names of the media he was referring to, he called them "bourgeois press," "information mafias," "unscrupulous businesses," "de facto powers," "media dictatorships," "corrupt press," "mercenaries," and "traitors to the homeland." He also subjected them to public scorn, with actions that could put the personal safety and lives of journalists at risk by showing their photographs on television screens and asking viewers to engrave in their minds the names and images of the "enemies of the people and of the Citizens Revolution."[4]

To this campaign to discredit journalists and the media he added economic extortion and judicial persecution, in order to strangle them financially and bankrupt them. To this end, he ordered public institutions, including state enterprises, not to advertise in the press that was an "enemy" of the government. In addition, he prohibited ministers and senior officials from granting interviews to them, in order to reduce the interest of their readers, viewers, and listeners and, in turn, the media outlets' popularity and advertising revenues.

The newspaper *Hoy* was one of the main targets of this policy of persecution of private media even though a few months earlier President Correa had asked it to monitor compliance with the Law on Transparency and Free Access to Public Information. Since Correa had not been able to intimidate the newspaper so that it would abandon its criticism of government authoritarianism, it was subjected to administrative, judicial, fiscal, economic, and labor-related harassment that eventually plunged it into bankruptcy. Before that happened, Correa had repeatedly announced that it would happen soon. For that purpose, he had prohibited public entities from advertising in its pages and the TAME airline from buying and distributing copies on its flights. As he could not cancel the newspaper's contract to publish English textbooks for primary and secondary schools, he eliminated the study of that language in order to make the textbooks unnecessary. He tried to do the same thing with the newspaper *El Universo*, when he got unprincipled judges to force it to pay him a compensation of tens of millions of dollars for the moral damages it had allegedly caused him.

Journalists targeted by Correa for having been notable defenders of democratic institutions and for investigating and denouncing corruption and criticizing authoritarianism were forced to leave the media in which they worked, due to pressures and threats against their owners and directors. This is what happened to journalist Emilio Palacio of *El Universo* and to Jorge Ortiz, Carlos Jijón, and Janeth Hinostroza of Teleamazonas.

The case of journalists Juan Carlos Calderón and Christian Zurita was the most illustrative. In the newspaper *Expreso*, they published an investigative report on the business done by Fabricio Correa during his brother's government, through contracts that he was awarded for the construction of physical infrastructure. The president sued the writers, accusing them of having libeled him by affirming that he knew that his brother had received state contracts, a fact that his brother had confirmed. In the lawsuit for nonpecuniary damages, he demanded that the journalists be ordered to pay a compensation of US$20 million. In order to pressure the judges, Correa attended the hearings accompanied by aides and police guards and by Alexis Mera, the legal secretary of the President's Office. After being found guilty, the journalists were "pardoned" by the "magnanimous" Correa.

Until the arrival of the Citizens Revolution, for decades the state had only had one media outlet: Radio Nacional. During Correa's government, however, there came to be sixteen, including newspapers, magazines, and radio and television stations, with which he formed a media empire unprecedented in the history of Ecuador. Some were set up with fiscal resources and others via the seizure of television and radio stations from the Isaías family.[5] They were called "public" media even though they did not fulfill that function. They did not serve the country, society, and the general interest but rather became instruments of government propaganda.

The progovernment media were born to dispute the readership and audiences of the private media, to win them over, and to supplement the government's propaganda campaigns to praise the dictator and his administration. They did not manage to achieve this purpose even among their supporters, not even during the years when Correa had the approval of two-thirds of Ecuadorians. For that reason, they had to receive substantial subsidies that came from taxpayers. Had Correa succeeded in this effort, he would have abandoned the passionate crusade he waged against private media.

This vast and persistent smear campaign against the free press, despite Correa's high credibility, did not produce the expected results: citizens who rejected his autocratic ideas and practices continued to read, listen, and watch and thus maintained the influence of those outlets. As for Correa's followers, over months and years, they decreased rather than increased, according to surveys that measured his popularity and based on the lower numbers he garnered in elections and popular consultations.

When he failed to silence the independent press through abusive persecutory measures, the autocratic president pushed for a punitive Communication Law. The bill presented to the legislature in 2010 by an assembly member from Alianza PAIS did not come to a vote thanks to the battle waged in favor of freedom of expression by opposition legislators and private media, but above all because the government could not assemble a majority. Nor did the bill pass when it was presented again after the issuing of such a law had been approved in the 2011 popular consultation.

Alianza PAIS won the 2013 legislative elections by a wide margin thanks to a change introduced in the Election Law to reward the majority party in an unconscionable way. Approval of the change was facilitated by Alianza PAIS's absolute majority in the National Assembly. Without any parliamentary debate, the Communication Law was voted on at the beginning of the new legislature, in a brief session that lasted only a few hours, and the president enacted it without modifications, announcing that "the party was over" for the media. Such was the arbitrariness with which the assembly members from Alianza PAIS proceeded that they introduced institutions and articles not included in the original bill, which had been discussed by the previous legislature but not reviewed and debated in the sitting assembly.

This law defined communication as a public service and established the conditions under which it should be provided. The state was empowered to control it, prohibiting the disclosure of confidential information; regulating the content of news and commentaries; and establishing the subsequent liability of journalists, managers, and owners for what the press, radio, and television wrote or said. It established new offenses such as "media lynching," unprecedented in any legislation and consisting of the persistent scrutiny of an individual's conduct in matters of public interest. This eliminated the possibility that officials' arbitrary or dishonest acts could be tracked. Because they were drafted in an obscure, confusing, and ambiguous manner, some rules allowed for their discretionary application, depending on the interpretation that the corresponding official wished to give them; others, because of their malicious wording, left the impression that they were protecting a right when in fact they were restricting it. All of these violated constitutional provisions and breached international treaties.

Intentionally, the law did not clearly establish the scope of its application, which is why public media were in fact excluded. The law only applied to private media, as if public media were immune to the transgressions typified in the Communication Law and did not have the same obligations as private media. This is further evidence that the purpose of issuing it was not to guarantee media transparency but rather to contain, threaten, and silence the private press.

Using an arbitrary practice whereby laws could be reformed by lower-level legal mechanisms contrary to the constitution, regulations extended their scope to digital media based on Internet services. At the same time, the government, through Spanish company Ares Rights, among others, managed to have videos and publications that could affect the image of the president of Ecuador censored on social networks.

For the application of the new body of laws and regulations, a regulatory council and a superintendency were created. Civil-society representatives, who were included in the original bill, were marginalized from the council so that it would only include people from the government sphere. Known for his submissive relationship with Correa, journalist Carlos Ochoa, a news director and interviewer for one of the progovernment channels, was appointed to head the superintendency. The superintendent was in charge of monitoring, investigating, and sanctioning the offensive media and those who worked for them, and the council was in charge of judging them. None of the members of these bodies had the virtues of an independent, impartial, and fair authority. In this regard, Catalina Botero, the Inter-American Commission on Human Rights rapporteur for freedom of expression, said, "Ecuador, after Cuba, has the most restrictive legislation on freedom of expression" in Latin America (*El País* 2014).

The repressive Communication Law and the submissive position of those who applied it, strengthened, deepened, and multiplied the persecutory actions that had been restricting free expression—with the advantage that they could now be presented as the application of regulations complying with a legal mandate. In order to avoid the payment of onerous fines, the media self-censored and refrained from publishing information and commentaries referring to government authoritarianism and acts of corruption. In order not to be liable to lawsuits and the conviction of owners, directors, journalists, and editorialists, they hired lawyers who were charged with approving or rejecting the news and editorials to be published or broadcast the following day. Once Correa had succeeded in silencing the free press, he could put an end to the holy war he had been waging against it since he took office.

So unrestrained was the way Correa exercised his excessive power and so little was the consideration he had for those who served under him that he became accustomed to publicly stating the name of the media outlet, journalist, or editorialist to be investigated, prosecuted, and sanctioned. Superintendent Ochoa would immediately open a file, and regardless of the objections of those affected, they were invariably found guilty. The proceedings resulted in fines, suspensions, shutdowns, imprisonment, and the mandatory publication of rectifications. The newspapers *La Hora, El Universo, Hoy,* and *El Comercio*; some radio stations; the magazines *Vistazo*[6] and *Vanguardia*; and the television station Teleamazonas were all found guilty.

Teleamazonas was subjected to ongoing harassment, and the dictator went so far as to request that it be "sanctioned and closed down permanently." After Correa described journalist Jorge Ortiz as a "twerp" and Teleamazonas as a "sewer with antennas" (*El Universo* 2009), Ortiz broadcast a recording in which Correa was heard discussing changes that had been introduced into the 2008 constitution after it had been approved. According to the NGO Fundamedios, while there was a total of twenty-two aggressions against freedom of expression in 2008, before the Communication Law, they increased exponentially after it was issued, to 283 in 2014, 499 in 2015, and 491 in 2016.

The long arm of repression of freedom of speech extended beyond national borders. Through foreign law firms paid with public funds, the government managed to have incriminating videos removed from the social network YouTube. These videos, which the Ecuadorian media did not dare to publish, denounced and offered proof of corruption, abuses of power, and other outrages. For this purpose, the lawyers hired by the regime argued that they "violated the president's copyrights" by using his images without the corresponding authorization. Meanwhile, Correa, through his Saturday broadcasts and the pamphlets of the government's propaganda apparatus, did not hesitate to put on display and stigmatize images of his opponents and critics.

So serious and repeated was the bullying of the media and those who worked for them that respectable international organizations called attention to the abuses suffered by freedom of expression in Ecuador.

The IACHR's special rapporteur for freedom of expression criticized President Correa's stigmatization of private media and journalistic work. Media outlets were called "corrupt press" and "ink hitmen," radio stations were shut down, and the official television and radio networks interrupted news programs. Furthermore, civil-society organizations that defended freedom of expression, such as Fundamedios and the National Journalists Union (Unión Nacional de Periodistas, UNP), were delegitimized.

A spokesman for the U.S. State Department called for the protection of "the life and freedom" of journalists threatened and intimidated by the government, especially Janeth Hinostroza of Teleamazonas, Martín Pallares of *El Comercio*, and Miguel Rivadeneira of Ecuador Radio. He added that the U.S. government asked the Ecuadorian government "to respect freedom of the press as a vital component of a democratic society and to guarantee that journalists can work without fear of reprisals."

The independent organization Freedom House (2013) reported that Ecuador had dropped seventeen points in its press freedom index over the last five years, "one of the most dramatic declines in the world," placing it in the low category of a country with a "partially free press." This decline was due to "prolonged threats to freedom of speech," restrictions on press coverage of electoral processes, and "President Correa's order to withdraw government advertising from the private media critical of his administration."

The same persecutory treatment was suffered by opposition legislators who in the National Assembly denounced or investigated the arbitrariness and corruption of members of the government.

The most shameless and perverse persecution was that of assembly member (deputy) Galo Lara. Since he had become the main government watchdog, on two occasions Alianza PAIS tried to deprive him of his parliamentary immunity so that he could be criminally prosecuted for slander. When they did not succeed, the Attorney General's Office incriminated him in a triple murder that took place in his province, Los Ríos, the intellectual authorship of which was attributed to his partner, Carolina Llanos. The accusation was based on the testimony of an individual with a criminal record. Lara was sentenced to ten years in prison and his partner to twenty. For that reason, he requested political asylum in Panama, alleging that he had suffered judicial persecution by the Ecuadorian government. The request was accepted even though the attorney general, the justice minister, and other officials traveled to Panama to demand Lara's deportation. Lara finally ended up in jail when the Panamanian government revoked his asylum in exchange for the Ecuadorian government's release of a Panamanian ship captured in the territorial sea while carrying out illegal activities.[7]

Years later, in late 2021, after a review of the unjust and manipulated court proceedings, the National Court of Justice unanimously declared Galo Lara and Carolina Llanos innocent. They had been unjustly imprisoned, the former for four years and the latter for eight, and she lost the child she was carrying because of the beating she received. According to the victims, the criminal proceeding was orchestrated by government minister José Serrano and Attorney General Galo Chiriboga; however, that conspiracy could not have been conceived and executed without approval from dictator Rafael Correa.

By means of an unconstitutional decree, and not a law as it should have been, Correa placed civil society under government control, giving himself the power to determine the activities of NGOs, monitor their programs, request information, scrutinize their financing, and supervise them. The government could dissolve them, among other reasons, for submitting insufficient information, failing to dispel concerns, engaging in "partisan political activities," criticizing public policies, and "undermining the internal and external security of the state or peace." Under penalty of dissolution, they were obliged to accept anyone who applied for membership.

It seems that the intention was to silence civil-society organizations and not to decimate them, as feared, since only a few NGOs were persecuted and only one was dissolved: Pachamama, linked to the Indigenous movement, whose leaders had staged a violent protest against the granting of oil concessions in the Amazon. The United States Agency for International Development (USAID) was forced to leave the country, as was the Konrad Adenauer Foundation of the German Christian Democrats, when it protested the government's intention to control its programs. Having lost their sources of funding, some NGOs reduced or suspended their programs. Others, faced with the risk of being dissolved, opted to refrain from criticism and to moderate their positions.

No longer were only journalists, media, legislators, and NGOs discredited and persecuted but also ordinary Ecuadorians and the organizations to which they belonged. Those targeted were mainly Indigenous people, workers, employees, women, businessmen, academics, professors, professionals, politicians, members of religious groups, and diplomats. Some were targeted because they denounced acts of corruption, criticized decisions, pointed out injustices, or challenged government authoritarianism, others because they disputed the veracity of a fact, a figure, or a statistic presented to public opinion by government officials. Instead of demonstrating the validity of his statements and the accuracy of his figures, the president personally attacked those who had disagreed, showering them with insults and defamations. Other measures included inspections related to tax, labor, social security, and superintendency issues; obstacles to professional, academic, or business activities; graffiti, threatening phone calls, and anonymous letters, messages, or emails.

The repressive nature of the regime can also be seen in the judicial and police persecution of Fernando Balda, one of the many young people who had joined Correa's presidential campaign but later distanced themselves. An email in which he said that there was an espionage center in the President's Office (the Intelligence Secretariat) was enough for the government to initiate a criminal trial accusing him of threatening state security. To avoid being found guilty, he went into exile in Colombia, where undercover Ecuadorian agents tried to kidnap him to take him back to Ecuador. When this conspiracy failed, the Ecuadorian government managed to get the government of President Juan Manuel Santos to arrest and deport him even though he was a political refugee. He was taken to Ecuador on an air force plane, criminally prosecuted, and sentenced to one year in prison for threatening state security and two years for libel.

After Correa's administration ended and when the Attorney General's Office and the judicial function regained their independence, a criminal trial was initiated to clarify these facts. In a third-instance ruling, National Intelligence Secretariat Director Pablo Romero was sentenced to nine years in prison for the crime of kidnapping. Former president Correa, who had ordered the kidnapping of Balda, could not be brought to trial, however, because he was a fugitive living outside the country. Since the crime had been carried out using public resources and the National Intelligence Secretariat had participated, the ruling ordered the Attorney General's Office to investigate Correa for the crime of misappropriation of public assets.

During Correa's decade in office, the right to free speech was not the only constitutional guarantee violated; the right to participate in public demonstrations and acts of protest was also restricted. This occurred even though, when they were the opposition, Alianza PAIS leaders and sympathizers had made social mobilizations the weapon with which they fought against all the democratic governments before theirs. Furthermore, in Article 98 of the Montecristi constitution, they consecrated the revolutionary "right to resistance" of individuals and collectives "against actions or omissions of public power."

Those who attended acts of protest and demonstrated in streets, on squares, and along roads were harshly repressed, and their leaders were criminally prosecuted, accused of carrying out acts of sabotage, terrorism, and rebellion against state security. However, the violent mobs mobilized by the government to storm the Electoral Tribunal, the Constitutional Court, and the National Congress at the beginning of its term of office had not been accused of these crimes, let alone prosecuted. Meanwhile, Correa refused to label the FARC terrorists, even though for decades those Colombian insurgents had committed, and continued to commit, countless crimes, the victims of which were often unarmed civilians. Hundreds of social and Indigenous leaders were charged for having blocked highways and city streets, and they were met with police repression, sometimes excessive, during protests and demonstrations.

Known as the "Luluncoto Ten" after the name of the Quito neighborhood where they were arrested, young people from the MPD (a party with a long history of violence, at the service of Correa in his first year of office) were criminally prosecuted for manufacturing and using explosive devices. When the president incriminated them, they had only been accused of placing "bombs" and calling for "armed struggle." Since no evidence was presented in the court hearing that they had carried out terrorist acts, despite pressure exerted by the government on the judges, the young people were only sentenced to one year in prison, not for the crime that had led to the criminal case but for "belonging to subversive groups."

While participating in acts of protest, which included demonstrations, students from the Central Technical School of Quito were also arrested and tried, accused by the government of the crime of rebellion, which was punishable by one to six years in prison. They were acquitted by the judge because the prosecutor who investigated the events refrained from charging them, finding no evidence that they had committed the crime of which they were accused. The president protested on the grounds that he had in his possession videos, photographs, and police testimonies of the crime they had committed. Another prosecutor immediately issued a new charge of rebellion, and a judge initiated the corresponding criminal proceedings. To general surprise, the trial ended with a light sentence of twenty-one days in jail, less than the penalty established by law, as though the judge had wanted to appease the dictator without causing disproportionate harm to the accused.

On a dozen occasions, as if he were a police officer or a judge, Correa personally ordered jail time for citizens who shouted disapproving remarks or made inappropriate gestures while the presidential motorcade was moving through the streets of Quito. The most notorious case was that of singer Jaime Guevara, whom Correa, after getting out of the car, rebuked and challenged to a fistfight. The following Saturday, after humiliating and insulting Guevara, Correa accused him of having acted under the influence of drugs and alcohol. The accusation turned out to be false since Guevara did not consume drugs or alcohol, according to testimony from members of the government who had shared revolutionary struggles and been in street protests with him.

In view of these and similar episodes, his former allies in the revolutionary Left were not unreasonable in accusing Correa of having "criminalized social protest" in order to prevent people from expressing their discontent in the streets. In 2018, the Focus portal estimated that seven hundred judicial proceedings of this nature were brought during Correa's government (*Focus News Ecuador* 2018).

For the same persecutory and repressive purposes, Correa promoted issuing a new penal code. A vote could not be taken in the first legislature because deputies from the opposition and some from Alianza PAIS deemed that the proposal limited constitutional freedoms. Once the government gained control of the National Assembly in the 2013 elections, the new code was immediately approved, without the thoughtful discussion merited by a complex legal text with more than four hundred articles that merged the former penal, penal procedure, and sentencing codes.

The new code made legal persons and natural persons over sixteen years of age subject to charges of criminal offenses, created numerous offenses, stiffened prison sentences and fines, required those convicted to apologize to those affected,[8] established fourteen forms of insults against authorities, and punished the same offense differently if the affected person was the head of state. It criminalized twenty tax offenses, including omissions, arrears, and nonfraudulent errors. It treated as criminal offenses the media's refusal to reveal their sources, measures to boycott authorities, popular protests and demonstrations, incitement of unrest, professional (medical) malpractice, disclosure of secrets even if they were not related to national security, statements causing economic panic, offenses to the president of the republic, noncompliance with administrative provisions, unjustified enrichment in private-sector activities, failure to affiliate workers to the social security system, failure to treat patients in emergency situations, deception regarding the identity or quality of a product, damages to nature, media lynching, and preaching of hate—which Correa did on a daily basis and with impunity. It also stipulated that the companies that provided telephone and Internet services should store users' information, data, communications, and other electronic documents for at least six months so that the state could conduct any investigations it wished.

Prominent jurist Ernesto Albán Gómez, professor of criminal law and former judge on the Supreme Court of Justice, said that the code was inspired by "doctrinaire gibberish" and was "repressive and plagued with legal inconsistencies." He also said that it included right-wing and extreme right-wing positions advocating for the thesis that citizen safety and security would improve if penalties were toughened. He concluded by saying that, if approved, the code would place Ecuador in one of the lowest rankings among countries with a similar culture (*Hoy*, August 26, 2012). According to Enrique Herrería, the director of the Rights and Justice Observers Group (Observatorio de Derechos y Justicia), the penal code was used by Correa "to scorn and humiliate with full severity any citizen who protested."

A National Intelligence Secretariat (Senain) was created in the President's Office, to which the equivalent services of the armed forces and the national police were made subordinate. Senain was directed by officials with personal ties to the dictator, as in the case of his bodyguard, Ronny Vallejo. Senain created files with private information on citizens, information taken from state offices and other sites. It also accessed personal documents; carried out undercover police operations; intercepted telephone, electronic, and written communications; recorded private conversations; and intimidated government opponents with anonymous threats—all of this with the knowledge of the president of the republic.

Even though these activities were extremely sensitive due to their potential impact on the constitutional rights of citizens, the secretariat was not subject to political oversight by the assembly and to public scrutiny. Disclosure of its large budget was forbidden since its expenditures were classified as secret. Senain agents infiltrated press conferences, seminars, conferences, colloquiums, meetings, and demonstrations in order to film, record, and photograph those who participated in them. They collected financial, salary, tax, and background information on individuals and on the institutions in which they worked. Some of these materials were used by Correa to silence government opponents. Undeterred, during his Saturday broadcasts Correa disseminated tax information and other information of a personal nature obtained by the intelligence service. He even went so far as to say that, thanks to intelligence agents who had infiltrated state agencies, he had verified the negligence of public employees, whom he punished by firing them.

By means of these procedures that violated rights, liberties, and constitutional guarantees, the government succeeded in frightening citizens. Many stopped freely attending protests and demonstrations, refrained from expressing their opinions publicly, and moderated their criticism when they did say something. Journalists and media outlets self-censored.

Repressive laws, restrictions on freedom of expression, defamation campaigns, judicial persecution, criminalization of social protests, interference in the private lives of individuals, restrictions on the work of civil society, and the daily sowing of fear were authoritarian practices present in the Ecuadorian and other Latin American dictatorships and in totalitarian regimes in other parts of the world during the nineteenth century and most of the twentieth century. All this was also seen in the twenty-first century, during the ten years that dictator Rafael Correa governed Ecuador.

According to the digital portal *Plan V*, in the decade of Correa, the reasons for the deaths of sixteen people who denounced acts of corruption were not clear, as well as for four who denounced incidences of drug trafficking and sixteen who died during social protests. The death that received the greatest attention in public opinion was the murder of General Jorge Gabela, the first air force commander in Correa's government. During his time in that post, he opposed the purchase of helicopters from a firm in India, four of which suffered accidents; when he left that post, he made repeated denouncements about their inadvisability. Common delinquents were investigated and convicted for his murder.

NOTES

1. They belonged to banker Fernando Aspiazu and the Isaías family, with businesses in banking, industry, commerce, insurance, and agriculture. Even these media had a certain openness to national political diversity.

2. Interview published in the Lima newspaper *La República* and reprinted by the Quito newspaper *Hoy* on June 12, 2010.

3. The director of the Ecuadorian Association of Newspaper Editors, Diego Cornejo, and the director of Fundamedios, Cesar Ricaurte.

4. Martín Pallares, from the newspaper *El Comercio*, one of the journalists sued by Correa, received the following tweets from an Ecuadorian student named Andrés

Fabricio Asimbay: "Death to this dog and U.S. pawn, death or get out of the country, we're going to kill you." "I hope they kill you . . . people like you deserve to die."

5. The seizure, actually confiscation, of 195 companies belonging to the Isaías family was decided through a simple administrative action by the Agency for Deposit Guarantees (Agencia de Garantía de Depósitos, AGD) on July 8, 2008. The decision was later confirmed by the Constituent Assembly through a "mandate" prohibiting them from recurring to judicial recourses to defend themselves and prohibiting judges from accepting their claims under the threat of being sanctioned. They based their decisions on the accusation that brothers Roberto and William Isaías, owners of Filanbanco, had been detrimental to the depositors and unduly benefited economically during the banking crisis at the end of the twentieth century.

6. *Vistazo* was fined US$100,000 for having taken a position in favor of the no option in the consultation-referendum of 2011. The government-owned newspaper *El Telégrafo* took a position in favor of the yes option but was not investigated or sanctioned.

7. Without being asked to by assembly member Lara, I wrote a letter to the president of Panama, asking him not to revoke asylum because Lara was an innocent citizen persecuted by the regime's repressive apparatus.

8. Paragraph 4 of Article 82 of that body of law, written in the unintelligible language of the assembly members from Alianza PAIS, ordered the person in violation to make reparations to "the dignity, reputation, apology, and public acknowledgment of the acts and responsibilities, commemorations and tributes to the victims, teaching and disseminating the historical truth."

Chapter 15

Government Transparency

The norms and procedures inherent to democratic societies include the honest management of public resources, alongside the legal, economic, and political responsibility of the authorities that administer them; the oversight of expenditures made; the punishment of officials who steal or embezzle; and accountability. They ensure the trustworthy, scrupulous, and austere management of the money handed over to the state by taxpayers.

In order for these principles to become permanent elements of public life and for the corruption of those who ignore them to be addressed, Ecuador's constitutions have granted broad powers to the legislative and judicial functions and to the control and oversight bodies—the Comptroller's Office, the Attorney General's Office, and the Federal Prosecutor's Office—to supervise the actions of officials and punish those who commit crimes. These bodies were joined by the Commission for Civic Control of Corruption, created in 1995, made up of representatives of civil society, and incorporated into the 1998 constitution.

This institutional framework, the result of many years of national experience, was weakened in the 2008 constitution when the commission was eliminated. In its place the Council for Citizen Participation and Social Control (discussed in previous chapters) was created and entrusted with controlling corruption and guaranteeing the transparent use of fiscal resources. According to the discourse of the Constituent Assembly members from Alianza PAIS, this body was to ensure the faithful fulfillment of these objectives since its members were to come from social organizations and not from the questionable political parties. As soon as the cancer of corruption appeared, it would be extirpated by the CPCCS, and the guilty would be prosecuted, convicted, and imprisoned.

Article 208 of the 2008 constitution assigned the CPCCS the following responsibilities: to fight against corruption; promote well-prepared citizens; imbue the acts of public officials with honesty and transparency; establish accountability mechanisms; promote oversight by citizens; investigate allegations of corruption; issue reports on responsibilities; make recommendations; promote legal actions; act as a party in criminal cases (brought against the government); confiscate the personal assets of those convicted; protect those who report acts of corruption; and request information from state entities and officials and sanction those who refuse to provide it.[1]

The members of the CPCCS were not aware of the vast and complex powers given to them by the members of the Constituent Assembly of the Citizens Revolution, to fight, pursue, and eliminate atavistic corruption. In the annals of Ecuadorian constitutional law, it must be the only institution, of the many that were created over almost two centuries, that did not fulfill the duties that were stipulated by the constitution—in its case, in the field of public morals. In addition to not investigating and denouncing the numerous cases of corruption that appeared in the government of President Correa, it filed away the complaints that reached its secretariat, thus committing a criminal cover-up. Alianza PAIS, the National Assembly, and the government never reprimanded the members of the Participation Council for such a reprehensible omission. So a wide and well-lit path was opened up for hundreds and perhaps thousands of officials of the Citizens Revolution to enrich themselves with public money, including the president, the vice president, ministers, and managers of state-owned enterprises.

For his part, President Correa created the political, economic, administrative, and judicial conditions for corruption to worsen dramatically during his government and end up becoming a kind of public policy. He issued 114 decrees declaring a state of emergency or exception, depending on whether the 1998 or 2008 constitution was in force, as though the country had become submerged in natural disasters, external threats, and ongoing political unrest. In the new Public Procurement Law he approved, this power was extended to ministers of state and other officials who exercised it through ministerial agreements or simple administrative resolutions. During its validity, the officials could directly enter into contracts for the construction of works, the acquisition of goods, and the provision of services without a previous bidding process or tender, nor prior reports from the Attorney General's Office and the Comptroller's Office, because these reports were also eliminated by the aforementioned law.

This permissive legal framework favored large "turnkey" contracts, mainly with Chinese companies, for the construction of public works or the purchase of often unnecessary or nonpriority goods, without any studies of their feasibility, convenience, and usefulness and without the indispensable bidding process. In some cases, bidders offered to provide the corresponding financing, at supposedly moderate interest rates, which were largely offset through excessive fees for the projects or purchases, which were the source of bribes paid to the officials involved in the negotiation.

Correa conveyed the certainty that corrupt acts would never be discovered and, if they were, they would not be investigated and sanctioned and would remain in impunity. His collaborators did not doubt that this would be the case, as they had seen him defend them bravely, arguing that those who had committed crimes were victims of the "hatred" of their adversaries and of "media lynching" by the "corrupt press." In addition, Correa asked prosecutors and judges to criminally prosecute those who denounced acts of corruption and compelled them to pay millions of dollars in compensation, among other sanctions.[2] To personally express his solidarity with officials prosecuted for corruption, he even visited them in the prisons where they were being held. He also arranged for the appointment of prosecutors—lawyers who, because they owed him favors and had been subordinate to him, would be willing to meet his demands.[3]

Meanwhile, the authorities refused to cooperate with those from outside the government who were interested in pursuing corruption, even when their assistance was requested by members of the National Assembly. They did not provide documents requested, they impeded access to official records, and they refused to grant interviews requested by the press. Ministers and directors of public enterprises were prevented from attending the National Assembly to render accounts of their actions or to answer the legislators' questions in keeping with the provisions of the Law of Transparency and the Organic Law of the Legislative Function. The Comptroller's Office and the Attorney General's Office covered their eyes and ears so as not to see or hear the anomalies that were occurring in public contracting. The president never did anything about the public accusations of corruption, not even those that were sent to his office, but rather did everything he could to silence them, unleashing relentless persecutions and virulent smear campaigns against those who made accusations. Upon learning about the information disclosed by the U.S. Department of Justice, that the Odebrecht company had paid his government officials US$33.5 million in bribes between 2007 and 2016, Correa merely said that the government "will not accept" the version of those officials.[4]

Correa promoted issuing a persecutory Communication Law that would establish restrictions on freedom of expression and severe sanctions on the media involved in "media lynching." In fear of such reprisals, the press, radio, and television opted for self-censorship, as seen in the previous chapter.

At the same time, in the National Assembly, Alianza PAIS reduced the power traditionally held by the National Congress to oversee ministers and high-level officials and introduced complicated requirements and complex procedures that systematically prevented the successful prosecution of ministers and high-level officials. As a result, the complaints filed by opposition legislators were regularly shelved in the commission that heard them and could never be dealt with in the plenary of the National Assembly. This ploy worsened when AP came to have an absolute majority in 2013.

Some government officials reached the conclusion that the time had come to compensate themselves for the economic hardships suffered during their revolutionary militancy and to accrue capital that would allow them to survive in bad times, should Alianza PAIS lose power. Knowledge that the bribes would not be paid with taxpayers' money but would come from the excessive profits obtained by capitalists who exploited the people contributed to appeasing their consciences, as though the bribes were not financed with excessive prices for project contracts.

Some ministers and directors of public enterprises who lacked moral scruples did not care about the functions they would be in charge of and the services they could provide to the country, but rather only about the size of the budget they would manage to buy goods, provide services, and build public works. For these officials, the most appealing government offices were those involved in oil, electricity, mining, and the construction of physical infrastructure because they could collect juicy commissions when the respective contracts were signed.

The rise in oil prices, the doubling of the size of the state,[5] and the exponential increase in public spending contributed to the spread of corruption. As never before in the history of Ecuador, Correa's government had unlimited economic resources at its disposal to buy goods, build works, and hire whatever services his collaborators could think of, regardless of costs and needs. On the other hand, the statist economic policy introduced a series of controls and regulations for private-sector business activities, to be applied by officials at their discretion as a function of the bribes they received from the beneficiaries of their decisions.

Finally, a political axiom also came into play, an axiom confirmed by Latin American and Ecuadorian experiences of the last decades, that honest presidents are usually accompanied by honest ministers and officials and that corrupt presidents are accompanied by dishonest ones. In governments of the first type, corruption is an exception and is usually prosecuted and punished; in the second, in addition to becoming a daily occurrence, it is tolerated and protected by the head of state.

The members of the president-dictator's government not only charged commissions (kickbacks) on large contracts for highways, buildings, power plants, refineries, water pipelines, oil pipelines, ports, airports, and military and police equipment acquisitions. They also did so on medium and small contracts: purchases of all kinds of goods, including cleaning or office supply items; consultancies, often unnecessary, unsubstantial, or fictitious; the provision of all kinds of services, including advertising packages; editing of textbooks or informational and advertising materials; and so on.

They also recruited thousands of unnecessary and useless advisors known by the nickname "fat cats" (*pipones*); collected unjustifiable and outrageous per diems; had trips around the world paid for; submitted invoices for personal invitations to bars and restaurants; abusively used government planes, helicopters, and other vehicles; garnered part of the salaries of individuals they recommended for public-service positions; and took nepotism to the extreme by giving government jobs to spouses, partners, children, parents, siblings, aunts and uncles, and nieces and nephews.[6]

It was thus that Rafael Correa—first as the president and then as a dictator—implemented a kleptocratic regime unprecedented in the republican history of Ecuador. It was thus that young revolutionaries who enlisted in the Alianza PAIS political movement put aside the electoral slogan that they would govern "with clean hands and fervent hearts." And it was thus that the president, vice presidents, ministers, assembly members, public enterprise officials, and thousands of employees compulsively enriched themselves.

Despite the wall built by the government to make the discovery and persecution of corruption impregnable, it was impossible for it to prevent some crimes against public funds from coming to light. The Attorney General's Office and the Comptroller's Office had nothing to do with their discovery, but rather it was the diligent investigation of journalists, opposition assembly members, and members of civil society. It also had to do with the cooperation of the U.S. justice system and the U.S. Attorney General's Office, which discovered, arrested, tried, and convicted a dozen Correa government officials for corruption after they had accepted their guilt and named their accomplices. Many more have suffered the dreaded sanction of losing their visas to the United States.[7]

Before Rafael Correa left the Carondelet Palace, four corruption schemes shocked Ecuadorians. The Correa Delgado siblings came from an upper-middle-class family from Guayaquil that had become impoverished. However, it was not more than a couple of years after the inauguration of Rafael's government that his brother Fabricio bragged about having assets totaling "several million dollars," in a statement published by the Panamanian newspaper *La Prensa* (2017).

Taking advantage of his family relationships through an emporium of companies he formed in Ecuador and Panama, Fabricio Correa had managed to get the government to award him several contracts for the construction of public works, for an amount estimated to be between US$167 million and US$300 million. The exact amount could never be established, as the government agencies refused to hand over the documents requested. The fact was discovered thanks to an investigation conducted by two journalists from the newspaper *Expreso*, Juan Carlos Calderón and Christian Zurita. When the findings were made public, the president denied having known about such contracts. However, his statement was denied by Fabricio Correa; observers Pablo Chambers and Gerardo Portillo, who investigated the case; and Public Works Minister Jorge Marún.

Once the scandal came to light, Correa said that the contracts would be terminated, but that decision was not executed because he did not confirm it in writing to the corresponding officials. The aforementioned observers were judicially persecuted by the president for the purpose of silencing them, and when he did not succeed, they were sentenced to one year in prison for false testimony. The same thing happened with the journalists who uncovered the criminal connivance of the Correa brothers, who were also sentenced to pay compensation for the moral damages they had allegedly caused. Despite the evidence provided by the whistleblowers, which incriminated Fabricio Correa and the officials who awarded him the contracts, the Attorney General's Office did not initiate any investigation to prosecute them for corruption.

An investigation carried out by social activist Fernando Villavicencio and published on the digital portal Focus revealed that the repair of the Esmeraldas refinery, budgeted at US$187 million, ended up costing US$2.2 billion, more than ten times the initial price. Attorney General Galo Chiriboga took six months to initiate an investigation and only acted when the pressure of public opinion became compelling. Refinery manager Alex Bravo and former Petroecuador managers/former hydrocarbons ministers Carlos Pareja Yannuzzelli and Pedro Merizalde, as well as several private-sector business-men, most of whom are now fugitives, were convicted of corruption. Those involved stole more than one billion dollars.

Although supervision of the refinery project was the responsibility of Vice President Jorge Glas, he was not investigated by the Attorney General's Office nor implicated by the judges. When approached by the press to explain the criminal conduct of his collaborators, the president responded by saying that he "did not know Bravo"—yet this "stranger" had been put in charge of one of the government's most costly and emblematic projects.

Public bank COFIEC granted a credit of US$800,000, without sufficient guarantees, to an unknown Argentine citizen named Gastón Duzac who, together with other individuals of the same nationality, had offered to pro-vide technological advising to the Central Bank. The COFIEC directors approved the loan because of pressures received from Pedro Delgado, who was the president of the Central Bank and President Correa's second cousin. The beneficiaries had ties to the Ecuadorian president through an Argentine classmate he had had at the University of Illinois, whom he employed at the Central Bank and who used to introduce himself as Correa's advisor.[8] Once the conspirators obtained the loan, they transferred it to banks in Panama, Switzerland, and the United States and immediately left the country. At the same time, Delgado bought a house in Miami for US$385,000.[9] Only a year before, he had been practically destitute: in the declaration of assets he submitted to the Comptroller's Office he had cited assets of only US$39,150 and liabilities of US$36,560.

When the scandal broke, Correa offered his "full support" to Delgado, presided over a tribute in his honor, praised his virtues, and threatened the media that had disclosed the shady loan operation. For his part, Attorney General Galo Chiriboga did nothing to investigate Delgado and to prevent him from fleeing to Miami. At that time, it was verified that Delgado had falsified his degree in economics, which he had used to obtain several public functions, first as director of the No More Impunity Trust Fund and then as president of the Central Bank.

The directors of the lending bank were released by a criminal court after Correa proclaimed their innocence and visited them in prison. Through this daring audacity, he averted the risk that, in order to save themselves, they would tell the judges the names of the "officials" who, through Delgado, had ordered them to grant the fraudulent loan.

Electricity Minister Alecksey Mosquera was sentenced to five years in prison and had to pay an indemnity for the crime of money laundering. He had taken a US$1 million bribe from the Odebrecht company for awarding it a hydropower project. When this fact became known, the president justified the payment by saying that, since it was made after Mosquera had left the ministry, "it was an agreement between private parties." The minister, on the other hand, admitted that he had committed a crime and "apologized to Ecuador."

Once Rafael Correa finished his long term in office and moved to Belgium, the power structure he had set up to favor corruption, cover up its perpetrators, and clear them of blame began to crumble. This process began with the political distancing of his successor, Lenín Moreno, who had been handpicked by Correa to protect him. Under Moreno's government, democratic institutions were reestablished, including the division of power, the independence of the justice system, the oversight power of the National Assembly, and freedom of expression. These actions were followed by a split in Alianza PAIS, the reorganization of the National Court of Justice, the creation of an independent Constitutional Court, the replacement of the comptroller, and the appointment of Attorney General Diana Salazar.

Salazar's appointment was key in making progress in and completing the investigations into Correa's corruption and in convicting those who were guilty. During her successful tenure, the Attorney General's Office once again represented public vindication, to which her moral integrity, political independence, career as a civil servant, and the fact that she belonged to an ethnic minority and was also a woman contributed. Thanks to these virtues, she was able to investigate the countless acts of corruption that had occurred during the decade of Correa's administration and to obtain convictions of the guilty, including former president Correa and former vice president Glas. The judicial collaboration provided by the attorneys general of the United States and Brazil, as well as the testimonies of Odebrecht company officials, contributed to this outcome, but not the justice system of the People's Republic of China, the country that was the largest public works funder and contractor during Correa's term in office.[10]

Of the numerous corruption scandals uncovered after Rafael Correa left the presidency, I will refer only to those that involved the highest-ranking state officials and those in which the individuals responsible were convicted and the guilty verdicts stood with judges and courts at all levels.

Former vice president Jorge Glas was sentenced to serve six years in prison and to pay an indemnity of US$33 million for the crime of illicit association. Through his uncle Ricardo Rivera, whose employee and partner he had been in various businesses before being elected, Glas received a US$13.5 million bribe from Odebrecht so that the company would be awarded physical infrastructure projects. This occurred while he was the minister of strategic sectors between 2010 and 2012. The tax investigation and criminal trial could be initiated thanks to information provided by the U.S. Department of Justice.

The court that sentenced Glas requested that the Attorney General's Office also investigate him for the crimes of illicit enrichment, embezzlement, extortion, bribery, organized crime, money laundering, influence peddling, and serving as a frontman since there were indications in the court file that he had committed such crimes. Glas is now incarcerated in the Latacunga jail. Years before, legislator Andres Páez had sent President Correa and Attorney General Chiriboga documents showing that Glas's uncle had transferred US$22.8 million to banks in Hong Kong. Páez received no response from either of the two officials (*Ecuador en Vivo* and *El Universo*, March 16, 2008).

A chamber of the National Court of Justice, in first and second instances, sentenced former president Rafael Correa and former vice president Jorge Glas for the crime of bribery and sentenced them to eight years in prison, the loss of political rights for the same period, the payment of an indemnity of about US$14 million dollars, and the presentation of public apologies in the Independence Square in Quito.[11] The two had formed and directed a criminal structure to collect commissions from private businessmen, in cash or through cross-charging, in exchange for awarding contracts for the construction of public works. The economic resources obtained through these extortions, US$7.1 million, were used almost in their entirety to finance election campaigns and other Alianza PAIS political events. Also convicted for the same crime were former ministers María Duarte, Walter Solís, and Vinicio Alvarado; the president's influential former legal secretary, Alexis Mera; Assemblywoman Viviana Bonilla; and a dozen businessmen. Presidential advisors-secretaries Pamela Martínez and Laura Terán received lesser sentences because they collaborated with the justice system to shed light on the crime. The former incriminated Rafael Correa by confessing that, on behalf of the president, she kept records of the bribes received and their allocation, and she handed over those documents to the Attorney General's Office.

Comptroller Carlos Pólit, now a fugitive from justice, remained in office during the ten years of Correa's administration. That official, who was responsible for ensuring the suitable use of public resources and for investigating and reporting acts of corruption to the Attorney General's Office, received bribes for US$13 million and asked that US$8 million be paid in cash, according to Odebrecht official José Conceição dos Santos. The company paid him this amount so that he would rule in favor of Odebrecht regarding problems involving five projects it was executing in Ecuador.

In the judicial proceedings to punish this crime of extortion, Pólit was sentenced to serve six years in prison and, together with his son John, to pay a compensation of US$40.4 million. In addition, his son was dismissed by the National Assembly, to which he had been sworn in two months earlier to begin a third term. He had been reelected by the CPCCS, by virtue of the exceptional score he obtained in the competition in which he participated. In a polygraph test, Carlos Pareja Yannuzzelli, a former hydrocarbons minister and former Petroecuador manager, declared that he had personally delivered packages of dollars to Pólit and to Attorney General Galo Chiriboga, in a hotel suite in Quito, for their participation in several acts of corruption.

Later, in early 2022, Pólit was detained in the United States for having conspired to commit the crime of money laundering. In order to grant him the option of bail as Pólit requested, the judge for the penal proceedings brought against him set the amount as US$18 million, required him to surrender his passport, prohibited him from selling or mortgaging his assets, made him renounce opposition to his extradiction, and ordered that he wear a GPS-enabled ankle monitor.

If Odebrecht paid bribes for all the contracts it signed in Ecuador, surely the other companies, including Ecuadorian companies (large, medium, and small) that built projects, sold goods, and provided services to public entities proceeded in the same way—and especially Chinese ones, in this case due to the amounts involved and the lack of transparency in the contracts they entered into. There were probably a few exceptions, in negotiations of smaller amounts and in those involving companies from the United States, whose laws prohibit the payment of bribes.

Finally, it is necessary to estimate the magnitude of corruption during the decade in which Rafael Correa governed Ecuador. According to calculations done by Cordes, public investment totaled US$108.9 billion dollars between 2007 and 2017. If the businessmen who negotiated with the state paid a moderate bribe of 5 percent of the amount of the contracts they signed (usually the percentage was higher and in some cases as much as 20 percent), the bribes received by officials in the Citizens Revolution government would have amounted to the enormous sum of a little over US$5.4 billion dollars.[12]

This figure could be substantially higher. In a recent report submitted to the Federal Prosecutor's Office and the Attorney General's Office by the government of President Guillermo Lasso, the damages caused to the state are estimated to be approximately US$5 billion under the loan contracts signed with China and to be repaid through periodical oil deliveries. (So that they could not be investigated, these agreements were declared secret by Correa's government.) The corresponding oil shipments never arrived in China because various intermediaries diverted them to other destinations. According to a confession made to U.S. authorities, U.S. citizen Raymond Kohut, in representation of the Gunvor Group, paid bribes totaling US$70 million to Petroecuador officials. Ecuadorian businessman Enrique Cadena appears to have been involved in similar operations.

Sizeable, deep, and widespread corruption lasted for a long decade and encompassed all state entities; the highest-level officials were involved, and corruption ran rampant, unencumbered, and remained in impunity. This could not have happened without the knowledge and participation of the person who governed Ecuador with all the powers of the state. This is evidenced by the fact that president, and later dictator, Rafael Correa is now subject to a dozen tax investigations, along with his vice president and many of his ministers and close collaborators, for the crimes of illicit enrichment, embezzlement, extortion, organized crime, bribery, influence peddling, money laundering, procedural fraud, swindling, and serving as fronts. In one of them, as seen earlier, Correa has been convicted by all judicial instances, after having fully exercised his rights to defense, due process, and a fair trial.

In the face of such serious violations of public morals, proven through numerous and irrefutable pieces of evidence, the leaders of the parties that boosted Correa politically, participated in his government, and promoted his leadership have not condemned his corruption.[13] Nor have they asked for him to be sanctioned by disciplinary bodies, let alone requested his expulsion from their ranks, in order to at least wash away collective responsibility in the atrocious corruption that Correa unleashed in Ecuador. On the contrary, they have strongly defended the innocence of Correa and other convicted persons, alleging that they have been judicially persecuted and unjustly punished.

During the years they governed in Ecuador, they would justify their silence by saying that they were "organic," that is, loyal to the "revolutionary process," for which reason they should not give their enemies weapons to be used against them. In other words, party loyalty was to be above public ethics, and this disgraceful stance continues.

The explanation for this amorality among Correa's supporters is probably to be found in a wise phrase uttered more than a century ago: "Power tends to corrupt, and absolute power corrupts absolutely."[14]

The transparency of a democratic government is not limited to the honest administration of public assets. Officials must render accounts regarding their actions and respond to information requests from the opposition, citizens, and the media. The president ignored this obligation, with the excuse that every week he rendered accounts directly to the people through Saturday-morning radio and television broadcasts that lasted several hours. Although it was true that in these Saturday programs he talked about the government's achievements, his talks had more to do with propaganda and rhetoric than with a reasoned analysis of the results of his administration. The information he provided in these monologues was not reliable, due to his tendency to exaggerate and distort. Much of his time was devoted to recounting stories from his personal life, attacking his opponents, making false accusations, threatening them in all sorts of ways, and ordering judges and officials to prosecute them judicially and administratively.

When events occurred that affected the image of the government and called into question the actions of an official, the person involved slipped away until the matter was forgotten or no longer of interest to public opinion. Frequently, when ministers and other high-ranking officials met with journalists, they simply read a statement and then immediately left the room, without answering questions.

The government made it difficult for citizens to access state information and documents even though that right is enshrined in the constitution and in the Law on Transparency. For example, the finance ministers refused to report on the amount of public indebtedness, falsely arguing that "it was forbidden by law," as well as on the conditions of the loans granted by China, which the government considered secret.

Even though the authorities were obliged to respond to citizens' demands for information under a mandate of the Law on Transparency, they always refused to provide it. This is what happened when the media requested that the communication secretary specify the names of the media that the government considered corrupt and labeled as such in a smear campaign mounted against them. The government also remained silent when it was asked to inform about the contracts entered into with advertisers and TV stations or about public safety and security statistics.

The president's word did not lend certainty to the government's political, economic, and international decisions or to the information it provided to citizens. Contradictions were common throughout Correa's long term in office, even between what he said one day and what he said another day or even immediately after he said or wrote something. He was inconsistent in his treatment of issues, manipulated facts to suit his positions, used a double standard to judge the same issue according to his interests, and used personal disparagements against those who contradicted him instead of refuting their positions, figures, and facts. If he obviously exaggerated or stated an ostensible falsehood, he would not accept having said what he said and would hide his assertion with the excuse that he had been misrepresented by the corrupt press. In more than half a century of having participated in debates on public affairs, I have never heard an Ecuadorian politician lie so brazenly, not even the worst populists. Nonetheless, in a report to the National Assembly, he went so far as to say that he would die "for the love of truth."

Correa was also capable of saying anything. It is worth noting two of his most scandalous and widely circulated comments. On one occasion he famously blurted out, "I do not know whether gender equity improves democracy; what is certain is that it has impressively improved partying." Also, in the executive decree he issued upon the death of Hugo Chávez, he affirmed that "the Bolivarian Revolution he led should be replicated in Latin America and the world and be viewed as emblematic for all humanity."

NOTES

1. I have modified the wording of this unintelligible constitutional article so that readers can understand its content.

2. According to the Inter-American Court of Human Rights, indemnities should not enrich the victim and impoverish the convicted person.

3. Washington Pesántez had been at the University of Lovaine with Rafael Correa, Galo Chiriboga had been his personal attorney, and Carlos Baca was serving as a presidential advisor at the time of his appointment.

4. For other acts of corruption, most of which occurred in Petroecuador, the U.S. justice system has convicted a dozen Ecuadorians, some of whom have accepted their guilt, collaborated with prosecutors, and provided the names of their accomplices so that they can also be tried.

5. The state's participation in the economy went from 21 percent of the GDP in 2006 to 41 percent in 2012. Eighty institutions, including ministries, secretariats, and enterprises, were created (Hurtado 2017).

6. The most notable case was that of Carlos Marx Carrasco, who served as the director of the Ecuadorian Internal Revenue Service (SRI for its acronym in Spanish) for seven years. He came to employ sixteen relatives in various public positions (*Plan V* 2017a).

7. In mid-2020, U.S. Ambassador Michael Fitzpatrick reported that his country had withdrawn the visas of more than three hundred Ecuadorians investigated for corruption. "We don't want thieves or their money in my country," he added.

8. Argentine citizen Pedro Elosegui had commented positively on a compilation of essays published by Correa and titled *Ecuador: De la Banana Republic a la no República* (2009).

9. Univision TV news broadcast (October 20, 2009).

10. The Chinese credits total $18.4 billion, approximately 20 percent of the 2019 GDP. Almost all of these were granted during Correa's consecutive terms (Gallagher and Myers 2020).

11. When the penal proceedings began, Correa said that he would shoot himself if they found he had any ill-gotten gains.

12. This estimate has not taken into account the acquisition of certain goods and services catalogued as current expenses in the federal budget.

13. Alianza PAIS was Rafael Correa's party until he left the presidency in 2017. Upon losing it to Lenín Moreno, Correa founded another party in 2020, called Union for Hope (Unión por la Esperanza, UNES).

14. Famous phrase coined in 1887 by British historian Lord John Emerich Edward Dalberg-Acton.

Chapter 16

Political Pluralism

Unlike totalitarian societies and some dictatorial societies with a single way of thinking and a single party, a democratic society has coexisting political, social, and economic organizations with different ideologies. In the exercise of pluralism, which is inherent to a democratic regime of government, citizens tend to take part in the country's public sphere by expressing their thoughts with independence, autonomy, and freedom.

As was seen in previous chapters, Rafael Correa's government severely affected the freedom of expression whereby citizens' ideas and concerns about the problems of a society and the paths to follow to overcome them are usually conveyed. Nothing similar had happened during the governments that succeeded each other during the present democratic period. During the Citizens Revolution, although diverging ideas were not forbidden or abolished, as usually occurs in totalitarian regimes, the right to dissent was restricted. Journalists, social leaders, political leaders, the media, and citizens suffered. The right to observe and criticize government conduct was challenged and even seen as conspiratorial, especially if economic and social policies, authoritarian procedures, the failure to abide by the constitution and laws, and misuse of public funds were called into question.

The president and his spokespersons, especially the former, did not discuss the validity, relevance, and veracity of the observations made by his critics, nor were they interested in disproving them by presenting reasons, evidence, and arguments. They preferred to demean those who had expressed them—personally, morally, and politically. This intolerance and irrationality were even worse when the opponents made accusations. To silence them, the government used intimidating actions: threats; insults; allegations; smear campaigns; persecutions related to tax, economic, and labor issues; and criminal prosecutions or multimillion-dollar lawsuits for alleged moral damages caused to the president. Politicians, businessmen, academics, journalists, social leaders, and citizens were all vulnerable to these.

During his ten years in office, Correa sued twenty-five people for moral damages, and numerous citizens were jailed on his orders, accused of actions against the "majesty" (i.e., sovereign dignity) of the presidency by making gestures and yelling at him as he traveled along in his presidential caravan.

To the extent that the regime ignored the ideas of those who thought differently, repressed criticism, and closed the doors to the exchange of opinions, the dialogue and debate that give meaning to pluralism were affected, as was the ability to correct inappropriate behavior, rectify hasty decisions, revise misguided policies, and improve government programs and initiatives. To the extent that frightened citizens, journalists, opinion leaders, and the media remained silent, the country lost the guiding voices it needed to hear. Had it not been for their uncertainty about the persecution they would suffer, they would have openly voiced their criticisms and made their contributions instead of self-censoring.

Societies in which the circulation of ideas is not allowed or is restricted, in which those who think differently are persecuted, in which citizens are conditioned by fear, and in which the government imposes its truth as it pleases are not pluralistic.

It can be concluded that Ecuadorians were free to think what they thought during Correa's government but not to say it publicly, even less so if their remarks and criticisms were directed at the president of the republic.

The participation of political parties in the institutions that make up the state and in the debate of public affairs, particularly in the National Assembly, is a second way pluralism is expressed. Since it is the state body in which all political organizations are present, different ideologies coexist, and its members are elected by the people, its democratic nature and pluralistic form are fully accredited.

However, this was not the way President Correa and his followers thought. They believed that parties other than Alianza PAIS had nothing to contribute to the operation of the democratic system, to national development, to social equity, and to the definition of national interests in the international arena. This sectarian position was based on the belief that the ideas of Alianza PAIS (actually those of Correa), not those of the nation's ideological plurality, were the only ones that should count in defining and implementing public policies.

Political parties suffered the same treatment as ideas did. Although they were not banned or excluded from public life, the government hindered the formation of those averse to it and marginalized all of them from state bodies that they had always been part of. It proceeded in this way moved by the dogmatic and illusory belief that Alianza PAIS represented the whole of society and together with its leader embodied the Ecuadorian nation.

In this hegemonic vision of the exercise of power, a utilitarian consideration also came into play, motivated by the caudillista plan for Rafael Correa to govern Ecuador indefinitely. For this to occur, among other factors, it was necessary for Alianza PAIS to become an indisputable political organization, capable of winning any election, consultation, or referendum. In turn, for this to occur, it was necessary to endow it with privileges and advantages and, at the same time, to close the doors to other political organizations, mainly the doors to the institutions that compose the state.

An all-powerful party with a majority in the National Assembly, replete with electoral privileges and in control of all public-sector institutions, was going to be a determining political factor in realizing Correa's political ambitions. The most important one was to have a constitution tailored to his needs in order for him to exercise autocratic power and govern Ecuador indefinitely.

In order to achieve these undemocratic ambitions, he had a clear path after the collapse of the party system that had emerged during the political process leading to the restoration of democracy in 1979. When Rafael Correa appeared in Ecuador's public sphere in the early twenty-first century, there were still fragmented political organizations that were not representative and that lacked leaders who could threaten the brilliant leadership of the budding caudillo.

In order not to halt but rather to advance the debacle of the parties, the government mounted a vast campaign of disinformation and efforts to discredit political organizations, which it pigeonholed under the label "partyocracy."[1] Something similar was done with their leaders, but not with the partyocratic parties that put themselves at the service of the government or kept a colluding silence. As soon as these joined the government, they ceased to be partyocratic, overcame their shortcomings, and recovered their virtues, which allowed them to obtain candidacies, ministerial positions, diplomatic representations, and other posts. These were the cases of leaders from Pachakutik, the Democratic Left, and groups from the balkanized Marxist Left, such as the Socialist Party and the MPD.[2]

Correa immediately eliminated the party system formally by arbitrarily issuing the statute that called for a constituent assembly, depriving them of their legal status, and forcing them to apply for new registration. Without the latter, they could not participate in the election of members for the constituent assembly and later in the elections for president, legislators, mayors, and provincial prefects.

The 2008 constitution established a major barrier for parties to re-register by requiring them to have a number of members representing 1.5 percent of the voter registry. Since the same percentage of only sympathizers and supporters had to be met by political movements, all of them registered as such. The only one that could have gathered enough members to register as a party, Alianza PAIS, for tactical reasons preferred not to do so, since that label had become pejorative. Sociedad Patriótica, PRE, MPD, PSC, the Socialist Party,

PRIAN, Pachakutik, Suma, Ruptura, Creo, Avanza, and, naturally, Alianza PAIS were re-registered.

Such was the dictator's determination that there should be only one party in "his democracy" that he promoted a costly publicity campaign to urge citizens not to provide their signatures to the opposition parties. When some parties still managed to collect enough signatures, he accused them of having falsified signatures and ordered the CNE to invalidate them. After an illegal, cumbersome, and opaque signature review process, all parties, including Alianza PAIS, were found to have "falsified" signatures. In fact, most were duplicated or different from those appearing on identity cards. The only movement finally eliminated, in a clear act of political retaliation, was Concertación, whose leader, César Montúfar, had fought against the Communication Law that Correa intended to push through the National Assembly.

It is natural for governments to be formed with members of the political party that receives the majority vote of the citizens. For this reason, it is not possible to criticize the fact that only members or sympathizers of Alianza PAIS participated in Correa's government. However, it was incompatible with political pluralism to have other, independent state institutions, including the justice system, the Attorney General's Office, and oversight bodies, monopolized by members or sympathizers of only one party, that of the government, and to ban the participation of the others.

Traditionally, the election board had been made up of representatives of all parties that received the most votes. In addition to guaranteeing political pluralism, this approach respected the will of the citizens and, through the self- and reciprocal control of its members, guaranteed transparent electoral processes. Once the new constitution was issued, the National Electoral Council was formed exclusively with Alianza PAIS militants and sympathizers, and it maintained that composition until Correa left the presidency in 2017. During those years, by virtue of its not being pluralistic but rather single-party, the council became an electoral instrument of the government. Its main obligation was to ensure the triumph of the government's candidates and its plebiscite proposals, regardless of whether electoral processes were equitable and ballot counting was fair.

According to the 1998 constitution, the National Congress was to be presided over by the majority party, the first vice president was to come from the party that had obtained the second highest number of votes, and the second vice president from one of the minority parties. In the decade of Correa's administration, that did not occur: these positions in the National Assembly, including the president and vice presidents of the parliamentary commissions, were held by members of Alianza PAIS. Thus, a body that in all the democracies of the world is the utmost expression of political pluralism became the domain of a single player, the government party.

One of the novel political phenomena common to Western democracies at the end of the century was the proliferation of nongovernmental organizations (NGOs), known under the generic term *civil society*. They were mainly environmentalists, human rights defenders, advisors to social organizations, and academic centers. In general, they were seen as a new expression of pluralism and an enriching element of democracy. Some were critical of parties and hoped to replace them.

These organizations began to form in Ecuador in the last third of the twentieth century, many promoted by citizens who would later become part of the Citizens Revolution. They were utilized to oppose the governments at the end of the century, organize protests and demonstrations, and even overthrow governments, as occurred in the case of President Jamil Mahuad. Once they came to power, they changed their minds. NGOs that the government claimed were related to political parties or that carried out research and studies that questioned some of its policies suffered the same hostile treatment as ideas and parties.

The government took five measures to prevent this contemporary form of pluralism from expressing itself in Ecuadorian democracy. First, economic harassment was used to deprive them of financing and political harassment to force their representatives to withdraw from public debate or at least moderate their criticisms. Second, their legal status was not recognized so that they could not operate legally and were thus paralyzed and dissolved. Third, the representation they had in certain state agencies was eliminated. Fourth, parallel organizations were created, and the president turned them into his spokespersons. Fifth, people with similar activities could not be forced to join trade unions and professional associations.

Among the NGOs that the government was determined to exclude from the pluralistic debate on public affairs, the following are noteworthy. Fundamedios, persecuted by the government with the intention of dissolving it, fought a daily battle in favor of freedom of expression so that journalists and the media could work without restrictions; it sometimes even had to resort to international recourses. The environmental organization Yasunidos was prevented from promoting a popular consultation on oil exploitation in the Yasuní reserve, under the provisions of the constitution. The politicized National Union of Educators (UNE), an opponent of all governments, was dissolved and its members' savings fund transferred to a state bank (BIESS). The director of Participación Ciudadana, an organization that audited the government's propaganda spending, candidates' equal access to the media, and the reliability of polls, was threatened by the president with criminal prosecution for not calling the 2017 presidential election due to the narrow margin.

Through propaganda and disinformation campaigns, the Correa administration sought to discredit the leaders of the Indigenous confederation Conaie, whom he pejoratively called "golden ponchos." They were removed from the public functions they had held, some were prosecuted, the economic aid they received was cut, and the institutions they led were eliminated. It was paradoxical that the Indigenous movement suffered this treatment during a "revolutionary" government led by former allies whom it had promoted politically and electorally.

Some university leaders in the FEUE and college students in the FESE were criminally prosecuted for committing abuses similar to those they used to commit with impunity when they were allies of the government and helped to intimidate and dissolve the highest bodies of the state. At the same time, the government co-opted student leaders to form a progovernment organization called the National Coordinating Committee of University Students (Coneu).

The private- and public-sector workers' unions, which were initially favorable to Correa's government because they agreed with his socialist, nationalist, anticapitalist, and statist proposals, gradually distanced themselves from him. The public-sector unions did so because of the measures Correa took to curtail rights and privileges: union organizing, collective bargaining, forced purchase of resignations, elimination of disproportionate severance pay and family benefits, and the dismissal of twelve thousand workers. The private-sector unions protested because their demands were not being met and the government took measures that they described as "neoliberal." Fearing that the union movement would become an opposition force, the government sought to weaken its two main pillars, the FUT (workers) and the UNE (educators), by co-opting leaders and creating parallel organizations under the political control of the government, which it used to defend or justify its policies. These were the cases of the Confederation of Public Sector Workers in 2011, the Unified Workers Central (CUT) in 2014, and the Network of Teachers for the Education Revolution in 2015 (Hurtado 2017).

As it has been possible to see, ideological and political pluralism ceased to nourish Ecuadorian democracy during Correa's government. Any criticism, disagreement, or protest was seen as conspiratorial and not as the expression of pluralism in a republican regime. This was what happened with political parties, social movements, civil-society organizations, and business and professional associations. The treatment of citizens and organizations that the government labeled as opposition was even worse and ignored the fact that the opposition is an institution of democracy.

For many years before Correa, some people had criticized and condemned the "single-minded mentality" of those who believed that democracy and a market-centered approach should be imposed worldwide. However, during Correa's terms in office, those same people buried ideological and political pluralism and tried to impose the "single-minded mentality" of the Citizens Revolution and the "sole leadership" of Rafael Correa.

NOTES

1. This demeaning term was introduced into the political debate by *Vistazo* magazine's editorial writer Alfredo Pinoargote and later used by the press and Correa, all three without exceptions.

2. Former president Rodrigo Borja, founder and leader of the Democratic Left Party, was nominated by Correa as the secretary general of the Union of South American Countries (UNASUR for its acronym in Spanish). After accepting at first, Borja later excused himself when his request that other regional organizations be incorporated did not prosper. He was not the only leader from that party who formed part of Correa's government.

Chapter 17

Alternation in Power

Political alternation, understood as the succession of parties and leaders from different ideological tendencies in governing a state, is another characteristic of representative democracy. This principle was incorporated into the Ecuadorian constitutions of the nineteenth and twentieth centuries through the prohibition of the incumbent president's immediate reelection. Whoever completed his term of office could run for a second term after a term had elapsed. One exception was the "Carta Negra" of 1869, inspired by autocrat Gabriel García Moreno, in which continuous reelection was introduced for the first and only time.

The 1979 constitution absolutely prohibited reelection of the president, determining that a person could hold that office only once. Motivated by the five reelections of José María Velasco Ibarra (though not successive), those who drafted that document believed that it would put an end to recurrent caudillismo, strengthen political parties, and shape a political class—steps on which the democratic institutions' proper functioning would depend. This radical constraint did not last for even a decade because the 1998 constitution returned to the traditional formula whereby former presidents could be reelected after one term out of office.

Ecuadorian democracy's nonreelection stance changed with the triumph of the Citizens Revolution. As soon as the leaders of Alianza PAIS realized that they had a caudillo in their ranks, they changed their minds, accepted his request, and introduced the immediate reelection of the president of the republic in the 2008 constitution, for the first time in 138 years. Curiously, it was twenty-first-century revolutionaries who resurrected an institution originating among mid-nineteenth-century conservatives. They added an ambitious transitory provision stipulating that Correa's first reelection (2009) would not be taken into account so that he could run again in 2013 for a third term, as in fact happened. When that term ended in early 2017, he became the first president to rule the country for more than ten consecutive years (in fact, two years and six months longer than dictator Ignacio de Veintemilla

(1876–1883), who until then had been the longest-serving Ecuadorian head of state).

Although the 2008 constitution opened up the possibility for an incumbent president to run for a new term, Article 144 established the limitation that "he may be reelected only once." This provision was approved with the favorable vote of Constituent Assembly members from Alianza PAIS, who held a majority. This limitation had been shared by Correa in 2007, when he said that "indefinite reelection was absurd since democracy implied alternation." He reiterated that opinion in 2012 when he announced that his third term "would be the last." In keeping with these categorical assertions, he asked his party colleagues to prepare for someone to succeed him in the leadership of Alianza PAIS and in the presidency.

Nonetheless, despite these firm statements against indefinite reelection, in mid-2013 he asked for it to be allowed, a surprising move that Alianza PAIS leaders learned about through the media. However, they hastily changed their position. The party's executive secretary, Galo Mora, assured that "the president's right" to reform the constitution in that regard would be accepted in the National Assembly since Alianza PAIS was a majority force. The president of the legislative body, Gabriela Rivadeneira, went further by saying that "no law, no article of the constitution, can be an obstacle to consolidating the political process that Ecuador is going through." Although Correa chose not to follow through on his initiative in light of the negative reaction of public opinion, he opened the door to taking it up again when political circumstances were propitious, with the certainty that his assembly members would support his request.

At the same time, he cunningly insinuated the opposite. He suggested that the presidency was a heavy burden, which he would be freed of if his voters did not support him and the leaders of Alianza PAIS were not loyal to him. "If they don't want me, I'll leave," he said. "I don't have to put up with anyone," he added. "If they don't like what I do, get someone else," he mused. "I'm tired of this." He concluded by saying that, if he were to resign, "I would go home with a clear conscience." Meanwhile, he praised himself, suggesting that there was no one better than him to govern Ecuador. He used these pitiful remarks to get controversial decisions—some of them contrary to the revolutionary ideals of AP—accepted by his party's legislators. Certainly, in his mind there was never even a remote possibility of following through on those complaints and threats.

In the following months he changed his mind again, spoke out several times against indefinite reelection, and reiterated that he would not run for a new term in 2017. He justified this by saying that he planned to retire from politics to attend to his "neglected family." It is worth quoting some of his contrite statements: "If I am reelected to the presidency, it will be my last four years, and I will retire from public life" (2012). "It is very detrimental when a person is so indispensable that it is necessary to change the Constitution to change the rules of the game" (2014). "It is not worth changing the Constitution for specific circumstances. I will fulfill my two [three] terms and I will go home" (2014) (Torres 2014).

In view of the unreliability of the president's words, after so many and such gross contradictions, many doubted that those statements were true. Indeed, a few months later, he changed his position again, saying that it was "his duty to review his sincere decision not to run for reelection because he had a duty to ensure that the process of the Citizens Revolution would be irreversible." He added that he felt obliged to "keep conservatives from returning" and from stalling or reversing the economic and social transformations initiated by his government. He concluded by saying that "it was up to the Ecuadorian people to freely choose the continuity or alternation of their leaders" (Torres 2014).

Alianza PAIS legislators immediately presented several constitutional reforms within the National Assembly, including the indefinite reelection of authorities elected by the citizens. Given Correa's ambition to govern Ecuador forever, those who inferred that the text of that reform had been written in the president's office and not by the leadership of Alianza PAIS were right. Meanwhile, the AP assembly members knew very well that, by having a winning presidential candidate in the next elections, those nominated for the assembly, mayorships, and prefectures would be carried along in his wake.

According to the constitution, reforms of this nature could be approved in a referendum or through amendments voted on by the National Assembly. It was surprising that the person who boasted that he had won every election in which he had participated, and all the consultations and referendums, should opt for the second alternative. Those who were familiar with the results of several polls—which coincided in that most citizens were against indefinite reelection[1]—knew that Correa had chosen the assembly approach due to the fear of being defeated in a constitutional referendum.

By proceeding in this way, he avoided consulting the people on a decision that affected the democratic principle of alternating power, that set aside the participatory democracy proclaimed by the Citizens Revolution, that substituted the vote of millions of voters with the vote of a hundred assembly members from a single party, and that opened up the doors to a presidency for life.[2] In the past, he had consulted the people on trivial matters, such as the prohibition of bullfighting and cockfighting.

A group of political organizations led by former presidential candidate Guillermo Lasso and grouped within the Compromiso Ecuador collective asked the National Electoral Council (CNE) for forms to collect signatures to call for a consultation of the people on the issue of indefinite reelection.

One day after the dictator said that such a petition should be denied, the CNE ruled accordingly.

The Constitutional Court ruled the amendments constitutional,[3] and the National Assembly approved the indefinite reelection of authorities elected by popular vote. In fact, it approved Rafael Correa's reelection with the vote of one hundred members from Alianza PAIS and its allies.

Although not included in the original proposal, a transitory provision was introduced at the last minute by the assembly, postponing indefinite reelection until May 24, 2017. Consequently, Correa could not run in the next presidential election but could in 2021. He justified his surprising relinquishment of the possibility of immediate reelection by saying that he had to attend to his family, an excuse he had used before. Then Bolivian president Evo Morales reported that Correa had "confessed" to him that this was the reason for excusing himself. Correa also posited that his presence would not be necessary for a political movement as powerful as Alianza PAIS to succeed, regardless of the presidential candidate.

There must have been other reasons, such as the well-founded fear of not being reelected in the first round of voting and being forced to go into a risky second round; the certainty that he would no longer have the enormous economic resources he had had during his governments, due to the fall in oil prices; and the advisability of avoiding the costly and unpopular responsibility of facing the serious economic and social crisis caused by his populist and statist policies.

The analysis done in the preceding pages regarding the deterioration of the republican institutions that occurred in the successive governments of Correa shows just how wise were the Ecuadorian politicians who systematically vetoed immediate presidential reelection for almost a century and a half, in the constitutions following that of 1869.

Utilitarian political considerations played a role in the dictator's eagerness to rule Ecuador indefinitely and in his followers' eagerness to please him. They were convinced that a dialectical turn of history had given them the opportunity to carry out a socialist revolution, a transforming process that could not be left halfway. They were alien to the way of thinking and acting of democratic politicians, for whom power was a transitory public service and alternation with the opposition was an element of republican regimes. Good Marxists, neo-Marxists, liberationists, and Chavistas had appropriated the Leninist precept that once power had been attained it could not be surrendered for any reason, much less to those who could hold them accountable for the abuses they had committed and the corruption in which they were mired. There were many who thought it was nonsense to give up the jobs, benefits, perks, prerogatives, comforts, attributes, privileges, and daily opportunities to enrich themselves that they had been enjoying at their leisure. Besides having succumbed to the thrills, privileges, wealth, and benefits that dishonestly and dictatorially exercised power tends to provide, Correa considered himself a paragon of virtues and an irreplaceable leader.

Once Correa concluded his third term and left the presidency, his successor, Lenín Moreno, called for a referendum on the indefinite reelection of the president of the republic and other popularly elected authorities. In the vote held in 2018, 64 percent of the citizens voted for its elimination. For that reason, the constitution was reformed accordingly, and Correa will not be able to run for the presidency ever again.

In a visionary way, liberator Simón Bolívar, in his famous speech at Angostura, summarized the risks that democratic institutions run in governments led by autocrats:

> The continuance of authority in the same individual has frequently meant the end of democratic governments. Repeated elections are essential in democratic systems of government, for nothing is more perilous than to permit one citizen to retain power for an extended period. The people become accustomed to obeying him, and he forms the habit of commanding them; herein lie the origins of usurpation and tyranny. A just zeal is the guarantee of republican liberty. Our citizens must with good reason learn to fear lest the magistrate that has governed them long will govern them forever.

NOTES

1. According to polls, 80 percent wanted to be consulted on constitutional changes and 65 percent were against indefinite reelection.

2. He had a majority in the National Assembly since, as mentioned previously, even though Alianza PAIS had received only half the votes it ended up with two-thirds of the seats in the assembly thanks to a skewed election system.

3. Three years later, when Correa no longer governed Ecuador, the Constitutional Court changed its opinion and declared them unconstitutional.

Chapter 18

Free Elections

The Revolution of 1925 (or July Revolution) put an end to thirty years of domination by the Liberal Party and to the electoral fraud that had kept it in power for such a long time. From 1925 onward, except when dictatorships ruled, presidents were elected by the free vote of citizens, though with the limitations of the backward Ecuador of that time, when only a minority participated in public affairs. Most of the population was illiterate and lived in isolated rural areas.

The urbanization of the cities caused by peasant migration, some improvements in communication systems, the spread of handheld transistor radios, and the long political reign of caudillo José María Velasco Ibarra—who mobilized crowds with his fiery rhetoric—expanded the people's participation in electoral processes.

By the last third of the twentieth century, most Ecuadorians were voting, thanks to widespread access to education, growth of the urban population, integration of the national territory through a broad network of roads, the massive scope of radio and television, and the right to vote granted to the illiterate by the 1979 constitution.

In the electoral processes of the second half of the twentieth century and the beginning of the twenty-first century, presidential candidates only exceptionally won with support from the media. Something similar happened with the candidates that had abundant economic resources and access to unlimited publicity. At least five presidents were elected despite experiencing the animosity of important sectors of the press and despite having less financing than their opponents. Between the twentieth and twenty-first centuries, Alvaro Noboa, one of Ecuador's richest men, despite his electoral campaigns' high levels of spending, failed to be elected all five times he ran.

In general, incumbent governments did not support their preferred presidential candidate, and those that did so exceptionally did not use the power of the state in his favor. The meager backing these candidates received was of little use to them, with only one exception: the election of Camilo Ponce in 1956 was helped by the support given to him by President Velasco Ibarra.

With Rafael Correa's arrival in the presidency in 2007, governments' traditional election neutrality ended since the new leader of Ecuadorian politics became the main player in his party's electoral campaigns. He was elected for the first time in 2006, on his own merits and against the political establishment. However, in the following electoral processes, he tapped all the resources of the state, issued legal norms that benefited him, and made the body in charge of guaranteeing free and fair elections subject to his interests. He accompanied this with the rhetoric that he was freeing the electoral processes from the control of economic and political powers.

The result was misguided. While his own campaigns for the presidency or campaigns in support of consultations, referendums, and his party's candidates for local elections were surrounded by privileges, those of the opposition suffered from restrictions that affected the electoral equity that is inherent to the democratic system. Therefore, the will of the voters was not changed by altering results at the ballot boxes, as had occurred in the first decades of the twentieth century, but rather before voting took place, during the electoral campaigns.

In 2006, Rafael Correa participated in the presidential race under the protection of the election rules in place and strictly applied by the impartial Supreme Electoral Tribunal of the time, which was composed of representatives of the majority political parties. After losing in the first round of voting, he tried to justify his defeat by arguing that he had been affected by electoral fraud, without pointing out who was responsible or providing evidence that it had occurred. The same electoral authorities whom he had indirectly disparaged counted the votes in the second round and proclaimed his victory. In both campaigns he had economic resources provided by wealthy groups at his disposal, and the media gave ample publicity to his campaign activities. Although he had less publicity than Alvaro Noboa, the difference was more than compensated for by the generous coverage provided by the private press, television, and radio.

After taking office, Correa participated in eight elections and plebiscite campaigns: the popular consultation of 2007; the election of members for the Constituent Assembly that same year; the referendum approving the 2008 constitution; his first reelection in 2009; the consultation-referendum of 2011; his second reelection in 2013; elections of mayors, prefects, and other authorities in 2015; and the presidential election of Lenín Moreno in 2017. In none of these electoral events was the vote of citizens entirely free, as will be seen below.

Due to the perception that there were economic asymmetries in the electoral campaigns, the norms initially issued by the government and later included in the constitution and in the Democracy Code, to guarantee an equitable distribution of electoral expenses, were well received. These rules provided for the state to finance candidates' advertising under equal conditions and prohibited them from using their own economic resources or those of their contributors. Many believed that these provisions would put an end to the influence of money in politics since candidates would have equal economic resources to advertise. Supposedly, this public financing of election campaigns would democratize them since the candidates would not be limited by high campaign costs. In addition, the danger that those who made economic contributions could condition government decisions would be eliminated.

These virtuous effects did not materialize or were imperceptible; instead, electoral inequalities worsened. In addition to the partisan funding provided by the state, the president as a candidate spent as much money as he wanted on his campaigns and consultations, not from his own pocket or from his sponsors, but from the fiscal coffers.

In fact, Correa made ample use of government propaganda, which had become massive since the day he took office. In the weekly Saturday broadcasts, in advertising spots, and in mandatory television and radio broadcasts, the work of the government was praised and opposing politicians and candidates were discredited. This occurred in violation of the constitution and the Democracy Code. The latter stipulated that no advertising could be done before the start of an electoral campaign, or in the forty-eight hours prior to voting, and that the government could not advertise its work while voting was in progress. However, Correa even went further. In the 2007 referendum he issued propaganda for the yes vote on the day of the elections, even though it was forbidden,[1] and in the 2013 presidential campaign he held a Saturday session promoting his candidacy one day before the election. With his usual brazenness, he justified these abuses by saying that the government was not issuing propaganda but rather informing public opinion about the work it was doing for the good of the country.

Public assets such as airplanes, helicopters, automobiles, and tax money were put at the service of his electoral campaigns, paying for trips, lodging, meals, per diems, and transportation for rallies, as well as for publicists, journalists, advisors, cameramen, security personnel, and an army of activists and claques, either hired for that purpose or often taken from the ranks of public employees.[2] Thanks to these advantages, Correa was able to visit as many cities and towns as he wished, to make contact with a greater number of voters, and to get information about his electoral activities in the press and on radio and television. Lacking these instruments and means, other candidates found it impossible to attain the scope and impact of the government's election or plebiscite campaigns.

The same thing happened with the state media. Their information and interviews were given much more space than those that the opposition candidates had. At the same time, public radios and press broadcast the election rallies of Correa and Alianza PAIS live, fiscal money was distributed in a clientelistic and populist way, works were inaugurated or cornerstones were laid, and bureaucrats were forced to perform proselytizing tasks.

All of the above occurred despite the fact that Article 115 of the constitution prohibited "the use of State resources and infrastructure, as well as government advertising, for election campaigning at all levels of government" and mandated that "sanctions be established for those who fail to comply" with this provision. Both the National Electoral Council (CNE) and the comptroller not only allowed such abuses and illegalities to occur but also encouraged the presidential candidate and the Alianza PAIS candidates to illicitly use public resources in their electoral activities.[3]

Since the CNE was composed exclusively of Alianza PAIS members or sympathizers and was also dependent on presidential volition, not only did it not take any measures to prevent those violations and evident abuses from occurring, but it also did not impose sanctions. Nothing similar had happened before in Ecuador in the electoral campaigns of the second half of the twentieth century.

The privileges surrounding Correa's electoral campaigns did not end there. Taking advantage of its unlimited power and violating the Democracy Code, the government extorted companies working for the state and had them pay campaign invoices and make economic contributions. In exchange, it randomly awarded them contracts for public works, without bidding processes and with excessive prices, as seen in part III, chapter 15.

The other candidates sorely lacked those economic, political, bureaucratic, logistical, and budgetary resources that were so beneficial in the election campaigns of Rafael Correa and Alianza PAIS. Instead, they had to submit to the restrictions established in the election laws, strictly enforced by the CNE, regarding private financing; the number, time, and length of advertising spots; and the prohibition of advertising before the start dates of election campaigns. In the meantime, the government candidates did as they pleased.

In view of the decline of Correa's electoral capital and that of Alianza PAIS, these undemocratic advantages seemed insufficient for the presidential reelection of 2013. From 82 percent of the vote obtained in the 2007 referendum, he had fallen to 47 percent in the 2011 consultation-referendum.

In order to win again, Correa ordered a change in election rules, despite the fact that Article 117 of the constitution prohibited election reforms during the year prior to the date of an election. The supreme leader, taking advantage of certain reforms made to the Democracy Code by the National Assembly, issued an unconstitutional veto in which he included a provision that would allow Alianza PAIS to obtain legislative representation that did not correspond to the vote obtained by its lists. This veto also violated Articles 115, 116, and 138 of the constitution, regarding the right of minorities to have parliamentary representation and stipulating that the participation of the different parties in the National Assembly and municipal councils be proportional to the number of votes received at the polls.

With this reform, the mechanism for proportionately allocating seats in the National Assembly was modified, disproportionately rewarding the list of candidates that obtained the highest number of votes. Furthermore, it created new voting districts in the provinces of Guayas, Pichincha, and Manabí, which accounted for 51 percent of the national electorate. Through these malicious legal ploys, in the 2013 elections Alianza PAIS obtained 73 percent of the seats in the National Assembly with 53 percent of the votes.

The presidential veto was so arbitrary and abusive that, contrary to the provisions of Article 115 of the constitution, it suppressed the legal prohibition for authorities to use official advertising and public resources in election campaigns for the benefit of government candidates. It also added a provision never reviewed or discussed by the National Assembly and left its application to the discretion of the biased CNE. This provision prohibited the media—obviously private media because the official media were not subject to any regulation—from publishing news and reports that could directly or indirectly promote the different candidates. Journalists' unions and political groups denounced the unconstitutionality of these election reforms. For several months the Constitutional Court did not issue a ruling; it finally did so the day before elections were called but without objecting to the unconstitutionality of the articles contained in the presidential veto.

In an equally unconstitutional manner, the CNE issued ad hoc regulations and approved resolutions that interfered with the work of political parties and movements and accommodated the electoral process to the interests of the government. It ordered CNE delegates to oversee the selection of candidates even though that matter was the sole responsibility of the political organizations. Voting districts were zoned to favor Alianza PAIS, including some rural voters controlled by the government's clientelist programs. The CNE determined that the advertising expenses incurred by the candidates prior to the call for elections were to be imputed to the maximum amounts they could spend in their campaigns, for the clear purpose of harming the opposition since the president as a candidate was politically proselytizing 365 days a year. It also forced the political movements to re-register, without any legal basis to justify doing so, in order to delay the start of their election campaigns. Thanks to the negative reaction from public opinion, the intention to control social networks and prohibit the early disclosure of election results before the CNE reported the official figures was thwarted.

Not only election rules were adapted to the political interests of the president and his party due to the authoritarian exercise of power. The adaptations also had to do with the single-party composition of the CNE, with members or sympathizers of Alianza PAIS and former government officials—instead of a pluralistic composition with the participation of the majority parties, as had been the case for several decades.

These two factors led to the elimination of the traditional independence of the CNE. Such was its submission that many times the dictator publicly ordered which decisions were to be made, and these were immediately issued by its members. To justify this ominous political dependence, one of the CNE presidents, Domingo Paredes, said that "morals and ethics obliged it to act outside the law." He was referring to the illegal resolution for political parties and movements to re-register. After confessing that presidential authority outweighed electoral authority in certain cases, he acknowledged his submission by saying, "Thanks to your inspiration, Mr. President," I have been able to perform my duties.

For the aforementioned reasons, in election campaigns, popular consultations, and referendums, there was a marked asymmetry of resources, means, and instruments between the campaigns of the ruling party and the opposition. The CNE applied legal norms to opposition candidates and let the president-candidate and his cronies do whatever they wanted. All of this prevented the electoral processes from being free, equitable, and fair as required by democratic principles.

These electoral inequities, privileges, and injustices, which appeared as soon as Rafael Correa took office as president, were manifested for the first time in the popular consultation of April 2007; were repeated in the elections, consultations, and referendums of the following years; worsened in the presidential elections of 2013; and were ubiquitous in the elections of mayors, prefects, and other officials in 2014 and in the presidential election of 2017. Even though Correa was not a candidate in the last two, he acted as if he were and worried about the risk of losing them because of the decline in his popularity. He got involved in election campaigns and used his power and influence in such a disproportionate way that many voters voted for Lenín Moreno while thinking of Rafael Correa. As he had been doing for a decade, Correa put all the state's means, instruments, resources, and propaganda at the service of Moreno's campaign.

Thus, the economic "monopoly" denounced by Correa, which in previous voting had supposedly prevented competitive elections and the free expression of the citizens' votes, was replaced by the illegal, undemocratic, and overwhelming political "monopoly" of the government. The president and his party proceeded in this way, moved by the Leninist conviction that, once they had attained power, they had to keep it whatever the price. According to his own discourse and his party's, this was so that the Citizens Revolution would not be interrupted. In reality, it was so that the dictator-president could rule Ecuador for life and Alianza PAIS could remain in power. Since Correa and his party had taken office through the power of the electorate, and not by the strength of arms, to remain in office they needed to win every election, consultation, or referendum they participated in. They therefore believed that the electoral bodies, rules, and procedures should be aligned in that direction.

Rafael Correa's charismatic personality, his populist rhetoric, the economic boom, and a propitious political situation influenced his electoral wins in 2006, 2007, and 2008. The legal, political, economic, administrative, and publicity structure he had set up through his dictatorial use of power also played an important role in his subsequent victories.

In the elections, consultations, and referendums, citizens were not prevented from voting, nor were they coerced while approaching the polls or excluded from the voter registry. At the polling stations there was a predominance of independent representatives or members of parties other than Alianza PAIS. In many voting precincts, journalists and representatives of the different political movements watched over the opening of the ballot boxes and the counting of the votes, and the number of voters usually coincided with the number of ballots deposited in the ballot boxes. It could thus be said that the voting precincts acted properly and that results were not altered during the voting and the first, on-site counting.[4]

The same cannot be said of the provincial electoral tribunals and particularly of the CNE or of the vote centralization and count verification centers and the bureaucratic staff that worked in this organization and the officials that conducted the final count using electronic processes.

In the past, the Supreme Electoral Tribunal (TSE), which oversaw the first election of President Rafael Correa, had been made up of representatives from the majority parties. It was therefore an independent and reliable body. However, as seen in part II, chapter 9, a few weeks after the inauguration of the government of the Citizens Revolution, most of the members of the tribunal and particularly its president, Jorge Acosta, had put themselves at the service of Correa and his ideology. Acosta did not reject the unconstitutional call for a popular consultation made by the president of the republic. In fact, he called the consultation despite the National Congress's resolution that restricted it, and he abusively removed some fifty deputies. Furthermore, both in the popular consultation and in the constitutional referendum, he was complaisant about the government's use of public resources.

Since the CNE was composed in keeping with the 2008 constitution, solely with members or allies of Alianza PAIS, this body became the diligent executor of the government's orders, so that the government could win any election, consultation, or referendum, regardless of the legality of the means used for that purpose. To the extent that these procedures affected the free expression of the popular will, the regime of the Citizens Revolution participated in an underhanded form of electoral fraud. Something similar happened in all the electoral events of the following years, as was seen in preceding pages.

Some of the questions of the 2011 referendum would have been rejected by the voters if the requirement that the yes option must obtain an absolute majority of votes had not been eliminated. The unconstitutional system of legislative seat allocation and the introduction of additional voting districts in the most highly populated provinces made it possible for Alianza PAIS to obtain two-thirds of the members of the National Assembly in the 2013 elections, without the voters' having that intention.

In the 2006 presidential elections, Correa won neatly thanks to his high levels of popularity, but not in subsequent elections in which he used the means and power of the state, manipulated election laws, and relied on the CNE to support him in his aim of winning every election, consultation, and referendum. It can therefore be concluded that during Correa's administration—since there were no fair election campaigns, no equal rights and responsibilities for the candidates, and no independent and fair electoral tribunals—the election results were not fair and reliable but somehow fraudulent.

These were the conditions in which the presidential campaign, first- and second-round voting, and ballot counting were conducted during the 2017 presidential election.

An exit poll conducted by Cedatos announced Guillermo Lasso's win with a seven-point lead over his opponent, Lenín Moreno. That pollster had been accurate in all its exit polls for presidential elections since 1978. Meanwhile, a rapid count by Participación Ciudadana estimated a virtual tie. The first reports of the CNE confirmed the results of the poll, and the trend continued for some time. In those circumstances, the report on the final count, to be broadcasted by all the media, was untimely suspended with the excuse that the computer system had broken down. Three hours later, when the CNE report was resumed, Moreno appeared in first place with 88 percent of the votes counted. Minutes later, when more than 95 percent of the votes were in, CNE President Juan Carlos Pozo confirmed Moreno's victory with 51.13 percent of the votes compared to 48.8 percent for Guillermo Lasso. These provisional results were ratified by the CNE two days later, and Moreno was proclaimed president-elect. Lasso's and other citizens' requests for an official recount were denied.

An OAS observer mission composed of former presidents with ties to Correa endorsed the official tallies. Ruth Hidalgo, the director of Participación Ciudadana, and Polibio Córdova, of the polling firm, were intimidated by Correa, who threatened them with criminal prosecution. The former was not prosecuted, but the latter was and, after a lengthy judicial proceeding, was acquitted. In several cities, especially in Quito, there were spontaneous popular demonstrations that lasted several weeks, in protest against the electoral fraud attributed to the National Electoral Council. The demonstrations in the capital surrounded the CNE headquarters and only ceased when the demonstrators were removed by the police and prevented from resuming their protests.

Months later, Nicaraguan Eduardo Mangas, the person who had been Moreno's assistant during his stay in Geneva and also during the presidential campaign and who was appointed the president's chief of staff, reported that Moreno's victory had been fraudulent. In a private conversation with Alianza PAIS leaders, recorded and leaked to the press, he confessed it in these terms: "We lost the first round, and we lost the second round as well." "There was no win."

The electoral fraud suggested by this statement might well have occurred since the person who made the statement was very well informed and close to candidate Moreno. In addition, it is feasible because of the following facts.

As mentioned before, the CNE was composed solely of members from Alianza PAIS. This composition meant not having vigilant observers and dissenting voices in a position to investigate and denounce alterations of electoral results. The director of the technical department, the heads of the different units, and the officials in charge of collecting and digitally counting the results of thousands of polling stations also belonged to this political movement.

In September 2016, the CNE had issued a regulation that reformed the Democracy Code and made it possible to break the chain of custody for voting records. Instead of being delivered to the provincial electoral tribunal, they were sent to a scanning center. The tally obtained through this procedure was not announced as provisional but was rather considered definitive, without a count in the presence of the delegates of candidate Lasso, as had occurred in previous electoral processes.[5]

The possibility that electoral frauds of this nature could be carried out by manipulating digital procedures during the counting of votes had been demonstrated in Nicolás Maduro's 2013 presidential election. Years later, something similar was done by Evo Morales in Bolivia in the 2019 presidential election. In both cases, as also occurred in Ecuador, the information on election results was interrupted, claiming issues with the computer system. Once reports resumed, Maduro was in first place and was declared the winner; Morales, on the other hand, reached the percentage of votes that allowed him to avoid the second round of voting.

Not in vain, the grateful president-dictator, days before the end of his government, awarded CNE President Carlos Pozo the Grand Cross of the National Order of Merit (Gran Cruz de la Orden Nacional al Mérito), a medal that Correa bestowed on Pozo at a ceremony held at the Carondelet Palace. Correa also got Pozo out of the country by obtaining a position for him in the OAS offices in Washington, D.C.

NOTES

1. I recall that radio stations were profusely broadcasting propaganda in favor of the yes option when I went to vote that morning.

2. In the 2008 referendum, the Alianza PAIS representative to the Supreme Electoral Tribunal, Eduardo Paredes, even said that it was "an obligation of the employees working for the regime to campaign for the yes option" (*El Comercio*, August 27, 2008).

3. When the National Electoral Council, after the 2011 referendum and consultation and at the insistence of public opinion, asked Correa to render accounts on electoral expenses, he refused to do so, and one of his ministers said that he had not spent a cent. The CNE did not take any measures to compel him to submit that information.

4. In the 2009 presidential election won by Correa, however, opposition candidates, particularly former president Lucio Gutiérrez, denounced electoral fraud, but the CNE did not authorize an investigation.

5. Sol Borja interviewed former National Electoral Council member Fausto Camacho on April 4, 2017. He concluded by saying that "the CNE did whatever it wanted."

PART IV

Perspectives on Authoritarianism

Chapter 19

The International Community

The international community did not pay due attention to the early-on dictatorial drift of the governments of Hugo Chávez, Evo Morales, Rafael Correa, and Daniel Ortega, despite their habitual authoritarian behavior and their gradual takeover of state entities.

Upon inaugurating their mandates, the first three ignored the constitutional order in place and announced that they would replace the constitution with a new one to be drafted by a constituent assembly convened for that purpose. Although the last of the four took a different path, all of them intended to diminish the attributions of the other functions of the state, weaken the independence of the justice system, and concentrate absolute power in the presidency—in short, to eliminate key elements of the democratic system. During the first months of their terms, they restricted freedoms, particularly freedom of expression, and persecuted those who criticized their authoritarianism. As time passed, they would violate human rights, and Maduro and Ortega would commit crimes against humanity.

Their authoritarian practices, which undermined the rule of law, did not initially attract the attention of Latin American governments, the Organization of American States, the international press, regional political leaders, and human rights organizations. As a result, very few thought of calling them undemocratic governments. Some did not simply because they had been elected by the people and there was a constitutional order, at least formally, and the republican institutions continued to function, others because the authoritarian actions had been occasional and legitimized by the vote of the citizens, and still others because these governments did not fit the traditional model of dictatorship since they had not overthrown a constitutional government and had not come to power through a military coup. Many did not consider these governments undemocratic because they seemed to be aiming at correcting long-standing social injustices through a social revolution that justified all their excesses; most, because they were supposedly progressive leaders who had replaced corrupt politicians and parties that had served the oligarchies and imperialism.

The military dictatorships that had ruled in some countries in previous decades had not enjoyed the same tolerance that the international community was allowing the new autocracies emerging in Latin America. All of the former had been criticized, denounced, and fought by political, social, and intellectual sectors that still held the same beliefs but were reacting differently.

However, the fact that the twenty-first-century dictatorships had won elections, popular consultations, and referendums could not justify their abuse of democratic institutions or their disregard for the constitutional order, even for the constitutions they themselves dictated. Besides, it is neither legitimate nor democratic for fundamental elements of the republican regime to be abolished or denaturalized because citizens have chosen a particular option, nor for freedom of expression to be restricted, human rights violated, and opponents and demonstrators judicially persecuted. Years ago, governments that indulged in these abuses of power were considered dictatorial, and some were overthrown—among many others, those of the Somoza family in Nicaragua, Alfredo Stroessner in Paraguay, and the brutal Augusto Pinochet in Chile, and even others elected by the people and not at all repressive, such as those of Abdalá Bucaram, Jamil Mahuad, and Lucio Gutiérrez in Ecuador.

Nor was it possible to justify the disappearance of the rule of law with the excuse that these governments were undertaking a social revolution that would eliminate poverty and put an end to unjust inequalities. First, because Latin America's important advances in the economic and social realms had been achieved by governments that respected democratic institutions and protected citizens' freedoms and guarantees. Second, because it was not legally and morally justifiable to defend abuses of power and disregard for the constitutional order with the excuse that a social revolution was being pursued. Third, because the economic and social results initially achieved were rather modest if one takes into account the enormous economic resources at the disposal of these new dictators, thanks to the favorable international economic situation. Fourth, because when the international economic situation turned against them and the negative consequences of their misguided economic policies became apparent, unemployment grew and poverty and destitution worsened in Venezuela, Ecuador, and Nicaragua, reaching catastrophic levels in the first of these.[1]

In this regard, it is worth mentioning the reflection not of conservative politicians but rather of former leaders of the communist youth in Chile during the government of Salvador Allende, leaders who later abandoned revolutionary militancy and renounced Marxism-Leninism. After saying a mea culpa, they say they have "learned that any political formula that subjugates human beings is not valid as a path of social redemption"; they accept that "no type of authoritarianism or totalitarianism deserves to be presented as a progressive alternative"; they acknowledge that the bloody aftermath of the overthrow of Allende's socialist government made them "reflect seriously on pluralism and the so-called formal democracy as permanent values and not as tactical phases to be overcome by a popular or proletarian democracy." They conclude by affirming that "no egalitarian dream that involves weakening or suppressing [formal democracy] can be considered acceptable" (Ottone and Muñoz Riveros 2018, 18, 110, and 148).

As seen previously, there were many reasons for the international community, particularly Latin America's governments and its political, social, intellectual, and civil-society leaders, to express their concern about the dictatorial drift of Venezuela, Bolivia, Ecuador, and Nicaragua.

The countries of the Americas and the Caribbean had committed themselves to defending democracy and protecting its institutions when they unanimously signed the Inter-American Democratic Charter.[2] They envisioned it as an international legal instrument that would help safeguard democratic institutions, prevent the return of dictatorships, and punish states that deviated from its principles and norms. To this end, they determined the elements that a political regime had to meet to be considered democratic, enshrined the immutable nature of human rights, and empowered the governments of the Americas and the Caribbean to act collectively to prevent the violation of "essential elements of representative democracy." All of this was happening regularly in the governments of Chávez, Morales, Ortega, and Correa since the day they assumed power.

For several years, the mandates contained in the Inter-American Democratic Charter[3] were set aside by Latin American governments and the regional entity representing them, the Organization of American States. Even though the process whereby the aforementioned presidents were methodically tearing down democratic institutions and replacing them with those of an autocratic regime was advancing relentlessly, the bodies of the Organization of American States were not convened at the initiative of any country or by Secretary General José Miguel Insulza,[4] even when in the four countries, particularly in Venezuela, the rule of law had disappeared and the norms of the Inter-American Democratic Charter were being blatantly and systematically violated. It was paradoxical that members of the U.S. Congress, spokespersons of the U.S. State Department, and civil-society organizations in that country denounced the abuses to democracy and freedom occurring in Venezuela and in the other twenty-first-century dictatorships and put them under the magnifying glass of the Inter-American Democratic Charter[5] while, on the other hand, the "Latin American brothers," represented by their governments, congresses, politicians, academics, and civil-society organizations, remained silent. Politicians from the Southern Cone countries, who had received protection and assistance from Venezuelan democracy during the years in which they were persecuted by the military dictatorships in their countries, were part of this tolerant silence.

With the tragic and even criminal outrages against democracy and human rights during the government of Nicolás Maduro, and the economic, social, political, human, and moral disaster in Venezuela, some promoted dialogue between the opposition and the government so that together they could find a solution to the political crisis. Former Spanish president José Luis Rodríguez Zapatero, closely linked to the Maduro government, was the most diligent of these intermediaries. Due to the Venezuelan government's refusal to reinstate democratic institutions, however, the initiatives that took place for this purpose did not yield results; instead, they helped the dictatorship overcome critical circumstances that had threatened its ability to remain in power.

Four events changed the contemplative position of Latin America, its governments, political leaders, public opinion, and the regional organization in the face of the twenty-first-century dictatorships. The first was the death of Venezuela's president, the influential, popular, and prodigious benefactor of the Bolivarian Revolution. The second was the replacement of the governments that had supported him by presidents interested in the return of democratic institutions and respect for human rights. The third was the election of a new secretary general of the OAS, committed to reestablishing republican institutions and critical of the tyrannical drift of the Maduro and Ortega dictatorships. Finally, there was the extreme deterioration suffered by democracy and freedom in Venezuela and Nicaragua, countries in which electoral fraud, criminal repression of popular demonstrations, and the torture and murder of opponents had become daily occurrences.

The international community's first reactions to these fateful events were twofold.

In 2015, numerous former presidents,[6] concerned about the democratic regression in Latin America, formed the Democratic Initiative of Spain and the Americas (IDEA for its acronym in Spanish), to contribute to restoring the rule of law and effectively protecting human rights. With that aim, they published manifestos, organized conferences, and participated in forums to address the problems affecting democracy, freedoms, and human rights in the aforementioned Latin American countries, mainly in Venezuela.

Faced with the OAS's inability to handle the Venezuelan political crisis, American countries (2017)[7] formed the Lima Group to monitor developments and seek a peaceful solution to the crisis. The first pronouncements were aimed at defending the legitimacy of the National Assembly and the government of Juan Guaidó, seen as the political players that could guide the reestablishment of democratic order. At the same time, they challenged the legitimacy of Maduro's second presidency and of the constituent assembly he had convened, and they denounced his abuses and crimes.

This new and propitious international political context was used by certain Latin American governments to broach within the OAS the need for the regional organization to assume the responsibility for finding a peaceful solution to the Venezuelan political crisis.

The election of Uruguayan Luis Almagro as secretary general (2015) marked a turning point in his predecessor's policy of appeasement. Almagro's positions were surprising and unexpected since he had been the foreign minister for President José Mujica and a member of the left-wing party Broad Front (Frente Amplio), both linked to the governments of Chávez and Maduro. Turned into an interpreter of Latin Americans and concerned about the dictatorial and then tyrannical drift of the Venezuelan government, Almagro has been a tenacious challenger of that regime as well as an outspoken ally of those who, inside and outside the country, are fighting for the recovery of democratic institutions.

Almagro cited the dictatorial nature of Maduro's government, which he treats as such in his public statements, and the illegitimate nature of the constituent assembly that Maduro convened. At the same time, he recognized the National Assembly and President Juan Guaidó as legitimate heads of the executive and legislative functions. Subsequently, he expressed similar positions on Ortega's dictatorship in Nicaragua. Almagro's actions, consistent with the Inter-American Democratic Charter, have given the regional organization a strong voice in the battle that the democracies of the American continent are waging to put an end to the dictatorships in Venezuela and Nicaragua.

The same thing did not occur with the Bolivian and Ecuadorian dictatorships, whose governments continued to be considered democratic by the international and regional communities.

Despite the fact that Evo Morales had taken over all the powers of the state, although without reaching the extremes of Venezuela and Nicaragua, the secretary general and the bodies of the OAS ignored the Bolivian president's authoritarian behavior and the violations of democracy and freedom contrary to the Inter-American Democratic Charter. Almagro even justified the nomination of Evo Morales for a fourth term in office, despite the fact that it was prohibited by the constitution and the people had voted against a fourth term in the referendum Morales called. However, Almagro's position was different when Morales tried to win the presidential election by means of election fraud, which the secretary general condemned in the strongest terms.

The deterioration suffered by Ecuadorian democracy was no different since President Rafael Correa, years before, had already taken over all the powers of the state; imposed severe restrictions on public freedoms, especially those of expression and protest; and judicially persecuted his opponents. Maliciously, he had managed to get the National Assembly, controlled by him and not the people, to approve the indefinite reelection of the president of the republic, although at the last minute he decided not to run for a fourth term.

In early 2019, the Permanent Council of the OAS resolved not to recognize the illegitimate reelection of Nicolás Maduro for a new term in office and called for electing a legitimate president through free, transparent, and reliable voting overseen by an independent electoral body, so that Venezuela could have "an authentically democratic government" (OAS 2019a). The General Assembly of the Organization of American States, meeting in Medellín in 2019, resolved to recognize the person who had been appointed by the National Assembly as Venezuela's representative to the OAS, until new presidential elections were held and a democratically elected government was in place. At the same time, it urged "that free, fair, transparent and legitimate presidential elections be called."[8]

The OAS has challenged Maduro's illegal reelection and the unconstitutional meeting of the constituent assembly convened by him and recognized the decisions made by the National Assembly and President Juan Guaidó, whom it considers legitimate representatives of the Venezuelan people. It has also condemned arbitrary detentions; the murder of opponents; extrajudicial executions; torture and sexual assaults; the existence of political prisoners; the obstruction of protesters' access to medical care; state terrorism practiced by police and paramilitary forces; and the criminalization of political and social leaders, protesters, journalists, and human rights defenders.

In October 2020, the OAS General Assembly did not recognize the Venezuelan National Electoral Council's call to hold parliamentary elections on December 6, 2020, to renew the National Assembly in office. The OAS resolution on the lack of minimum democratic conditions (AG/RES. 2963 [L-O/20]) cited "minimum conditions for guaranteeing the organization of democratic electoral processes in keeping with international standards" and stated that voting should meet the requirements, then nonexistent, of "freedom, justice, impartiality, and transparency, with guarantees for the participation of all political actors and citizens . . . and with independent and credible international electoral observation." At the same time, it urged "the calling, as promptly as possible, of free, fair, transparent, and legitimate presidential elections" and expressed its concern that the legitimate National Assembly presided over by Juan Guaidó might no longer be recognized as valid.

These and other actions deployed by the international community to have the Maduro regime replaced by a democratic government have not brought about the fall of the Venezuelan dictatorship, even though Juan Guaidó was recognized as the president by fifty-nine countries and was treated as Venezuela's head of state by the governments that weigh the most in world politics—something totally unusual. This fact, alongside the increasingly serious abuses of power and human rights violations, led some thirty countries to impose sanctions, mainly economic, on the Venezuelan government for the purpose of weakening it.[9]

The severest sanctions, imposed by the United States, are equivalent to those imposed on North Korea, Syria, Iran, and Cuba. They have led to a sizeable cost (billions of dollars) to the Venezuelan economy and affected hundreds of people in Maduro's government, including family members, high-ranking government officials, military commanders, prosecutors, and judges.[10] All of them were banned from entering the United States and had their mostly ill-gotten funds in bank accounts, investments, businesses, and properties in U.S. territory frozen. The same thing has occurred with government-owned or government-related companies. Third parties or companies that carry out transactions to produce and export oil, gold, minerals, and other goods also run the risk of suffering similar economic sanctions.

Such sanctions have been imposed by U.S. presidents Barack Obama, Donald Trump, and Joe Biden when serious human rights violations, punitive repression of peaceful popular demonstrations, and election frauds occurred, and when the unconstitutional constituent assembly was convened and met and a new National Assembly was formed. In addition to these sanctions, the United States has added openly direct support to those fighting to reestablish the rule of law[11] and has recognized Juan Guaidó and the National Assembly as the legitimate representatives of Venezuelan democracy.

The European Union initially hoped that the Venezuelan conflict could be resolved through dialogue. Disappointed by the failure of that option, the constant deterioration of democratic institutions, the repeated and serious violations of human rights, and the bloody repression of popular demonstrations, the European Union opted to apply various sanctions against the Maduro government. These consisted of the seizure of weapons and equipment used by police and paramilitary forces to repress demonstrators, the seizure of assets held by high-ranking Venezuelan dignitaries in EU territory, and the prohibition of their entry into the EU. It has recognized the National Assembly as the valid legislative body and Juan Guaidó as president of Venezuela. For its part, the European Parliament has said that, if the Venezuelan situation does not change, "it will use all the instruments at its disposal" in order to find a peaceful and negotiated solution.

U.S. Attorney General William Barr, invoking the United Nations Convention against Transnational Organized Crime (UNCTOC), issued arrest warrants against a dozen officials of the Venezuelan dictatorship. The list includes President Nicolás Maduro, Constituent Assembly President Diosdado Cabello, Supreme Court of Justice President Maikel Moreno, and Defense Minister Vladimir Padrino. The charges brought by the Attorney

General's Office include the crimes of terrorism, drug trafficking, and money laundering. The rewards offered for information leading to these officials' capture and bringing them to justice are fifteen million dollars for the first and ten million dollars for the others. The U.S. attorney general's decision places the leaders of the Venezuelan dictatorship among the most wanted criminals within the Venezuelan justice system and means that there is no statute of limitations on the crimes committed by them.

When a call was made to elect a new National Assembly in Venezuela and when elections were later held in December 2020, the United States, the European Union, the United Kingdom, the Lima Group, and the OAS first spoke out against the results and then refused to recognize them, considering them illegal, undemocratic, and fraudulent. The Europeans hardened their position by imposing new sanctions for "human rights violations and crimes against humanity" committed by the Venezuelan government. In addition to freezing assets, these sanctions prohibited European entities from being involved with Maduro's government and prohibited officials and employees of the Venezuelan regime from entering EU territories.

Meanwhile, the White House has also announced that it is suspending and restricting some members of the Nicaraguan government's entry into the United States, including Ortega's wife, military commanders, judges, and prosecutors. It has grounded these sanctions on the persecution of opponents, the corruption of regime officials, and the attacks on democracy and human rights. The day that Ortega was sworn in, it canceled the visas of 116 Ortega supporters because of their complicity in undermining democracy and human rights. Furthermore, the U.S. Department of the Treasury has frozen the deposits of nine high-level government officials.

After the fraudulent Nicaraguan presidential elections of November 2021, with the "triumph" of sole candidate Daniel Ortega, the U.S. Congress passed the RENACER Act, as the result of a bipartisan consensus, to contribute to the reestablishment of democratic institutions through free and competitive elections. The act grants President Biden broad powers to impose new and harsher sanctions on Nicaragua, which could include exclusion from the Free Trade Agreement with the United States and the limitation of loans from Washington-based multilateral agencies. He also has the power to extend and toughen those sanctions already applied to the Ortega–Murillo family, high-level officials, and police and army commanders involved in acts of corruption, human rights violations, and obstruction of free elections.[12]

For its part, the European Union extended the economic sanctions it had imposed on the president and the vice president to include two other children, officials close to Ortega, the president of the Supreme Electoral Council, police commanders, and directors of the Telecommunications Institute, for a total of twenty-one people and three entities. The United Kingdom and

Switzerland have also imposed economic sanctions on members of the Nicaraguan government and on certain public institutions and companies, as well as on Vice President Rosario Murillo.

The international community has never before mobilized in such a broad and committed way to defend and restore democracy, freedom, and human rights in Latin America, specifically in Venezuela and Nicaragua. This is a remarkable twenty-first-century expression of world solidarity, committed to defending the humanist principles and values that inspire the peoples of the West. This international battle to put an end to the dictatorships of Nicolás Maduro and Daniel Ortega has been led by the United States, not by Latin America.

With few exceptions, governments, politicians, political parties, intellectuals, and civil-society activists belonging to the Latin American Left, even non-Marxists, have identified ideologically and politically with the dictatorships of Hugo Chávez, Nicolás Maduro, Evo Morales, Rafael Correa, and Daniel Ortega. The ones who did not remained silent looked the other way or shielded themselves behind vague or ambiguous remarks. Quite a few continued to defend them, even though the governments of Venezuela and Nicaragua had become tyrannies that ruthlessly violated human rights, committed crimes against humanity, and stayed in power by means of scandalous electoral frauds. In recent years, because such outrages have become evident and commonplace, even when individuals and groups have not explicitly censured the dictatorships of Maduro and Ortega, they have begun to distance themselves from those regimes.

The governments of Presidents Evo Morales and Luis Arce (in Bolivia), Tabaré Vázquez (in Uruguay), Alberto Fernández (in Argentina), and Andrés Manuel López Obrador (in Mexico) have even abstained from supporting OAS resolutions condemning the dictatorships of Maduro and Ortega for organizing fraudulent electoral processes and preventing citizens from freely expressing their will at the ballot boxes. To justify their stance, they have used the excuse that "external interference cannot be allowed" in the affairs of a state and "the principle of nonintervention cannot be set aside"—as though the Inter-American Democratic Charter, of which their countries are signatories, did not oblige them to act collectively when there is an unconstitutional alteration of the constitutional regime that seriously impairs the democratic order in a member state.[13]

Former Brazilian president Lula da Silva has stated that it was "shameful that the self-proclaimed president [Guaidó] was recognized" and "such a low blow should be erased from history" (teleSURtv.net 2019). With regard to Ortega, Lula da Silva said that he advised him "not to abandon democracy because when a leader in power considers himself irreplaceable, a little dictatorship creeps in" (*Confidencial* 2021). To justify indefinite presidential terms in office, he asked: "Why can Angela Merkel be in power for sixteen years and Ortega not? Why can Margaret Thatcher be in power for twelve years and Chávez not?" (*Cronista* 2022). In mid-2019, former Uruguayan president José Mujica accepted that the Venezuelan government was "a dictatorship" but that the Caracas protesters "should not get in front of the little tanks" (*El Comercio* 2019b). Later on, in 2021, together with some one hundred intellectuals from the Latin American Left, he signed a letter repudiating Ortega's government.

Regarding Ortega's reelection, the Communist Party of Chile said, "The Nicaraguan people massively went to the polls to democratically elect officials, and they have done so in peace, in accordance with their institutions and the laws in force."[14] The Workers Party of Brazil celebrated "Ortega's victory" as a "popular and democratic" act and affirmed that the results demonstrated "the population's support for a project whose main objective is the construction of a socially just and egalitarian country."[15]

Behind the Left's political connivance with authoritarian and tyrannical regimes lies the moral superiority with which some of its members tend to credit themselves. This posturing leads them to justify all kinds of violations of freedom of expression, electoral frauds, widespread corruption, extrajudicial executions, judicial persecution, repression, imprisonment, dictatorship, and totalitarianism if those who commit these outrages are their comrades and propose to effect a social revolution—in which case such actions are not only justifiable but also laudable.

In the face of the barbaric repression of the Venezuelan and Nicaraguan peoples, the cruel tortures inflicted on those imprisoned, the extrajudicial executions of protesters, and the widespread abuses of human rights, Pope Francis has remained surprisingly silent.

When these criminal abuses extended to places of worship, churchgoers, priests, missionaries, and bishops in Nicaragua, twenty-six former Latin American presidents took an inventory and in August 2022 called for the pope to take "a firm stance in defense of the Nicaraguan people and their religious freedom." After stating that he was following the situation in Nicaragua closely, "with concern and sorrow," the pope limited himself to expressing his conviction and hope that, "through open and sincere dialogue, the basis for a respectful and peaceful coexistence can still be found" (*Vatican News* 2022).

The pope took a similar position on the tyrannical dictatorship of Maduro, whom he welcomed at the Vatican. The few pronouncements he has made on Venezuela have basically encouraged "peace, coexistence, agreements, reconciliation, and unity" to prevail and have condemned "the arrogance of the powerful," without naming the powerful. Meanwhile, he has criticized and opposed "any outside intervention" in Venezuelan affairs. He has not openly referred to the economic, social, human, and migratory tragedy experienced by the peoples of either Venezuela or Nicaragua.

In his first official visit to South America (2014), Pope Francis visited dictator Rafael Correa in Ecuador and dictator Evo Morales in Bolivia and the following year Fidel Castro in Havana. He has claimed to have a "human relationship" with the latter's brother Raúl, but he has not referred to the inhuman repression and draconian convictions of the young Cubans who protested in the streets in 2021, demanding democracy and freedom.

Nonetheless, bishops and episcopal conferences in Venezuela and Nicaragua have criticized and denounced the abuses and crimes of those illegitimately in power and called for them to respect human dignity and integrity and the fact that humans are entitled to exercise fully their rights and freedoms.

In this somber panorama of Latin American democracy, there have been important legal advances that could contribute to joining forces to address one of the major issues. Colombian president Iván Duque requested that the Inter-American Court of Human Rights determine whether "the prohibition of indefinite reelection is compatible with the American Convention on Human Rights." The court determined that indefinite reelection "does not constitute an autonomous right protected by the American Convention nor by the *corpus iuris* of international human rights law" and that "it is contrary to the principles of a representative democracy." Therefore, "its prohibition prevents persons who hold elected office from perpetuating themselves in the exercise of power" (IACHR 2021).

NOTES

1. As indicated previously, this was not the case in Bolivia. In that country, the economy was managed with relative sensibility.

2. Approved by the General Assembly of the Organization of American States in Lima on September 11, 2001. The signatories included President Hugo Chávez on behalf of Venezuela.

3. Since it is an international treaty also recognized by all the countries in the Americas, compliance with it is mandatory, and it takes precedence over the legislation of individual countries.

4. Insulza called attention to Chávez's authoritarian excesses when Chávez enacted laws through decrees for over a year and when he shut down private media outlet Radio Caracas Televisión. In 2019, he called Maduro a dictator and added that Chávez "wasn't one." When Chávez died, the Permanent Council of the OAS offered him a "posthumous tribute." Insulza's predecessor, César Gaviria, was interested in seeing that the referendum to revoke Chávez's mandate was transparent and the results accurate, but he was unable to achieve those goals.

5. President Barack Obama, in a speech given on World Press Freedom Day, referred to the "threats and harassment" to which Ecuadorian journalist César Ricaurte had been subjected and said that this persecution had produced "a chilling effect" on freedom of expression.

6. Among others, Óscar Arias, José María Aznar, Felipe Calderón, Laura Chinchilla, Vicente Fox, Eduardo Frei, César Gaviria, Felipe González, Osvaldo Hurtado, Luis Alberto Lacalle, Jamil Mahuad, Andrés Pastrana, Jorge Quiroga, Miguel Ángel Rodríguez, and Álvaro Uribe.

7. Argentina, Brazil, Canada, Chile, Colombia, Costa Rica, Guatemala, Honduras, Mexico, Panama, Paraguay, and Peru, and later also Guyana, Haiti, St. Lucía, and Bolivia.

8. This resolution did not have the votes of Uruguay, Mexico, Nicaragua, Bolivia (then governed by Morales), and certain Caribbean countries.

9. Among these, the United States, Canada, Switzerland, Panama, and the European Union's member countries.

10. Maduro's wife and children, the president of the Constituent Assembly, the vice president of Venezuela, the president of the Supreme Court of Justice, the defense minister, the heads of intelligence and security, and their frontmen, among others.

11. In early 2020, Juan Guaidó was welcomed as the president of Venezuela by President Donald Trump at the White House and received an ovation from both Democrats and Republicans in the U.S. Congress.

12. He added a harsh and unusual comment: "The Ortega–Murillo family, long unpopular and now lacking a democratic mandate, governs Nicaragua as autocrats, no different from the Somoza family against whom Ortega and the Sandinistas fought four decades ago."

13. Before the OAS could remove Nicaragua by applying Article 21 of the Inter-American Democratic Charter, Daniel Ortega decided to withdraw from that regional organization.

14. Following its publication, presidential candidate Gabriel Boric deauthorized it, and the president of the Communist Party only said that responsibility for the government's foreign policy fell to the president (*La Tercera* 2021).

15. Just as in the previous case, the party simply took down the statement posted on its website and said that it rejected "external interference" and that democracy should be respected by "the government and the opposition" (*El País* 2021a).

Chapter 20

Causes of the Dictatorial Drift

The political events that occurred in Venezuela, Bolivia, Nicaragua, and Ecuador between the late twentieth and the early twenty-first centuries, and the most recent events in El Salvador—all discussed in the three previous parts of this book—have been examined as a function of the elements comprised by a democratic political system. These events illustrate how constitutional governments can be transformed into dictatorial governments under the leadership of authoritarian politicians.

From the day Hugo Chávez, Evo Morales, Daniel Ortega, Rafael Correa, and Nayib Bukele began their mandates, the rule of law languished, only to disappear in the following months and years. Presidents who had been elected by the people to govern their countries according to constitutional precepts installed dictatorships through the malicious use of democratic institutions. As soon as they assumed power, through the procedures that will be examined below they undermined and then eliminated the key components of the democratic system: the rule of law; separation of powers; judiciary independence; accountability; transparency on the part of officials; political pluralism; alternation in government; free elections; and citizens' freedoms, guarantees, and rights.

In the cases of Venezuela, Bolivia, and Ecuador, the meeting of an unconstitutional constituent assembly was the starting point of this authoritarian process that culminated in replacing a democratic regime with a dictatorial one. In the cases of Nicaragua and El Salvador, it was a systematic takeover of the powers of the state by the president of the republic, by means of actions taken or constitutional reforms. Once gathered, the constituent assembly members declared themselves sovereign. As such, they dismissed the National Congress, removed the National Court of Justice, and replaced the heads of the other independent state bodies with officials aligned with the new administration. The same thing was done by those in power in Nicaragua and El Salvador, but through constitutional reforms, biased interpretations, or acts of force.

The constitutions they issued or reformed strengthened the authority of the president of the republic and undermined the attributions of the legislative and judicial functions through self-interested and malicious interpretations of constitutional articles and the laws conceived with the separation of powers in mind. These legal instruments were used by the twenty-first-century dictators to restrict freedom of expression; crush social protests; favor the ruling party electorally; limit the action of opposition organizations and leaders; hinder the work of civil society; control, divide, and weaken social movements; and affect private-sector economic activities.

When they voted in presidential and legislative elections, consultations, and referendums, the people allowed this power-concentrating process to take its first steps, advance rapidly, and culminate successfully. Therefore, it could be said that the more elections held, the more democracy was undermined and authoritarianism advanced. A majority of citizens, initially more than two-thirds, elected presidents who set out to demolish republican institutions, and citizens continued to vote for them despite tangible evidence that they were eroding democracy. Those who approved the authoritarian constitutions tailor-made for the virtual dictators, as well as the reforms they proposed to consolidate their power and extend it to all state agencies, were the citizens themselves. Their overwhelming number of votes came not only from the popular sectors but also from the middle class and even from the upper class, at least initially—that is, the voters' economic status and educational level made no difference.

First the most well-informed sectors, and later citizens in general, belatedly realized that the enormous power bestowed on the new presidents had not served to improve democracy but rather had made it worse by degrading its institutions and restricting rights, liberties, and constitutional guarantees. By then, the dictatorships had advanced so far that, when the people decided to express their rejection of the autocratic regime at the ballot boxes by voting against those who oppressed them, the dictators turned their election defeats into victories by means of fraudulent practices.

In massive demonstrations, people took to the streets to express their disenchantment, protest government outrages, and demand respect for the will of the people. Demonstrators were met with brutal repression that left hundreds and thousands dead and wounded. As good Leninists, the twenty-first-century socialist leaders were convinced that once they had reached power they should not leave it for any reason, regardless of the abuses, outrages, and crimes they had to commit to keep it.

With all the limitations, shortcomings, and mistakes that democracy, the parties, and the politicians of the five countries studied may have had, nothing similar had happened during previous governments.

Republican institutions were fully operational, constitutions and laws governed the actions and functions of government offices, and officials were accountable for their performance and were supervised by representatives of the people in congresses and assemblies and by oversight agencies. Human rights were respected, and if any official committed an excess, it was corrected and the person responsible was sanctioned. Elections were free, campaigns were relatively equitable, and ballot counting was transparent, thanks to the supervision of independent electoral bodies made up of representatives of the main political forces. No president sought to become a vice president; many presidents had only one term in office, and if any sought to be reelected arbitrarily, they did not succeed due to the timely intervention of bodies responsible for ensuring respect for democratic institutions. Government actions contrary to the norms of the rule of law were exceptional, and when they did occur, the separation of powers (with its system of checks and balances) allowed them to be rectified and the perpetrators punished.

Why, then, did citizens who had enjoyed rights, guarantees, freedoms, and other benefits provided by democratic institutions not defend them? Why were presidents who had been elected by the people to govern their countries constitutionally allowed to do so dictatorially? Why did citizens allow all the powers of the state to be abusively subjected to presidential authority and allow autocratic governments to be established?

According to Samuel Huntington, a democracy is institutionalized when the people and their leaders and authorities value it as part of their lives, submit to its procedures, share the principles of the political community, believe that the political system is legitimate, respect disagreements, have a shared vision of public interests, overcome differences through agreements, comply with the mandates of the law, obey the orders of authorities, and contribute their efforts to achieving collective objectives (Huntington 1972, 13–32).

These civic virtues, on which the functioning, good health, and long life of a democratic system depend, have not been present in the culture of the inhabitants of the countries being studied herein—that is to say, in the minds, beliefs, ideas, attitudes, practices, habits, and daily behavior of Bolivians, Ecuadorians, Nicaraguans, Salvadorans, and Venezuelans, regardless of their ideologies, race, age, gender, religious creed, level of education, economic position, and social status, nor in those of political leaders, economic and social leaders, intellectuals, and members of the media. Although some have displayed superior cultural values, as a minority they were not in a position to define the character of democratic institutions, to ensure they functioned correctly, to contribute to strengthening them, and to have a constructive impact on the countries' day-to-day politics.

Jorge Luis Borges, in an essay on the history of tango, wrote that "an Argentine, unlike North Americans and almost all Europeans, does not identify with the state" and "he is an individual, not a citizen" (Borges 1974, 162). Based on the information provided in the first three parts of this book, the same could be said of other Latin Americans. Scholars of the U.S. Founding Fathers have determined that the term *virtue* is mentioned more than the term *liberty* in their writings. One would be hard-pressed to find something similar in the writings of Latin America's intellectuals and politicians.

This deficit of cultural values and civic virtues has not been taken into account by the political scientists and sociologists who have studied the weaknesses and failures of Latin American democracy. This has occurred despite the fact that this deficit had conspired against democracy's sound performance since the day the republics were founded two centuries ago and despite the meager results of the new constitutions issued and the innumerable constitutional reforms introduced to perfect democratic institutions and improve their functioning.

This lack of a civic culture was expressed in the absence of values, principles, and beliefs consistent with a democratic form of government—among a large number of the members of political society, both citizens and their leaders and government officials—alongside the presence of behaviors and practices that were instead contrary to it. These ways of being, thinking, and acting of those who governed and those who were governed prevented democracy from being considered a greater good, to be cultivated, protected, and defended from those who sought to violate it, no matter how negative the political circumstances and no matter how commendable the objectives sought by those who wanted to replace it.

Among high percentages of the population there was no culture of legality, a central element of the democratic system. Such a culture usually takes shape when citizens believe that their actions must always be lawful, that is, framed within the mandates of the law. This presupposition is usually present in their minds when they are preparing to make a decision, promote a certain action, or join any initiative. This holds true even when the legal norm is contrary to their interests and purposes, when there is no authority or law enforcement official to enforce observance, or when they are unlikely to be discovered or be subject to sanction.

From the time their countries were established as independent republics, this behavior was not, and had not been, commonplace for Bolivians, Ecuadorians, Nicaraguans, Salvadorans, and Venezuelans in their daily lives and in their relations with the state.

Like other Latin Americans, the peoples of the countries studied herein inherited a culture of illegality, structured over hundreds of years, dating back to the colonial period, and reproduced and strengthened in the republican period. Since the law had not guided the acts of individuals during generations, citizens became accustomed to not abiding by it or to accommodating it to their ends. Conquerors and colonists carried out their economic activities outside the legal norms established by the Spanish monarchs in the Laws of the Indies. If authorities considered them unadvisable or inconvenient, they were empowered to violate them by reciting the sacramental chant, "I obey, but I do not comply." When the republics were established, popular wit mischievously changed this solemn monarchical saying to, "If there's a law, there's a way to get around it."

Due to this cultural deficiency, when a twenty-first-century dictator disregarded the constitution, citizens were not shocked and did not mobilize to defend it and prevent the breakdown of the democratic order. Moreover, they popularly legitimized the dictator's arbitrary actions by casting their votes in favor of those who had proceeded arbitrarily, reelecting them or voting blindly for their plebiscite proposals, without stopping to think that they would use the support received in the elections to increase their power and overthrow the democratic order, taking all the functions of the state into their own hands.

In light of the avalanche of public support, even institutions, authorities, and government bodies and offices that, by constitutional mandate, were obliged to defend the rule of law did not do so. Undaunted or fearful, they let abusive presidential power have its way by approving its decisions and requests.

More than half a century ago, the father of Latin American sociology, José Medina Echavarría, attributed the authoritarianism and paternalism of political society to the oppressive, arbitrary, and despotic way large landowners exercised power on their haciendas, ranches, farms, and estates. There the landowners established a system of lordly domination based on relations of subordination, obedience, loyalty, and violence. Not only were their servants and those who depended on their favors or influence subject to them, but so too was the surrounding population, including those living in neighboring towns and cities (Medina Echavarría 1964, 32–25).

The landowner's authority extended to areas other than farming and raising livestock on his land. In addition to attending to these activities, he supervised the religious practices of his workers; settled personal, family, and community conflicts; and intervened in local and national public affairs.

The rigid social hierarchies that separated the landowning class from the rest of society, the economic importance of agricultural production, and the presence of a mostly rural population all contributed to the extent of the landowner's authority—as did the fact that the hacienda owners did not live in the countryside but in the cities and usually performed important public functions.

For the aforementioned reasons, the model of power that the people knew and learned was the arbitrary and authoritarian behavior of the large landowners, who gave orders, demanded compliance, and punished those who disobeyed them.

The authoritarian and undemocratic way government leaders exercised power in the nineteenth and early twentieth centuries, regardless of their political orientation, was reproduced by the dictators of the twenty-first century when they were elected and became presidents. Presidents elected by the people, with the intention that they would exercise their power democratically, found ways to amass unlimited power and rule abusively, going outside the constitution, ignoring laws, marginalizing or subjugating the other branches of government, and restricting rights and freedoms.

Such authoritarianism did not bother or attract the attention of the peoples of Bolivia, Ecuador, El Salvador, Nicaragua, and Venezuela. It seemed natural, and even advisable, for the presidents to proceed in this way, even if they eliminated the democratic state. Even though in the second half of the twentieth century millions of Bolivians, Ecuadorians, Nicaraguans, Salvadorans, and Venezuelans managed to improve their level of education, become integrated into the modern economy of the cities, achieve social mobility, and become informed about public life, authoritarian leaders continued to be to the liking of the electorate.

If the presidents were to vindicate the exploited, settle accounts with the exploiters, put an end to injustice, and bring about the social revolution promised, they had to use the power given to them by the people. This way of thinking was no different in wealthy sectors, for whom a strong hand to bring order and discipline seemed indispensable for the countries' progress.

Culture also played a role in the return of the old Latin American caudillismo, a phenomenon that had dominated the political life of almost all the countries of the region throughout the history of the republic and prevailed over the incipient parties and the disparate ideas among mainly conservatives and liberals. Among the numerous and dissimilar caudillos who governed in the five countries studied for long periods—in some cases almost three decades—the following are noteworthy: Mariano Melgarejo in Bolivia, Eloy Alfaro in Ecuador, Maximiliano Hernández in El Salvador, Anastasio Somoza García in Nicaragua, and Juan Vicente Gómez in Venezuela. So important were these and other caudillos that the history of their countries during the nineteenth and early twentieth centuries could be summarized in the events surrounding their rise to power, their time in office, and their decline.

Many of the characteristics of these traditional caudillos were reproduced in the presidents elected to govern Venezuela, Bolivia, Nicaragua, Ecuador, and El Salvador in the twenty-first century. However, unlike the power of their predecessors, theirs was not based on their wealth, the leadership of unruly groups, or the command of armies but rather on their strong personalities, unbreakable will, effort and sacrifice, demagogic rhetoric, high degree of popularity, and repeated election triumphs. The magic of their charismatic personalities and people's universal access to mass media contributed to the ability of their passionate rhetoric to win the hearts of voters. This was not the case of drab Daniel Ortega, however.

All of the new caudillos considered themselves exceptional beings. They were not committed to oligarchic economic powers, and they thought they had been called by history or Providence to save the homeland, refound the country, and give birth to a new society at the service of the neediest. Thanks to their enlightened wisdom, they knew what the country's problems were, what the people's needs were, and how these should be addressed and solved. The citizens' perception of their merits, knowledge, bravery, courage, and character was no different. Citizens felt that, because these new caudillos possessed such virtues, were motivated by revolutionary convictions, and had an unbreakable will, they would defeat the enemies of the people in no time and lift the dispossessed out of their poverty and destitution.

By the end of the second millennium, many (not only academics) thought that this political phenomenon had been overcome in Latin America by virtue of the economic, social, and political changes that had taken place in the region, some of them profound, and by virtue of the broad relations that its inhabitants had established worldwide. Democracy ruled in all the countries of the subcontinent, a representative middle class had been formed, the living conditions of the popular sectors had improved, illiteracy had disappeared, women had access to higher education, and there were representative political parties. As for suffrage, in addition to being universal and free, the electorate tended to be informed thanks to better educational levels and the scope of the media, particularly radio and television. Nevertheless, caudillismo resurfaced in a surprising and unusually strong way with the election wins and successive reelections of Hugo Chávez, Evo Morales, Daniel Ortega, Rafael Correa, and later Nayib Bukele.

The economic and social conditions of the five countries, and the mood of their citizens, were fertile ground for the revolutionary discourse and generous offers of the twenty-first-century populist caudillos to bear fruit. Two lost decades in the fields of economic and social development had multiplied the unsatisfied needs of broad sectors of the popular and middle classes, affected by unemployment and the deterioration of salaries and real income, many in situations of poverty and indigence.[1] These problems were serious in the slums and shantytowns in peripheral areas of the cities—expanded by internal migration—due to their inhabitants' lack of or limited access to basic public services, including education and health care.

On the other hand, the ancestral paternalism, still present in the minds of many and not only in the minds of the poor, led people to expect protection and shelter from the state and those in power, that is, the opportunity to earn a living through a job or in the informal economy and access to the goods and services they needed. Furthermore, there were social and even ethnic resentments accumulated over centuries of exploitation, deprivation, and marginalization, and these were exacerbated by the wealth amassed by the affluent groups.

The sum of a paternalistic culture, unsatisfied needs, and social resentments created conditions for the populist discourse to thrive once again and to resonate with voters. The discourse of Chávez, Morales, Ortega, Correa, and Bukele was vindictive, accusatory, committed, and promising, and it was used to their advantage with people who had been voting for populist leaders for many years.

Insofar as they responded to felt needs, the populist policies and clientelist programs with which the new rulers responded to social demands covered day-to-day needs, reached a significant number of families, and thus aroused widespread popular support. The most noteworthy policies and programs were regulatory wage hikes, greater labor benefits, free public services, expansion of social benefits and higher numbers of beneficiaries, housing programs, increase in public employment, redistribution of wealth, and creation of all kinds of subsidies. Because these programs were indiscriminate, they also benefited the middle and even the upper classes.

All of this was facilitated by the notable increase in public revenues thanks to the boom in exports and the higher levels of foreign debt. The adverse international economic situation of the 1980s and 1990s coincided with the reestablishment of democratic institutions in Ecuador, Nicaragua, Bolivia, and Nicaragua. This was not the case in Venezuela, one of the few Latin American countries with a long-standing constitutional regime. Faced with the need to correct macroeconomic imbalances—Ecuador hastily and the others more slowly—the governments adjusted their economies to the constraints derived from lower fiscal revenues and the suspension of the easy credits they had been receiving from international banks. These adjustments had to be repeated when new international crises broke out and export prices, particularly those of petroleum and petroleum products, became volatile. The measures were aimed at putting the economy in order, recovering growth, and improving employment by reducing the large fiscal deficit, renegotiating the foreign debt, controlling inflation, and stabilizing the foreign exchange market.

These economic programs, labeled as neoliberal, were rejected by societies that had enjoyed a long period of economic stability and relative social progress since the 1950s, during which employment improved, inflation was controlled, and public benefits were expanded. The general discontent, fueled by the intransigent opposition of populist and revolutionary parties and the protests of social organizations, was burned into the minds of the citizens because of the coverage these events received in the media, especially on television. Even in the ruling classes, few considered such economic decisions advisable and inevitable in order to bring the economy in line with the depleted economic resources available and to avoid greater evils for the people. This was what happened in countries whose governments did not apply the highly criticized austerity programs: that of Hernán Siles in Bolivia (1982–1985) and that of Daniel Ortega in Nicaragua (1985–1990).[2]

Democracy, parties, and politicians were the scapegoats of popular frustration. Since such negative events had taken place under the aegis of republican institutions, impoverishing sectors of the popular and middle classes, they were easy to discredit because the impugning discourse reached ears willing to listen to it. Also, since a good number of the party organizations and their most important leaders had been part of the governments that succeeded each other over a long period of more than twenty years, none of them could escape blame. All of them ended up sharing the disparagement of the political class, contemptuously called the "partyocracy," which activists, candidates, and leaders of twenty-first-century socialism, and later Nayib Bukele, would trample on.

For these reasons, when they appeared on the political scene and ran for various offices, the most important of which was the presidency, the new players found the table served. There were no parties and leaders in a position to confront them in the public debate, defeat them at the polls, and later at least compel them to exercise power in a constitutional and democratic way.

Except in Venezuela, the parties had not become representative political organizations that could bring together majority currents of opinion. Therefore, rather than joining their ranks, citizens preferred to follow the new leaders who appeared on the political scene. Because their members were not militants determined to support the parties in good times and in bad, the members abandoned them when difficulties arose. Alongside these intrinsic weaknesses of the party systems, there were episodes of corruption, internal struggles, and the prevalence of personal interests over those of the party and those of the party over those of the country.

These situations were seen by public opinion as common to all parties and politicians, due to the generalizations made by journalists, media, intellectuals, civil society, business associations, and social organizations.[3] As no distinctions were made between politicians who were honest and corrupt, capable and inept, serious and demagogic, tolerant and dogmatic, democratic and authoritarian, public opinion formed the idea that "they were all the same." Very few believed that the weakening of the parties would be followed by a crisis of the democratic system, the rise of messianic caudillos, and the emergence of dictatorial governments.

Venezuela had had a solid, pluralistic, and representative party system, formed by Acción Democrática (1941) and COPEI (1946), organizations that in the second half of the twentieth century led public life, won the presidency several times, and achieved a majority or significant representation in the National Congress. This political hegemony was lost at the end of the century, affected by dissidence, divisions, and internal struggles so irresolvable that they led to the removal of their historical leaders: Carlos Andrés Pérez and Rafael Caldera.[4] The political void left by the collapse of the two-party system was filled by Hugo Chávez and the revolutionary groups that surrounded him. Prevailing over fragmentation and dissidence, he took over the political and electoral stage and imposed his omnipotent will, without hesitation. Nicolás Maduro later did so by means of shameless election frauds and barbaric abuses of power.

Founded in 1942, the Revolutionary Nationalist Movement (Movimiento Nacionalista Revolucionario, MNR) had dominated Bolivian politics for more than half a century, since the first presidential election of Víctor Paz Estenssoro in 1952. During this long period there were no party forces that could dispute the hegemony of the influential majority-holder MNR. In addition to getting its founder reelected three times, it brought other leaders to power. However, before the end of his second term, Gonzalo Sánchez de Lozada was assailed with bloody popular demonstrations and forced to resign. This sealed his political demise. He was displaced by a new force, MAS, led by his bitter opponent, Evo Morales, whose repeated candidacies were supported by all sectors of the Bolivian Left while the democratic forces became fragmented.

Of the numerous parties that emerged in Ecuador during the years of democratic transition (1977–1979), the most important was the Concentración de Fuerzas Populares (CFP) featuring the populist leader Assad Bucaram. However, it did not manage to become consolidated, and no party was able to become a majority party. The parties' influence was so limited that they did not manage to win the presidency more than once over a quarter of a century.[5] The volatility of the electorate ended with the election of Rafael Correa in 2006 and his two subsequent reelections, which were achieved in the first round of voting. The electoral grouping that sponsored him, Alianza PAIS, was constituted as a party after the inauguration of his first term in office, mainly with sectors of the balkanized Left. At the same time, the weak party system of old was disappearing, which meant that Correa was able to enjoy an uncluttered political arena.

The National Opposition Union (Unión Nacional Opositora, UNO), formed by a dozen political movements opposed to Sandinismo, won the presidency of Nicaragua in 1990 with Violeta Chamorro. This first defeat of Daniel Ortega was followed by his 1996 and 2001 defeats by Arnoldo Alemán and Enrique Bolaños, sponsored by conservatives and liberals. The division among democratic forces and a self-interested constitutional reform facilitated by Alemán, which lowered the percentage of votes necessary for a candidate to win in the first round, made Ortega's reelection possible in 2006. In exchange, Alemán received political protection from Sandinismo in the corruption trials against him. Ortega was subsequently reelected in 2011, 2017, and 2021, through electoral frauds.

The Salvadoran civil war, fought by the armed forces and the guerrilla groups of the Farabundo Martí National Liberation Front (Frente Farabundo Martí para la Liberación Nacional, FMLN) between 1979 and 1992, ended with the signing of the Chapultepec Peace Accords. The demobilized insurgents and other leftist groups transformed the FMLN into a partisan organization and became integrated into democratic life. Meanwhile, right-wing groups turned the Nationalist Republican Alliance (Alianza Republicana Nacionalista, ARENA), founded in 1981, into the party of the Right. ARENA governed between 1989 and 2009, and then FMLN governed until 2019. The ARENA–FMLN bipartisanship was terminated by Nayib Bukele and his party, New Ideas (Nuevas Ideas), in the presidential elections of 2019 and reduced to a minimum expression in the parliamentary elections of 2021.

In addition to the aforementioned cultural, structural, and situational causes, the high prices enjoyed by their countries' exports in the early years of the twenty-first century, due to the prolonged boom of the international economy, contributed to the consolidation of the initial governments of Chávez, Morales, Correa, and Ortega, which maintained their popularity and were reelected. Thanks to these exceptional circumstances, they had enormous budgetary resources at their disposal to expand the coverage of public services and finance all kinds of populist and clientelist programs that had an enormous impact on poor and indigent social sectors. Ortega also counted on the billions of dollars gifted to Nicaragua by Chávez for six years.

Finally, as examined in the first and second parts of this book, the twenty-first-century dictators were able to remain in office for long periods of time due to the immense power they were able to concentrate by submitting all state functions and offices to their authority, the attributions of which they assumed and exercised either directly or indirectly through officials under their command. When they lost their popularity and faced the risk of being defeated at the polls, they used their unlimited powers to impose their will and maintain themselves in office through electoral frauds. At the same time, they incapacitated, repressed, and persecuted the leaders of the helpless opposition forces, and with all kinds of ploys they thwarted their opponents' political initiatives, sometimes by means of cruel repression.

NOTES

1. In the first five years of the twenty-first century, poverty in Ecuador was significantly reduced.

2. For this reason and with the application of a statist, interventionist policy, Bolivia's economy became chaotic. One example of this was the annual hyperinflation of 18,171 percent in 1985. Something similar occurred in Nicaragua, which saw a hyperinflation of 33,547 percent in 1988.

3. In that regard, the national and regional scandal that led to the collapse of the government of Venezuelan president Carlos Andrés Pérez serves as a good illustration. Initially accused of corruption (embezzlement), he was actually convicted and sentenced to over two years in prison for the misappropriation of public funds. As his second-term cabinet minister Beatriz Rangel told me, when Pérez visited the White House in the spring of 1990, President George Bush expressed concern about a report of the U.S. intelligence services, which had detected the risk that a radical Sandinista group could carry out an attempt to oust Nicaraguan president Violeta Chamorro. In view of her vulnerability, since Nicaraguan law enforcement was controlled by the Sandinistas, Pérez decided to fund a protection team with money from the president's secret slush fund, in the amount of some seventeen million dollars. This was Pérez's "corruption."

4. Pérez was expelled from the Democratic Action (Acción Democrática) party after the National Congress voted for his removal (1993) for the aforementioned reason. Caldera left COPEI and set up another party in order to run for his second term (1994–1999), which he won through an alliance with other political organizations.

5. Founded in 1978, the Popular Democracy (Democracia Popular) party as the heir to Christian Democracy (Democracia Cristiana), founded in 1964, put two presidents in office: Osvaldo Hurtado (1981–1984) and Jamil Mahuad (1998–2000). I was elected vice president and, as such, succeeded President Jaime Roldós after he perished in an airplane crash.

Chapter 21

The Arduous Path of Democracy

Dictator Francisco Franco, upon reaching the end of his life and after having ruled Spain for thirty years, announced in his 1969 Christmas message that he was leaving everything "all tied up [with a bow]." With this expression, he wanted to assure his worried followers that after his death nothing would change, that everything would remain the same in the autocratic regime he had imposed after winning the civil war waged against the military forces of the republic decades before.

When presenting his last Report to the Nation (2017), Ecuadorian dictator Rafael Correa, after having governed Ecuador for more than ten years and having then resolved not to run for a fourth term, could well have said the same.

Correa was succeeded in the presidency by the person who had accompanied him as vice president in his first two terms, and he saw to it that Jorge Glas, his friend, lackey, and confidant, would be the vice president. In the ceremony in which Lenín Moreno was nominated, Correa handed him the government plan to be implemented during Moreno's administration, and he later added a more comprehensive document to that plan. The Alianza PAIS legislators and the presidents and vice presidents who would lead the National Assembly and its commissions had also been selected under Correa's supervision. The members of the new president's ministerial cabinet, some of his advisors, and the managers of public enterprises had all been close collaborators of Correa. The heads of the National Court of Justice, the Constitutional Court, the National Electoral Council, the Attorney General's Office, the Comptroller's Office, and other oversight bodies had served him as well.

The constitution then in effect had been written according to Correa's economic positions and political interests. Reforming it required a prior opinion from the Constitutional Court, and some articles were very complex. In addition, because certain important laws had been declared organic, modifying or repealing them required a two-thirds vote in favor by the National Assembly.

These political, constitutional, and legal fetters—which were difficult, if not impossible, to loosen—were not the only ones that gave rise to the widespread belief that the autocratic regime installed by Correa would last. Vice President Moreno's subordination to presidential authority had been notorious, and he had always been seen to identify strongly with the ideas of the Citizens Revolution and to reiterate his oaths of loyalty. As for the first authoritarian and then dictatorial way his predecessor exercised power, Moreno had never disagreed with him and, worse yet, had never challenged him, not even when the excesses became extreme. Although his attitude was rather tolerant and conciliatory, Moreno's government would be conditioned by the intricate legal and political authoritarian structure and by high-level officials personally and politically linked to Correa.

The pessimistic predictions that Moreno's government would be similar to what would have been a fourth Correa term did not come true. A first sign was the announcement, on the day he took office, that he would not continue his predecessor's highly criticized weekly broadcasts on radio and television channels, popularly known as "sabatinas."

Once installed in Carondelet, Moreno confirmed his democratic openness. He called for a national dialogue that included meetings with local authorities, political leaders, business associations, and social organizations such as the Indigenous confederation. He returned to Indigenous federation Conaie its institutional premises, taken away by the Correa government, and repealed executive decrees that had placed civil-society organizations under state control. Confrontational language, malicious propaganda, and the judicial persecution of adversaries, opponents, journalists, and citizens also disappeared from the political scene. Freedom of expression was reestablished, and the government media became independent.

Four months after beginning his mandate, President Moreno proposed the reform of the untouchable constitution of the Citizens Revolution through a popular consultation. In the referendum held on February 4, 2018, voters approved the elimination of the indefinite reelection of the president and other authorities, the permanent suspension of officials guilty of corruption from holding public office, and the creation of a Transitory Citizens Participation Council. This body, once formed, replaced the heads of the main state agencies—which Correa had trusted would follow his instructions—with citizens chosen for their merits, moral integrity, and experience, in such important institutions as the ordinary, constitutional, and electoral justice systems, the Comptroller's Office, and the Attorney General's Office.

Thus, in the brief period of just over a year, the country recovered the elements that define a political regime as democratic: the division and independence of the powers of the state; the rule of the constitution and laws; the independence of the constitutional, ordinary, and electoral justice systems;

citizens' liberties, rights, and guarantees; alternation in power; and political pluralism.

These changes eliminated the autocratic system neatly woven by Rafael Correa, but other unexpected political events also eroded his influence and weakened his leadership.

In late 2017, Vice President Jorge Glas was removed from office when he was prosecuted, convicted, and sent to prison for corruption. He had been chosen by Correa to represent the former president's interests, impose his agenda on Moreno's government, and eventually succeed Moreno. Likewise, Rafael Correa and a dozen ministers and close collaborators became fugitives from justice, were given the same sentence, and were banned from holding public office. The dismantling of Correa's tremendous power did not end there. At the hands of Moreno, he also lost the political party that he had founded and that had helped him win the presidency on three occasions. He was barely able to save a minority faction.

For Ecuador to reach the full reestablishment of democratic institutionality, it will be necessary to replace the 2008 constitution or to reform it profoundly. This possibility seems remote due to the complex procedures established therein. From this perspective, the most important change will be returning to the National Assembly the power to appoint the most important state officials; this power is currently in the hands of the so-called Citizens Participation and Social Control Council, formed without the universal vote of citizens.

In the second round of voting in the 2021 presidential elections, Correa's candidate was defeated, and one of his opponents, banker/businessman Guillermo Lasso—who had tried to defeat the then candidate and president of the republic on two previous occasions—was elected. However, Correa's party managed to earn more than one-third of the seats in the National Assembly.

As was seen in chapter 5, the Bolivian people mobilized to prevent Evo Morales from obtaining a fourth consecutive term, which would have circumvented an express constitutional prohibition and would have ignored the citizens' rejection of a fourth term, as voiced in the popular consultation Morales had called. Aided by ploys of the National Assembly and the Constitutional Court, bodies dependent on his will, Morales managed to get his participation in a new election arbitrarily approved. In the face of the general outcry caused by such an abuse of power, he called for a popular consultation so that the people could voice their opinion on his unconstitutional intention. Even though he had promised to abide by the popular verdict, he failed to comply with his pledge and, with the complicity of the Supreme Electoral Tribunal, registered his candidacy. When he did not get his way at the ballot boxes, he tried to turn his defeat into victory by means of electoral fraud. Faced with a popular revolt motivated by his ambition to govern Bolivia forever, he ultimately resigned and left the country.

Since the government was left without a head due to the resignation of all the officials that could constitutionally succeed Morales, the senate's second vice president, Jeanine Áñez, assumed the presidency. Her government did not live up to the historic responsibility that the Bolivian people placed in her hands, so a former economic minister and Morales protégé, Luis Arce, was elected in the 2020 presidential elections. Thus, the old autocratic regime was reestablished, albeit with a different president, but under the tutelage of the coca growers' caudillo. The most visible evidence of this anomaly is the judicial persecution suffered by former president Áñez. Despite the clear evidence cited above, politicized prosecutors and judges accused her of having "deposed President Morales by means of a coup d'état." These abuses of power and violations of constitutional rights demonstrate that the justice system in Bolivia continues to be under the control of the ex-dictator and is used to settle accounts with his adversaries.

President Luis Arce's first year in office has not been auspicious. He has not managed to carve out his own identity and leadership or to display political strength. Morales's presence in the government, in public affairs, in the justice system, and in the streets is notable. The confrontations between members of Bolivian Indigenous communities from the Andean region and the eastern lowlands are weakening the social base that put Arce in office and that sustained the governments of his predecessor. His party (MAS) has lost mayoral positions in important municipalities, including the electoral stronghold of El Alto. Mobilizations of major and diverse social sectors have forced him to revoke an important economic law in order to safeguard the stability of the government. The growing middle class continues to be aligned with the opposition. So extreme is the political polarization that Arce's opponents in the National Assembly prevented him from delivering the traditional annual Report to the Nation in peace.

The subsistence of the authoritarian regime he inherited and the political use of the justice system to persecute its adversaries and opponents must have weighed in U.S. President Joe Biden's decision not to invite President Luis Arce to the Summit for Democracy held in December 2021. There, 110 countries discussed the challenge that authoritarianism, human rights violations, and corruption represent to their principles and values.

The same can be said of Nayib Bukele, whom President Biden did not invite to the summit either. With that exclusion, Biden wanted to send a signal that the United States does not consider the government of El Salvador democratic, as could be seen in the corresponding chapter of part I.

El Salvador's transformation from a democratic government to a dictatorial one has made it possible to confirm that authoritarianism has nothing to do with political ideologies, since Nayib Bukele—unlike Chávez, Maduro, Morales, Ortega, and Correa—does not belong to the so-called twenty-first-century socialism. It also confirms that the authoritarian phenomenon existing in the region for two centuries is due instead to vertical personal, business, trade-union, and political relationships, regardless of the activity, social status, and ideology of the parties involved. For this reason, there may very well be right-wing autocrats and left-wing autocrats, as well as right-wing dictatorships and left-wing dictatorships.

In Venezuela and Nicaragua, the dictatorships of Nicolás Maduro and Daniel Ortega have tightened their dictatorial grip on democracy and freedom. Their governments have become cruel tyrannies, perhaps worse than those that Latin America had previously experienced during its troubled history. Hundreds of Nicaraguans and thousands of Venezuelans, mainly young people, including military personnel, have been imprisoned, tortured, and murdered for having dared to fight for the recovery of democracy and freedom.

This is evident in reports issued by the United Nations, the OAS, the Inter-American Commission on Human Rights, the Inter-American Court of Human Rights, the Office of the Prosecutor of the International Criminal Court, and numerous international nongovernmental organizations. All of them agree that human rights are being seriously violated in Venezuela and Nicaragua; some have even accused these countries of crimes against humanity.

Both dictators have refused to heed the demands of their peoples and the international community to restore their citizens' right to freely elect their presidents, to guarantee their constitutional freedoms, and to allow them to live in societies governed by democratic institutions. In order to shut out the clamor of their peoples and the international community, the dictators have covered their ears, closed their eyes, and blocked their consciences. Deaf, blind, and oblivious to the humanitarian demands and ready to maintain power at any cost, they have exacerbated their abuses, outrages, and crimes using the repressive apparatuses of their governments.

This has not been the only suffering that the people in these two countries have had to endure, especially in Venezuela.

In Venezuela, the poverty, indigence, unemployment, life expectancy, infant mortality, education, malnutrition, and social inequality indexes have worsened dramatically. After having been the richest society in Latin America, today it has the highest percentage of poor people in the region. During its time of prosperity, Venezuela received hundreds of thousands of immigrants, but now it has triggered the exodus of millions.

In Nicaragua, hundreds of citizens have been imprisoned, tortured, and victimized for demonstrating in the streets against the Ortega–Murillo regime and calling for their resignation. To escape police and judicial persecution, thousands of women and men, mainly young people, have left their homeland to seek refuge in neighboring countries. In the last presidential elections, all potential opposition candidates were imprisoned to prevent them from registering their candidacies, and they are being given long sentences for supposedly having committed crimes typified in the repressive laws issued by Sandinista legislators.

In the second half of the twentieth century, dictatorships that at one time or another governed various Latin American countries were overthrown, as happened recently in Bolivia. Their fall was brought on by serious economic and social crises, attacks on citizens' rights and freedoms, violations of democratic institutions, and popular protests and mobilizations. Despite the numerous huge protests in Venezuela and Nicaragua, such measures have not succeeded in overthrowing the dictatorships of Maduro and Ortega.

This failure has been mainly due to the bribery and co-optation of the high command of the security forces. In both countries, military and police officers have stopped serving the state, the nation, and the people, in exchange for enriching themselves, benefiting from perks, and benefiting from power, particularly the members of the high commands. Patriotic, democratic, and honest officers, soldiers, and policemen who did not submit or become corrupt have been silenced, imprisoned, tortured, or eliminated by the ruthless intelligence services.

Not even the proclamation of Juan Guaidó as the legitimate president of Venezuela and his recognition by more than fifty countries, including the most important countries in the world, with the exception of China and Russia, have led to the collapse of the Maduro government. A constitutional manipulation underpinned this shrewd initiative, for Guaidó had been elected a member of the National Assembly and then named its president by his colleagues. The response of Maduro's government was to assemble an unconstitutional and fraudulent constituent assembly, whose first decision was to deprive the legislative function of all its powers, thus turning it into a mere figurehead. In order to politically nullify Guaidó, top Chavista leaders have requested that the attorney general "speed up the application of justice to Juan Guaidó and his accomplices" for "attacking the patrimonial assets of the nation, bankrupting the public treasury," and even "conspiring against democracy and the rule of law."

The harsh economic sanctions imposed by the United States and the European Union on Venezuela and Nicaragua have affected both countries, several public institutions, the highest-ranking state officials and their families, as well as military and police commanders, prosecutors, and judges. The sanctions have especially had a major impact on Venezuela due to the negative collateral effects they are generating on economic activities, particularly exports, imports, and financing. At some point but not immediately, they could well lead to unsurmountable economic crises or force some kind of political negotiation in exchange for their repeal.

This impasse could eventually be overcome if the International Criminal Court were to issue a ruling convicting dictator Maduro, several of his ministers, and military and police commanders for crimes against humanity. Such a conviction would be possible in view of the innumerable crimes of this nature committed by the Venezuelan dictatorship, the fact that court prosecutor Karim Khan has initiated an investigation, and the fact that the former prosecutor accepted the existence of such criminal conduct.

It will be interesting to follow the political repercussions the arrests of two major players from the Chávez and Maduro regimes—currently under investigation by the United States justice system—may have in Venezuela, Latin America, and the international community. These players are Alex Saab, a Colombian businessman closely involved in the secret financial operations of Maduro's government and identified by former Venezuelan officials as Maduro's front, and Hugo Carvajal, a former military counterintelligence head in the governments of Chávez and Maduro, who is awaiting extradition to the United States from Spain.

The failure of opposition initiatives and the uncertain outcome of the international sanctions aimed at putting an end to the Maduro dictatorship encouraged seeking a formula acceptable to both parties, to be reached through a negotiation process. This alternative has not borne fruit either, since the talks that were initiated for that purpose were abandoned without reaching any agreement. This was surely because the obvious and reasonable request that the conflict be resolved by calling elections for president and legislators—elections organized and endorsed by an independent and pluralist electoral tribunal—has been unacceptable to the Venezuelan tyranny for the simple reason that no dictator relinquishes power voluntarily to face an uncertain future. In the case of Maduro, his future would involve being tried for crimes against humanity in national or international criminal courts.

The reflection made in the preceding paragraphs could also apply to the Nicaraguan dictatorship of the Ortega–Murillo family.

The analysis done throughout this book leads to a worrisome conclusion: the prospects for the removal of the tyrannical dictatorships of Nicolás Maduro and Daniel Ortega are not encouraging, at least in the short term. However, it is worth bearing in mind that, in the unpredictable politics of Latin America, anything is possible.

References

ABC Internacional. 2018. "Nicolás Maduro, en las elecciones: 'Tu voto decide, votos o balas, patria o colonia, paz o violencia.'" May 20. https://www.abc.es/internacional/abci-nicolas-maduro-elecciones-voto-decide-votos-o-balas-patria-o -colonia-o-violencia-201805201514_noticia.html?ref=https:%2F%2F%20www .google.com%2F/.

Academic. n.d. "Conflictos entre el gobierno de Rafael Correa y la Prensa de Ecuador." Wikipedia Español. https://es-academic.com/dic.nsf/eswiki/1283749.

Aguiar, Asdrúbal. 2005. Memorandum sent to André Dupuy, the papal nuncio in Caracas, by Asdrúbal Aguiar, an opposition representative for negotiations with the government regarding the referendum. April 25.

———. 2009. *De la Revolución Restauradora a la Revolución Bolivariana*. Caracas: Universidad Andrés Bello-Diario Universal.

———. 2012. *Historia inconstitucional de Venezuela 1999–2012*. Colección Estudios Políticos 6. Caracas: Editorial Jurídica Venezolana.

———. 2016. *El problema de Venezuela 2008–2016*. Colección Estudios Políticos 14. Caracas: Editorial Jurídica Venezolana.

———. 2018. *Civilización y barbarie. Venezuela 2015–2018*. Colección Estudios Políticos 16. Caracas: Ediciones EjV Internacional.

———. 2020. *Más allá de nuestra historia*. Miami: Fundación IDEA-Democrática.

Andrade, Francis. n.d. *La nueva Ley de Comunicación y su aplicación para el ejercicio periodístico y el derecho a la libertad de expresión en el Ecuador*. Serie Investigación 6, Centro de Derechos Humanos, Facultad de Jurisprudencia. https://www.uasb.edu.ec/documents/62017/1434654/La+nueva+Ley+de+Comunicació n+y+su+aplicación+para+el+ejercicio+periodístico.pdf/d68bf7ed-d741-4137-8fb9 -1cf850896d76.

Ayala Corao, Carlos M. n.d. *Venezuela: De la Constituyente de 1999 a la reforma constitucional de 2007*. Instituto de Investigaciones Jurídicas, UNAM. https://archivos.juridicas.unam.mx/www/bjv/libros/6/2728/13.pdf.

Ayala Mora, Enrique. 2015. "Así cayó la Corte Suprema de Justicia en el 2004." *Plan V*, September 29. https://www.planv.com.ec/historias/politica/asi-cayo-la-corte -suprema-justicia-el-2004.

Basabe-Serrano, Santiago. 2009. "Ecuador: Reforma constitucional, nuevos actores políticos y viejas prácticas partidistas." *Revista de Ciencia Política* 29 (2): 381–406. https://www.flacsoandes.edu.ec/sites/default/files/agora/files/1275502992 .ecuador_reforma_constitucional.pdf.

BBC (British Broadcasting Corporation). 2018a. "Nicaragua, 'la dulce y explosiva cintura de América' en palabras de Sergio Ramírez, premio Cervantes de Literatura." April 24. https://www.bbc.com/mundo/noticias-america-latina-43880109.

———. 2018b. "Muerte de Fernando Albán en una comisaría del Sebin: 3 incógnitas del caso del opositor que falleció en Venezuela." October 10. https://www.bbc.com /mundo/noticias-america-latina-45817059.

———. 2018c. "Evo Morales: el Tribunal Electoral de Bolivia lo habilita como candidato presidencial tras haber perdido el referéndum por la reelección." December 5. https://www.bbc.com/mundo/noticias-america-latina-46450251.

———. 2019a. "Crisis en Venezuela: qué medios tiene el ejército del país para responder a una intervención de EE.UU." February 19. https//www.bbc.com/ mundo/noticias-america-latina-47248371.

———. 2019b. "Revolución sandinista: 4 claves para entender la última revolución armada de América Latina y lo que queda de su legado en Nicaragua." July 18. https://www.bbc.com/mundo/noticias-america-latina-49035196.

———. 2019c. "Evo Morales: cómo hizo el presidente de Bolivia para poder presentarse a un cuarto mandato presidencial si la Constitución solo permite una reelección." October 20. https://www.bbc.com/mundo/noticias-america-latina-49926169.

———. 2020. "Guaidó en la Casa Blanca: qué consecuencias puede tener el encuentro del líder opositor venezolano con Trump." February 5. https://www.bbc.com/ mundo/noticias-america-latina-51393978.

Benavides Llerena, Gina. n.d.. *Estados de excepción en 2012, Programa Andino de Derechos Humanos*. Quito: UASB. http://repositorio.uasb.edu.ec/bitstream/10644 /4114/1/Benavides-Estados.pdf.

Bolivia Decide. 2013. "OEA confirma que 2006–2010 fue acordado como 'primer mandato.'" June 14, 2013. https://boliviadecide.blogspot.com/2013/06/oea -confirma-que-2006-2010-fue-acordado.html.

Borges, Jorge Luis. 1974. *Obras Completas 1923–1972*. Buenos Aires: Emecé Editores.

Brewer-Carías, Allan R. 2001. *Golpe de Estado y proceso constituyente en Venezuela*. México: UNAM. https://www.corteidh.or.cr/tablas/13677.pdf.

———. 2007a. "El inicio del proceso constituyente en Ecuador en 2007 y las lecciones de la experiencia venezolana de 1999." *Iuris Dictio* 7 (11): 71–94.

———. 2017b. "Crónica constitucional de una inconstitucionalidad: Las ejecutorias de la Asamblea Nacional Constituyente agosto-octubre del 2017." *Revista de Derecho Público* 151–152 (July–December): 165–224.

———. 2018. *Usurpación Constituyente (1999, 2017): La historia se repite*. Colección Estudios Jurídicos 121, Caracas: Editorial Jurídica Venezolana International.

Calapaqui Tapia, Karla. 2016. *Criminalización de la protesta 2007–2015, las víctimas del correísmo*. Quito: Ediciones Opción.

CLACSO. 2007. *Ecuador. Cronología del conflicto social enero–abril 2007*. Buenos Aires: CLACSO.

CNN. 2020. "Gobierno de Trump acusa a Maduro de narcoterrorismo y ofrece US$ 15 millones por información que lleve a su captura." March 26. https://cnnespanol.cnn.com/ 2020/03/26/gobierno-trump-cargos-maduro-venezuela/.

"Comandante Eterno: ¡El modelo capitalista jamás nos mostrará los valores!" 2017. YouTube.com, November 24. https://www.youtube.com/watch?v=LrtUEfxVawo.

Confidencial. 2021. "Lula da Silva aconseja a Ortega: 'No abandone la democracia.'" August 2. https://www.confidencial.com.ni/politica/lula-da-silva-aconseja-a-ortega-no-abandone-la-democracia/.

"Constitución de la República Bolivariana de Venezuela." 1999. *Gaceta Oficial de la República de Venezuela* 127, month 3, no. 36: 860.

"Constitución de la República del Ecuador." 2008. https://www.asambleanacional.gob.ec/sites/default/files/documents/old/constitucion_de_bolsillo.pdf.

"Constitución de la República de Venezuela de 1961." 1961. http://americo.usal.es/oir/legislatina/normasyreglamentos/constituciones/Venezuela1961.pdf.

"Constitución Política del Estado Plurinacional de Bolivia." 2009. https://www.autoridadminera.gob.bo/public/uploads/normativa_juridic/estado.pdf.

Contraloría General del Estado. 2019. *Acciones emprendidas durante estados de excepción no contribuyeron a superar las emergencias*. https://www.contraloria.gob.ec/CentralMedios/SalaPrensa/23600.

Correa, Rafael. 2007. "Econ. Rafael Correa en la mitad del mundo." January 15. Speech when taking office as president. https://www.presidencia.gob.ec/wp-content/uploads/downloads/2013/09/2007-01-15-Discurso-Posesión-Presidencial-Mitad-del-Mundo.pdf.

"Correa perdona a El Universo." 2012. YouTube.com, February 27. https://www.youtube.com/watch?v=Wu5UJglGUxo.

Correa Delgado, Rafael. 2009. *Ecuador: De Banana Republic a la No República*. Bogota: Penguin Random House Mondadori, S.A.

CPCCS, Ministerio de Justicia, Derechos Humanos y Cultos. 2012. *Informe final de la Veeduría Internacional a la reforma a la justicia en el Ecuador*. https://www.academia.edu/5237061/Informe_final_final_veeduria_internacional.

Cronista. 2022. "Lula: ¿Por qué Angela Merkel puede estar 16 años en el poder y Ortega no?" January 6. https://www.cronista.com/internacionales/616473/.

"Daniel Ortega." 2022. Wikipedia. https://en.wikipedia.org/wiki/Daniel_Ortega.

"Denuncia de Ecuador en la Corte Internacional de La Haya, Documento Complementario." 2016. https://www.scribd.com/doc/316026941/Documento-Complementario-Denuncia-Ecuador-La-Haya.

DPLF (Due Process of Law Foundation). 2014. *Judicial Independence in Ecuador's Judicial Reform Process*. July 28. https://www.dplf.org/en/resources/judicial-independence-ecuadors-judicial-reform-process.

DW. 2015. "Corte Constitucional de Ecuador avala la reelección indefinida." December 17. https://www.dw.com/es/corte-constitucional-de-ecuador-avala-la-reelección-indefinida/a-18923501.

————. 2019. "Ideólogo del Socialismo del Siglo XXI: 'Maduro se rehusó a ver la realidad.'" January 31. https://www.dw.com/es/ideólogo-del-socialismo-del-siglo-xxi-maduro-se-rehusó-a-ver-la-realidad/a-47316573.

————. 2020. "Suiza sanciona a seis altos funcionarios del Gobierno de Daniel Ortega." June 24. https://www.dw.com/es/suiza-sanciona-a-seis-altos-funcionarios-del-gobierno-de-daniel-ortega/a-53932340.

El Comercio. 2010. "6 focos de conflicto de la Constitución." October 20. https://www.elcomercio.com/actualidad/politica/focos-conflicto-constitucion.html.

————. 2011a. "' . . . que pruebe su inocencia.'" March 9. https://www.elcomercio.com/opinion/pruebe-inocencia.html.

————. 2011b. "La amnistía a Floresmilo Villalta aumenta la polémica en la Corte Constitucional." March 9. https://www.elcomercio.com/actualidad/politica/amnistia-a-floresmilo-villalta-aumenta.html.

————. 2011c. "Correa depositó en Alemania el dinero de su demanda a Banco Pichincha." June 21. https://www.elcomercio.com/actualidad/politica/correa-deposito-alemania-dinero-de.html.

————. 2011d. "Polémica por el gasto electoral de Correa." August 3. https://www.elcomercio.com/actualidad/politica/polemica-gasto-electoral-de-correa.html.

————. 2011e. "Gobierno dice que no gastó ni un centavo en la campaña." September 2. https://www.elcomercio.com/actualidad/politica/gobierno-dice-que-no-gasto.html.

————. 2012a. "Veedores de contratos de Fabrico [*sic*] Correa esperan para mañana respuesta sobre asilo." May 15. https://www.elcomercio.com/actualidad/politica/veedores-de-contratos-de-fabrico.html.

————. 2012b. "Barack Obama expresa respaldo a César Ricaurte." May 3. https://www.elcomercio.com/actualidad/politica/barack-obama-expresa-respaldo-a.html.

————. 2014. "Según Cedatos, aumenta el número de ecuatorianos que quieren la consulta por la reelección." October 6. https://www.elcomercio.com/actualidad/cedatos-ecuador-consulta-reeleccion.html.

————. 2015a. "La vertiginosa era de Podemos y los 'think tank' españoles en Quito." May 15. https://www.elcomercio.com/actualidad/espana-quito-ecuador-politica.html.

————. 2015b. "Correa: Creo que no hay necesidad de presentarme como candidato en el 2017." December 5. https://www.elcomercio.com/actualidad/rafaelcorrea-enlaceciudadano-elecciones2017-presidente-candidato.html.

————. 2017a. "Exit Poll-Cedatos: Lasso 53.02–Moreno 46.98; Perfiles de Opinión: Lasso 47.8–Moreno: 52.2." April 2. https://www.elcomercio.com/actualidad/votacion-ecuador-exitpoll-guillermolasso-leninmoreno.html.

————. 2017b. "Participación Ciudadana ratificó el empate técnico y cuestionó amenazas." April 3. https://www.elcomercio.com/actualidad/conteorapido-participacionciudadana-elecciones-segundavuelta-leninmoreno.html.

————. 2017c. "Gerardo Portillo, indultado; Pablo Chambers aún clandestino." December 12. https://www.elcomercio.com/actualidad/gerardoportillo-indultado-pablochambers-justicia-leninmoreno.html.

————. 2017d. "Tribunal: Jorge Glas condenado a 6 años por asociación ilícita con Odebrecht." December 13. https://www.elcomercio.com/actualidad/tribunal -jorgeglas-condena-juicio-odebrecht.html.

————. 2018. "¿Rafael Correa no podrá volver a Ecuador hasta el 2022 o el 2027? El alcance del llamado a juicio por plagio." November 9. https://www.elcomercio .com/actualidad/prescripcion-juicio-correa-plagio-balda.html.

————. 2019a. "Rafael Correa: 'Si encuentran un centavo mal habido, me pego un tiro.'" July 19. https://www.elcomercio.com/actualidad/rafael-correa-cuentas -viajes-sobornos.html.

————. 2019b. "José Mujica tilda por primera vez de 'dictadura' al régimen de Maduro." July 29. https://www.elcomercio.com/actualidad/mundo/jose-mujica -dictadura-venezuela-maduro.html.

————. 2020a. "Cuatro delitos quedan por investigar en el caso Sobornos." April 9. https://www.elcomercio.com/actualidad/delitos-investigacion-caso-sobornos -sentencia.html.

————. 2020b. "Tribunal negó la apelación de Rafael Correa y confirma su sentencia de ocho años de cárcel por cohecho en el caso Sobornos." July 20. https://www .elcomercio.com/actualidad/apelacion-condena-correa-caso-sobornos.html.

————. 2020c. "Los bienes de canal de televisión crítico del gobierno nicaragüense fueron embargados." September 12. https://www.elcomercio.com/actualidad/ mundo/bienes-canal-critico-nicaragua-embargo.html.

El Deber. 2019. "'Perseguidos políticos' bolivianos envían una carta de res- paldo a Guaidó." February 5. https://eldeber.com.bo/bolivia/perseguidos-politicos -bolivianos-envian-una-carta-de-respaldo-a-guaido_40842.

El Diario.ec. 2011. "Serrano visitó a juez por el caso Carrión." June 23. https://www .eldiario.ec/noticias-manabi-ecuador/195990-serrano-visito-a-juez-por-el-caso -carrion/.

El Mundo. 2011. "'Evadas,' 100 frases 'célebres' de Evo Morales." June 14. https: //www.elmundo.es/america/2011/06/14/noticias/1308069851.html?cid=CM0803.

El Mundo.es. 2007. "Devuelven su cargo a 51 de los 57 diputados ecuatorianos suspendidos por el TC." April 24. https://www.elmundo.es/elmundo/2007/04/24/ internacional/1177367225.html.

El País. 2014. "Ecuador es, tras Cuba, el país más restrictivo en libertad de expre- sión." July 26. https://elpais.com/internacional/2014/07/26/actualidad/1406330612 _575671.html.

————. 2018a. "La resistencia de Radio Darío in Nicaragua." May 6. https://elpais .com/internacional/2018/05/06/america/1525560573_841224.html.

————. 2018b. "Despedidos decenas de médicos en Nicaragua que apoyaron las protestas contra Ortega." August 4. https://elpais.com/internacional/2018/08/04/ america/1533334159_403441.html.

————. 2018c. "El fraude electoral divide a Nicaragua." November 14. https://elpais .com/diario/2008/11/14/internacional/1226617201_850215.html.

————. 2018d. "Los expertos de la OEA denuncian 'crímenes de lesa humanidad' en Nicaragua." December 22. https://elpais.com/internacional/2018/12/21/america /1545415977_152844.html.

———. 2019a. "Abril es el mes más cruel." April 15. https://elpais.com/elpais/2019/04/15/opinion/1555331667_316236.html?ssm=whatsapp.

———. 2019b. "Estados Unidos golpea las finanzas de la familia Ortega en Nicaragua." December 16. https://elpais.com/internacional/2019/12/16/america/1576457941_905226.html.

———. 2021a. "Ortega y Murillo escriben su epitafio." November 4. https://elpais.com/opinion/2021-11-05/ortega-y-murillo-escriben-su-epitafio.html.

———. 2021b. "Bukele presenta una ley para acallar las voces críticas en El Salvador." November 11. https://elpais.com/internacional/2021-11-11/bukele-emula-una-de-las-leyes-represivas-de-ortega-para-acallar-la-critica-en-el-salvador.html.

El Telégrafo. 2011. "La presidenta de la Corte de Guayas fue destituida." November 24. https://www.eltelegrafo.com.ec/noticias/judicial/12/la-presidenta-de-la-corte-de-guayas-fue-destituida.

———. 2013. "La Ley de Comunicación del Ecuador se aprueba con 108 votos." June 14. https://www.eltelegrafo.com.ec/noticias/informacion/1/ecuador-ya-cuenta-con-nueva-ley-de-comunicación.

El Universo. 2004a. "León Febres-Cordero asegura que hay causales para enjuiciar al Presidente." September 3. https://www.eluniverso.com/2004/09/03/0001/8/176753EF41E54FA6B14F11D865986DFC.html.

———. 2004b. "Ex presidente Borja pide destitución de actual mandatario." October 18. https://www.eluniverso.com/2004/10/18/0001/8/87BC0EDC53C944BE89148EFF61D311BE.html.

———. 2007a. "Correa da plazo al TSE para impulsar consulta." February 11. https://www.eluniverso.com/2007/02/11/0001/8/CCEC6667C7F044A09D6D8E7F54BF4210.html.

———. 2007b. "Diputado golpeado y mujer herida en manifestación." March 9. https://www.eluniverso.com/2007/03/09/0001/8/C40450AA3C1D4B918B387008613F8F67.html.

———. 2007c. "La consulta fue prioridad en los tres meses del Gobierno." April 14. https://www.eluniverso.com/2007/04/14/0001/8/0FD56F5E1BD34D25A516D80913DEF565.html.

———. 2007d. "Rodrigo Borja acepta Secretaría de Unasur." May 9. https://www.eluniverso.com/2007/05/09/0001/8/3C94DD297EBB42459C772DD5B77BE922.html.

———. 2007e. "No se ha dado un paso real hacia una economía socialista." September 2. https://www.eluniverso.com/2007/09/02/0001/8/C0A0032D5222472CB016E00F354CBF91.html.

———. 2007f. "Correa va contra las fundaciones." December 9. https://www.eluniverso.com/2007/12/09/0001/18/D8A7D3F5D9D04E17824A2210C2DFD17F.html.

———. 2008a. "Laurel y chuquiragua." May 19. https://www.eluniverso.com/2008/05/19/0001/21/30B7D3EAC2AB4BC6A797475DDBDCE2FA.html.

———. 2008b. "Rafael Correa compró un departamento en Bélgica para su familia." June 23. https://www.eluniverso.com/2011/06/23/1/1355/correa-compro-un-departamento-belgica-familia.html.

————. 2008c. "Es 'obligación,' según PAIS, que burócratas promocionen el Sí." August 26. https://www.eluniverso.com/2008/08/26/0001/8/1FC5EEC39AC04C8 FB81EA86BB7341ACC.html.

————. 2008d. "Españoles redactaron textos para mesas." August 28. https://www .eluniverso.com/2008/08/28/0001/8/149495D767A04A8EBE0A9285A79F606A .html.

————. 2008e. "Presidente Correa ganó juicio al Banco del Pichincha." October 31. https://www.eluniverso.com/2008/10/31/0001/8/5E688F5443C34BFFAFF264DC E35700E3.html.

————. 2009. "Correa advirtió en agosto que pediría una cuarta infracción." December 23. https://www.eluniverso.com/2009/12/23/1/1355/correa-advirtio -agosto-pediria-cuarta-infraccion.html/.

————. 2010a. "Cinco organismos de Inteligencia fallaron el 30 de septiembre." October 4. https://www.eluniverso.com/2010/10/04/1/1355/cinco-organismos -inteligencia-fallaron-30-septiembre.html.

————. 2010b. "Doris Soliz negó golpe de Estado el 30-S." October 27. https://www .eluniverso.com/2010/10/27/1/1355/doris-soliz-nego-golpe-estado-30-s.html.

————. 2011a. "Con cambios, Corte Constitucional dio paso a referéndum y la consulta." February 16. https://www.eluniverso.com/2011/02/16/1/1355/cambios -corte-constitucional-dio-paso-referendum-consulta.html.

————. 2011b. "Preguntas de la Consulta y del Referéndum con sus anexos." February 16. https://www.eluniverso.com/2011/02/16/1/1355/preguntas-consulta -referendum-sus-anexos.html.

————. 2012a. "Presidente Rafael Correa asegura que no le importa lo que diga la CIDH." February 26. https://www.eluniverso.com/2012/02/26/1/1355/presidente -rafael-correa-asegura-le-importa-lo-diga-cidh.html.

————. 2012b. "El Ejecutivo vetó norma legislativa porque era 'mamotreto jurídico.'" April 22. https://www.eluniverso.com/2012/04/22/1/1355/ejecutivo -veto-norma-legislativa-porque-era-mamotreto-juridico.html.

————. 2012c. "Exjuez Luis Fernández: 'Somos el ejemplo: Quien no obedece es destituido por más que actúe en derecho.'" June 18. https://www.eluniverso.com /2012/06/18/1/1355/somos-ejemplo-quien-obedece-destituido-mas-actue-derecho .html.

————. 2012d. "Hijo de Abdalá Bucaram afirma que hay fotos de sus sesiones con Rafael Correa." August 9. https://www.eluniverso.com/2012/08/09/1/1355/hijo -abdala-afirma-hay-fotos-sus-sesiones-rafael.html.

————. 2012e. "Joffre Campaña: El caso Chucky Seven recién empieza, le quedan 9 años." September 16. https://www.eluniverso.com/2012/09/16/1/1355/joffre -campana-caso-chucky-seven-recien-empieza-le-quedan-9-anos.html/.

————. 2013. "La mayoría oficialista aprobó la Ley de Comunicación en Ecuador." June 14. https://www.eluniverso.com/noticias/2013/06/14/nota/1026696/mayoria -oficialista-aprobo-ley-comunicación.

————. 2015a. "La fiscalización, limitada por la ley y disposiciones oficiales." February 15. https://www.eluniverso.com/noticias/2015/02/15/nota/4556001/ fiscalizacion-limitada-ley-disposiciones-oficiales.

———. 2015b. "Secom dice que renuncia de Rafael Correa a la reelección es por motivos políticos." November 12. https://www.eluniverso.com/noticias/2015/11 /27/nota/5264640/secom-dice-que-renuncia-rafael-correa-reeleccion-es-motivos.

———. 2016. "Constructora Odebrecht pagó sobornos en Ecuador, anuncia Departamento de Justicia de EE.UU." December 21. https://www.eluniverso.com/ noticias/2016/12/21/nota/5965135/constructora-odebrecht-pago-sobornos-ecuador -anuncia-fiscal-estados.

———. 2017a. "10 años de Rafael Correa en 10 frases." May 22. https://www .eluniverso.com/noticias/2017/05/22/nota/6196054/10-anos-rafael-correa-10 -frases.

———. 2017b. "La honra de Rafael Correa volverá a debatirse judicialmente." June 26. https://www.eluniverso.com/noticias/2017/06/26/nota/6249835/honra-correa -volvera-debatirse-judicialmente.

———. 2017c. "Richard Proaño: Me destituyeron por fallo contra Ricardo Rivera." August 23. https://www.eluniverso.com/noticias/2017/08/23/nota/6343630/me -destituyeron-fallo-contra-ricardo-rivera.

———. 2017d. "Hubo 23 cambios a la Constitución vigente en 9 años." October 8. https://www.eluniverso.com/noticias/2017/10/08/nota/6420070/hubo-23-cambios -constitucion-vigente-9-anos/.

———. 2019. "Suman 101 decretos de estados de excepción y renovación desde 2007 en Ecuador." October 7. https://www.eluniverso.com/noticias/2019/10/07/ nota/7550306/suman-101-decretos-estados-excepcion-renovacion-2007/.

———. n.d. "Paulo Rodríguez: 'He liderado procesos que han marcado hitos.'" https: //especiales.eluniverso.com/justicia/funcionario/paulo-rodriguez/.

———. n.d. "Tania Arias: 'La Corte Nacional de Justicia es legítima.'" https:// especiales.eluniverso.com/justicia/funcionario/tania-arias/.

———. n.d. "Yavar se concentró en la depuración de los judiciales." https:// especiales.eluniverso.com/justicia/funcionario/fernando-yavar/.

Encovi. 2019–2020. *Encuesta Nacional de Condiciones de Vida 2019–2020.* https:// www.proyectoencovi.com/informe-interactivo-2019.

Envío digital. 2009. "Nicaragua. Informe final de Ética y Transparencia: Ante las ruinas de un proceso electoral viciado." March. https://www.envio.org.ni/articulo /3974.

Estrella Tutivén, Ingrid Viviana. 2018. "La transformación de la televisión ecuatoriana a raíz de la promulgación de la Ley Orgánica de comunicación." Doctoral thesis, Universidad de Málaga.

European Council. 2016–2020. "Venezuela: The Council's Response to the Crisis." https://www.consilium.europa.eu/en/policies/venezuela/.

Facebook. n.d. https://www.facebook.com/Creativeidias7/videos/558119504894517. Minute 1:37 [no longer available].

Focus News Ecuador. 2018. "El verdadero intocable: Alexis Mera." June 24. https://medium.com/focus-news-ecuador/el-verdadero-intocable-alexis-mera -11f587ffe68f.

Freedom House. 2013. "Middle East Volatility amid Global Decline. Freedom of the Press 2013." https://freedomhouse.org/report/freedom-press/2013/middle-east -volatility-amid-global-decline.

Fundación 1000 hojas. 2017. "Pablo Chambers: 'La persecución a los veedores se debe a que detectamos el vínculo de Fabricio Correa con OAS y Odebrecht.'" June 2. http://www.milhojas.is/index.php/612460-pablo-chambers-la-persecucion -a-los-veedores-se-debe-a-que-detectamos-el-vinculo-de-fabricio-correa-con-oas -y-odebrecht.html.

Fundamedios. 2012. "Tribunal Electoral multa a Vistazo con 80 mil dólares por artículo de opinión." September 28. https://www.fundamedios.org.ec/alertas/tribunal -electoral-multa-vistazo-con-80-mil-dolares-por-articulo-de-opinion/.

———. 2015. *Ecuador: La censura cabalga sobre el lomo de una ley. Informe de libertad de expresión 2014.* https://www.fundamedios.org.ec/wp-content/uploads /2015/03/Informe2014espaniol.pdf.

———. 2018. "Archivos inaccesibles, chatarra y deudas, a cuatro años del cierre de diario Hoy." August 28. https://www.fundamedios.org.ec/un-archivo-perdido -chatarra-y-deudas-a-cuatro-anos-del-cierre-de-diario-hoy.

Gallagher, Kevin P., and Margaret Myers. 2020. *China–Latin America Finance Database.* Washington, DC: Inter-American Dialogue.

Gamboa Rocabado, Franco. 2010. "Transformaciones constitucionales en Bolivia." *Colombia Internacional* 71 (January–June): 151–88. http://www.scielo.org.co/pdf /rci/n71/n71a08.pdf.

García Falconí, Ramiro. 2013. "Reflexiones y propuestas." *El Universo*, May 13.

Gehrke, Mirjam, Nelsy Lizarazo, Patricia Noboa, Davis Olmos, and Oliver Pieper. 2016. *Panorama de los medios en Ecuador. Sistema informativo y actores implicados.* DW Akademie. https://www.dw.com/downloads/30336831/panorama-de-los -medios-en-ecuador-pdf.pdf.

Gestión. 2019. "Declaratorias de estado de excepción en el Gobierno de Rafael Correa." https://revistagestion.ec/sites/default/files/import/legacy_pdfs/197_007 .pdf.

GK. 2017. "Fausto Camacho: 'El CNE hizo lo que le dio la gana.'" April 4. https:// elecciones2017.gk.city/2017/04/04/hubo-fraude-en-las-elecciones-presidenciales -de-ecuador/.

Human Rights Watch. 2014. "Letter on Judicial Independence in Ecuador." January 29. https://www.hrw.org/news/2014/01/29/letter-judicial-independence-ecuador.

———. 2018a. "Ecuador: Injerencia política en el poder judicial." April 20. https://www.hrw.org/es/news/2018/04/20/ecuador-injerencia-politica-en-el-poder -judicial#.

———. 2018b. "Venezuela. Eventos de 2018." https://www.hrw.org/es/world-report /2019/country-chapters/325542.

Huntington, Samuel P. 1972. *El orden político en las sociedades en cambio.* Buenos Aires: Paidós.

Hurtado, Osvaldo. 1998. *Una constitución para el futuro.* Quito: Fundación Ecuatoriana de Estudios Sociales.

———. 2008. *La dictadura civil.* Quito: FESO.

————. 2017. *Ecuador entre dos siglos*. Colombia: Penguin Random House Grupo Editorial S.A.S.

IACHR (Inter-American Court of Human Rights). 2018. *Gross Human Rights Violations in the Context of Social Protests in Nicaragua*. June 21. OAS. https://www.oas.org/en/iachr/reports/pdfs/nicaragua2018-en.pdf.

————. 2021. "Advisory Opinion OC-28/21 of June 7, 2021, Requested by the Republic of Colombia: Presidential Reelection without Term Limits in the Context of the Inter-American Human Rights System (Interpretation and Scope of Articles 1, 23, 24, and 32 of the American Convention on Human Rights, XX of the American Declaration of the Rights and Duties of Man, 3(d) of the Charter of the Organization of American States, paragraph 145." https://www.corteidh.or.cr/docs/opiniones/seriea_28_eng.pdf.

Icaza Gallard, Julio. 2016. "Fin del Estado de derecho: Principales reformas constitucionales y legislativas." In *El régimen de Ortega ¿Una nueva dictadura familiar en el continente?*, edited by Edmundo Jarquín Calderon. Managua: Pavsa.

ICN (*Iberomérica Central de Noticias*). 2012. "Ecuador: Correa ratifica que ministros no pueden hablar con medios de prensa privados." September 26. https://www.icndiario.com/2012/09/ecuador-correa-ratifica-que-ministros-no-pueden-hablar-con-medios-de-prensa-privados/.

————. 2019. "Escritor boliviano regresa al país luego de ser un perseguido político del régimen de Evo Morales." December 6. https://www.icndiario.com/2019/12/escritor-boliviano-regresa-al-pais-y-denuncia-la-persecucion-politica-del-evo-morales/.

Infobae. 2019. "Cómo es el sistema de trampas electorales que diseñó Daniel Ortega para ganar siempre." September 1. https://www.infobae.com/america/america-latina/2019/09/01/como-es-el-sistema-de-trampas-electorales-que-diseno-daniel-ortega-para-ganar-siempre/.

Jadán Heredia, Diego. 2013. "Los modelos de integración del Consejo de la Judicatura y su relación con la independencia del Poder Judicial." Master's thesis, UASB Ecuador.

Jarquín C., Edmundo. 2016. "Introducción." In *El régimen de Ortega ¿Una nueva dictadura familiar en el continente?*, edited by Edmundo Jarquín. Managua: Pavsa.

————, ed. 2020. *Nicaragua, el cambio azul y blanco. Dejando atrás el régimen de Ortega*. Managua: Funpadem.

Kornblithen, Miriam. 1996. "Crisis y transformación del sistema político venezolano: Nuevas y viejas reglas de juego." In *El sistema político venezolano: Crisis y transformaciones*, edited by A Álvarez, 1–31. Caracas: IEP-UCV.

La Hora. 2007. "En Rocafuerte, Policía salvó a diputados de linchamiento." March 16. https://lahora.com.ec/noticia/546807/en-rocafuerte-policia-salvo-a-diputados-de-linchamiento.

————. 2008. "Feneció la Corte Suprema de Justicia y nació la Corte Nacional de Justicia." October 21. https://www.lahora.com.ec/frontEnd/main.php?idSeccion=788546.

————. 2009. "Lucio Gutiérrez dice que exigirá suspensión de proceso electoral por fraude." April 28.

———. 2011a. "Correa conocía de los contratos de su hermano." February 4. https://lahora.com.ec/noticia/1101089880/correa-conocia-de-los-contratos-de-su-hermano.

———. 2011b. "Juez denuncia presión de Ministro." June 23. https://lahora.com.ec/noticia/1101162006/juez-denuncia-presión-de-ministro.

La Hora Loja. 2012. "Dalo Bucaram arremete contra Correa." August 9. https://issuu.com/la_hora/docs/diario_la_hora_loja_09_de_agosto_2012/9.

La Nación. 2019. "Venezuela terminó otro año como el país más violento de la región." December 27. https://www.lanacion.com.ar/el-mundo/venezuela-termino-otro-ano-como-pais-mas-nid2319281.

La Prensa. 2017. "Me convertí en el líder de los que callan por miedo." http://impresa.prensa.com/mundo/converti-lider-callan-miedo-correa_0_3353664669.html.

La República. 2010. "Con Perú, esto recién empieza. Lo mejor está por venir." June 10. https://larepublica.pe/politica/468292-con-peru-esto-recien-empieza-lo-mejor-esta-por-venir/.

———. 2012a. "Correa convoca a la Asamblea 'a trabajar con seriedad.'" April 17. https://www.larepublica.ec/blog/politica/2012/04/17/correa-convoca-a-la-asamblea-a-trabajar-con-seriedad/.

———. 2012b. "Destituyen a jueces que declararon inocente a Carrión." April 18. https://www.larepublica.ec/blog/politica/2012/04/18/destituyen-a-jueces-que-declararon-inocente-a-carrion/.

———. 2012c. "Bancos ecuatorianos triangulan dinero iraní por mandato presidencial." July 19. https://www.larepublica.ec/blog/opinion/2012/07/19/bancos-ecuatorianos-triangulan-dinero-irani-por-mandato-presidencial/.

———. 2013. "Correa llama 'mamotreto' a la Ley de Inquilinato y la veta totalmente." March 9. https://www.larepublica.ec/blog/economia/2013/03/09/correa-llama-mamotreto-a-la-ley-de-inquilinato-y-la-veta-totalmente/.

———. 2015a. "Juez de Cuenca renuncia porque dice que 'la justicia depende del poder político.'" January 8. https://www.larepublica.ec/blog/politica/2015/01/08/juez-cuenca-renuncia-justicia-depende-poder-politico/.

———. 2015b. "Alfredo Ruiz y Pamela Martínez presiden la Corte Constitucional." November 5. https://www.larepublica.ec/blog/politica/2015/11/05/alfredo-ruiz-y-pamela-martinez-presiden-la-corte-constitucional/.

———. 2017. "Mangas admite que voz de audio es suya pero dice que declaraciones están fuera de contexto." December 5. https://www.larepublica.ec/blog/politica/2017/12/05/eduardo-mangas-rechaza-grabacion-de-audio-y-dice-que-declaraciones-fueron-sacadas-de-contexto/.

La Tercera. 2021. "Gabriel Boric se desmarca del PC tras declaración sobre Nicaragua: pide que se 'retracten' de su apoyo a Ortega y califica de 'fraudulentas' las elecciones en dicho país." November 12. https://www.latercera.com/politica/noticia/gabriel-boric-se-desmarca-del-pc-tras-declaracion-sobre-nicaragua-y-califica-de-fraudulentas-las-elecciones-en-dicho-pais/JEONPLQXJFECPM6PYGSKFCK4OA/.

La Vanguardia. 2013. "Las frases célebres de Hugo Chávez." March 5. https://www
.lavanguardia.com/internacional/20130305/54369024984/frases-celebres-hugo
-chavez.html.

———. 2018. "Moreno logra el apoyo para cerrarle la puerta a Correa." February 5.
https://www.lavanguardia.com/internacional/20180205/44561794420/referendum
-ecuador-lenin-moreno-rafael-correa.html.

Latouche, Miguel Ángel. 2005. "Los dilemas del presidencialismo. Separación de
poderes y gobernabilidad democrática en la Venezuela contemporánea." *Revista
Venezolana de Análisis de Coyuntura* 11 (2): 245–65. https://www.redalyc.org/pdf
/364/36411214.pdf.

Ley Orgánica de participación ciudadana. 2011. https://www.oas.org/juridico/pdfs/
mesicic4_ecu_org6.pdf.

Loo Ríos, Evans Alberto. 2008. *El jacobino de la boina roja.* Panama: Biblioley.

Lucio-Paredes, Pablo. 2008. *En busca de la Constitución perdida.* Quito: Trama
Ediciones.

Magnet. 2018. "¿Han sido limpias las elecciones en Venezuela? Qué dicen Gobierno,
oposición y Zapatero." May 23. https://magnet.xataka.com/en-diez-minutos/
han-sido-limpias-las-elecciones-en-venezuela-que-dicen-gobierno-oposicion-y
-zapatero.

Martí Puig, Salvador, and Mateo Jarquín. 2021. "El precio de la perpetuación de
Daniel Ortega." *Nueva Sociedad*, June.

Mecanismo para el reconocimiento de personas presas políticas. n.d. Nicaragua.
https://presasypresospoliticosnicaragua.org/.

Medina, Echavarría José. 1964. *Consideraciones sobre el desarrollo económico.*
Buenos Aires: Solar y Hachette.

Melo Delgado, Rosa. 2015. *El estado de excepción en el actual constitucionalismo
andino.* Serie Magister 181. Quito: UASB Ecuador; Corporación Editora Nacional.

Miño, María Dolores, Martha Roldós, Ramón Muños Castro, and Luis Verdesoto.
2017. "Letter to the Special Rapporteur for the Independence of Magistrates and
Attorneys." October 31. United Nations Organization. Quito: RIDH, Fundación
1000 Hojas, Derecho y Justicia, Democracia y DD. HH. https://www.planv.com.ec
/sites/default/files/reporte_independencia_justicia_relator_nnuu_odj_mh_rd_pdh
.pdf.

Moallic, Benjamín. 2021. "El Salvador: un autoritarismo millennial." *Nueva
Sociedad*, September–October.

Neuman, Laura, and Jennifer McCoy. 2001. *Observing Political Change in Venezuela:
The Bolivarian Constitution and the 2000 Elections; Final Report.* Atlanta: Carter
Center. https://www.cartercenter.org/documents/297.pdf.

New York Times. 2022. "Explosion of Gang Violence Grips El Salvador, Setting
Record." March 27. https://www.nytimes.com/2022/03/27/world/americas/el
-salvador-gang-violence.html.

notimérica. 2007. "Ecuador—El ex presidente Rodrigo Borja pone condiciones
para asumir la secretaría de la Unión de Naciones del Sur." August 7. https://
www.notimerica.com/politica/noticia-ecuador-ex-presidente-rodrigo-borja-pone
-condiciones-asumir-secretaria-union-naciones-sur-20070807214325.html.

ntn24. 2013. "Momentos memorables del presidente Hugo Chávez." YouTube.com, March 6. https://www.youtube.com/watch?v=4A6z7KXjtww [no longer available].

OAS (Organization of American States). 2001. *Inter-American Democratic Charter*. https://www.oas.org/en/democratic-charter/pdf/demcharter_en.pdf.

———. 2015. "UN and IACHR Experts Condemn Moves to Dissolve Prominent Organization in Ecuador." September 17. https://www.oas.org/en/iachr/media_center/PReleases/2015/103.asp.

———. 2019a. "OAS Permanent Council Agrees 'to Not Recognize the Legitimacy of Nicolas Maduro's New Term.'" January 10. https://www.oas.org/en/media_center/press_release.asp?sCodigo=E-001/19.

———. 2019b. "OAS Permanent Council Approves Resolution on the Situation of Human Rights in Venezuela." August 28. https://www.oas.org/en/media_center/press_release.asp?sCodigo=E-058/19.

———. 2019c. *Final Report—Analysis of Electoral Integrity—General Elections in the Plurinational State of Bolivia*. October 20. https://www.oas.org/en/spa/deco/Report-Bolivia-2019/.

———. 2019d. "Statement of the OAS General Secretariat on the Situation in Nicaragua." November 17. https://www.oas.org/en/media_center/press_release.asp?sCodigo=E-104/19.

———. 2019e. "Report of the OAS High-Level Commission on Nicaragua." November 19. https://scm.oas.org/pdfs/2019/CP41661EREPORTCOMMISSIONONNICARAGUA.pdf.

———. 2020a. "Statement of the OAS General Secretariat on the Situation in Venezuela." January 5. https://www.oas.org/en/media_center/press_release.asp?sCodigo=E-116/20.

———. 2020b. "Proceedings Volume I AG/DEC. 102 (L-O/20) AG/RES. 2948 (L-O/20)–AG/RES. 2964 (L-O/20). Certified Texts of the Declaration and Resolutions, Fiftieth Regular Session, Washington, D.C., October 20–21."

Opinión. 2013. "La emboscada a policías era para matar al Zorro." August 4. https://www.opinion.com.bo/articulo/escenario-politico/emboscada-policias-era-matar-zorro/20130804023100444466.html.

Ortiz García, Pablo. 2012. "Decreto supremo." *El Comercio*, October 26. https://www.elcomercio.com/opinion/decreto-supremo.html.

Ottone, Ernesto, and Sergio Muñoz Riveros. 2018. *Después de la quimera*. Santiago de Chile: Random House Mondadori.

Our World in Data. n.d. https://ourworldindata.org.

OVV (Observatorio de Violencia en Venezuela). 2020. *Informe anual de violencia 2019*. https://observatoriodeviolencia.org.ve/news/informe-anual-de-violencia-2019/.

Página 12. 2007. "Hacia una democracia socialista." January 15. https://www.pagina12.com.ar/diario/elmundo/4-79109-2007-01-15.html.

Pásara, Luis. 2014. *Judicial Independence in Ecuador's Judicial Reform Process*. Due Process of Law Foundation. https://www.dplf.org/en/resources/judicial-independence-ecuadors-judicial-reform-process.

Peraza, José Antonio. 2016. "Colapso del sistema electoral." In *El régimen de Ortega ¿Una nueva dictadura familiar en el continente?*, edited by Edmundo Jarquín. Managua: Pavsa.

Periodismo de investigación. 2018. "El tío de Glas esconde millones en empresa vinculada a contratos estatales." September 14. https://periodismodeinvestigacion .com/2018/09/14/el-tio-de-glas/.

Plan V. 2013. "Mery Zamora y las educadoras estigmatizadas." https://sobrevivientes .planv.com.ec/mery-zamora-y-las-educadoras-estigmatizadas/.

———. 2015. "Los del círculo son intocables." April 24. https://www.planv.com.ec/ historias/politica/del-circulo-son-intocables.

———. 2017a. "Alianza PAÍS: Todo queda en familia." March 21. https://www.planv .com.ec/investigacion/investigacion/alianza-pais-todo-queda-familia.

———. 2017b. "Las muertes sin aclarar de la década correísta." June 11. https://www .planv.com.ec/historias/politica/muertes-sin-aclarar-la-decada-correista-1.

———. 2017c. "El top ten de la injerencia judicial durante el correato." September 25. https://www.planv.com.ec/historias/politica/el-top-ten-la-injerencia-judicial -durante-el-correato.

———. 2017d. "Mangas: la encrucijada de Moreno." December 6. https://www.planv .com.ec/ideas/ideas/mangas-la-encrucijada-moreno.

———. 2017e. "Así metió el gobierno Correa la mano en la justicia: Primera parte." December 11. https://www.planv.com.ec/investigacion/investigacion/asi-metio-el -gobierno-correa-la-mano-la-justicia-primera-parte.

———. 2017f. "Así metió el gobierno Correa la mano en la justicia (Parte 2)." December 18. https://www.planv.com.ec/historias/sociedad/asi-metio-el-gobierno -correa-la-mano-la-justicia-segunda-parte.

———. 2018. "Caso Balda: Las pruebas documentales contra Correa." November 12. https://www.planv.com.ec/investigacion/investigacion/caso-balda-pruebas -documentales-contra-correa.

"¿Rafael Correa dictador?" 2009. YouTube.com, March 7. https://www.youtube.com /watch?v=3RnJRGmK0Wg.

Regalado, Roberto. 2008. *Encuentros y desencuentros de la izquierda latinoamericana. Una mirada desde el Foro de São Paulo*. Querétaro: Ocean Sur.

Registro Oficial No. 653. 2015. "Enmiendas a la Constitución de la República del Ecuador. Quito: Registro Oficial." December 21. http://biblioteca.defensoria.gob .ec/handle/37000/2009.

runrun.es. 2020a. "UE incluye a presidente de Conatel y otros 10 nombres en la lista de sancionados." February 18. https://runrun.es/rr-es-plus/398805/156 -venezolanos-han-sido-sancionados-por-31-paises/.

———. 2020b. "Runrunes de Bocaranda: Alto—a confesión de parte." July 9. https: //runrun.es/runrunes-de-bocaranda/runrunes/414322/runrunes-de-bocaranda-alto-a -confesion-de-parte/.

Sábato, Ernesto. 1977. "Sábato, el anarquismo, el comunismo, Marx, Stalin, el Che y la democracia." https://www.youtube.com/watch?v=1mR3P7JnvRc.

Sánchez Berzaín, Carlos. 2013. *XXI Century Dictatorship in Bolivia*. Miami: Interamerican Institute for Democracy.

São Paulo Forum. 1990. *Declaración de São Paulo*. https://forodesaopaulo.org/wp-content/uploads/2014/07/01-Declaracion-de-Sao-Paulo-19901.pdf.

Tardío Quiroga, Fátima Elva. 2006. *El Estado boliviano como Estado Social de derecho.* Master's thesis, UASB Ecuador. https://repositorio.uasb.edu.ec/handle/10644/2607.

Teleamazonas. 2019. "Refrescándole la memoria al Mashi." January 1. https://www.facebook.com/edwin.navarrete.14/posts/10217220438644210.

teleSURtv.net. 2019. "Lula da Silva: Venezuela es un asunto del pueblo venezolano." June 6. https://www.telesurtv.net/news/lula-sobre-venezuela-entrevista-20190606-0026.html.

"Tomás Borge—Declaraciones en Telesur." 2009. YouTube.com, July 26. https://www.youtube.com/watch?v=WnzNZuGrbuk.

Torres, Rosa María. 2014. "Rafael Correa: Entre la renuncia y la reelección." *Otraeducación* (blog), June 2. https://otra-educacion.blogspot.com/2014/05/correa-entre-la-renuncia-y-la-reeleccion.html.

UCAB. 2020. "Universidad Católica Andrés Bello. Encuesta Nacional de Condiciones de Vida 2019–2020." https://www.proyectoencovi.com/.

UN Human Rights Council. 2019a. *Report of the United Nations High Commissioner for Human Rights on the Situation of Human Rights in the Bolivarian Republic of Venezuela* (A/HRC/41/18.Add.1). 41st session, July. https://www.ohchr.org/en/documents/comments-state/ahrc4118add1-report-united-nations-high-commissioner-human-rights.

———. 2019b. *Situation of Human Rights in Nicaragua—Report of the United Nations High Commissioner for Human Rights* (A/HRC/42/18). 42nd session, September. https://www.ohchr.org/en/documents/country-reports/ahrc4218-situation-human-rights-nicaragua-report-united-nations-high.

———. 2020. "Venezuela: UN Report Urges Accountability for Crimes against Humanity." September 16. https://www.ohchr.org/en/press-releases/2020/09/venezuela-un-report-urges-accountability-crimes-against-humanity?LangID=E&NewsID=26247.

———. 2021. *Report of the Independent International Fact-Finding Mission on the Bolivarian Republic of Venezuela.* 48th sess., September–October. https://www.ohchr.org/sites/default/files/Documents/HRBodies/HRCouncil/FFMV/A.HRC.48.69_EN.pdf.

United Nations. 2021. "Venezuela's Justice System Aiding Repression: Human Rights Probe." UN News, September 16. https://news.un.org/en/story/2021/09/1100122.

UNODC (United Nations Office on Drugs and Crime). 2020. "Datos sobre homicidios." February 25. https://public.tableau.com/profile/unodc.rab#!/vizhome/Homiciderates_15826327950430/Homicide-rates.

———. n.d. "UNODC: Bolivia Debe Reducir Cultivos Ilegales De Coca Hasta 2019." February 26. https://www.unodc.org/bolivia/es/stories/bolivia_debe_reducir_cultivos_de_coca.html.

Valenzuela, Pablo A. 2014. "Caída y resurgimiento. La evolución de la oposición política venezolana durante el gobierno de Hugo Chávez." *Política y gobierno* 21 (2): 379–408.

Varela, Alejandro. 2021. "Daniel Ortega, el guerrillero nicaragüense que ni sabía ni quería mandar." SWI, November 4. https://www.swissinfo.ch/spa/elecciones -nicaragua-ortega_daniel-ortega--el-guerrillero-nicaragueense-que-ni-sabía-ni -quería-mandar/47084520.

Vatican News. 2022. "Pope expresses sorrow for Nicaragua, says dialogue should be basis for a respectful coexistence." August 21. https://www.vaticannews.va/en/ pope/news/2022-08/pope-expresses-sorrow-for-nicaragua.html.

Veeduría Internacional. 2012. *Informe final de la Veeduría Internacional para la reforma de la función judicial del Ecuador*. December 13. https://periodismodeinvestigacion .com/wp-content/uploads/2018/08/veeduria-internacional-informe-final-LF.pdf.

Velásquez, Uriel, and Claudia Rivas. 2019. "La fortuna del FSLN amasada de fraude en fraude." *Despacho 505*, February 6. https://www.despacho505.com/la-fortuna -del-fslnf-fraude/.

Vera, Leonardo V. 2008. "Políticas sociales y productivas en un Estado patrimoni-alista petrolero: Venezuela 1999–2007." *Nueva Sociedad* 215:111–29. https://nuso .org/media/articles/downloads/3525_1.pdf.

Voz de América. 2019. "OEA aprueba resolución que desconoce segundo mandato de Maduro en Venezuela." January 10. https://www.vozdeamerica.com/a/oea-consejo -permanente-busca-condenar-a-venezuela-mientras-maduro-se-reelige/4736994 .html.

Zemmouche, Florent. 2021. "Elecciones legislativas y municipales en El Salvador." Fundación Carolina. https://www.fundacioncarolina.es/wp-content/uploads/2021 /03/AC-8.-2021.pdf.

Index

281

About the Author

Osvaldo Hurtado is both a scholar and a politician, which is an unusual combination in Latin America.

He has written numerous essays and papers on Latin America, some of which have been included in compilations or journals in the fields of social sciences and political sciences. He has also had twelve books published in Spanish about his country's economic, social, and political issues. The most recent of these was *Ecuador entre dos siglos* (2017). In addition to this book, two of his previous texts have also been translated into English: *Political Power in Ecuador* (1980 and 1985) and *Portrait of a Nation: Culture and Progress in Ecuador* (2010), the former now having more than twenty editions in Spanish and the latter fifteen.

Hurtado served as both vice president of Ecuador (1979–1981) and president (1981–1984), as well as president of the 1998 Constituent Assembly. His life and work in the public sphere have been characterized by seeking to bolster national economic development, institutionalize democracy, defend rights and freedoms, and fight against military and civil authoritarianism.

Since 1984, Hurtado has headed a Quito-based think tank, the Corporation for Development Studies (Corporación de Estudios para el Desarrollo, CORDES).

More information is available at www.osvaldohurtado.com.